D0354468

Palestinians Born in Exile

PALESTINIANS
BORN IN EXILE
Diaspora and the Search for a Homeland

JULIANE HAMMER

UNIVERSITY OF TEXAS PRESS ⬥ AUSTIN

"In the Deserts of Exile" by Jabra Ibrahim Jabra, on pages
61–62, is from Mounah A. Khouri and Hamid Algar, eds., *An
Anthology of Modern Arabic Poetry* (Berkeley: University of
California Press, 1974), 225. The Regents of the University of
California. Reprinted with permission.
    Poems on pages 50, 62, 64–65, and 82–83 are from Salma
Khadra Jayyusi, *Anthology of Modern Palestinian Literature*
(New York: Columbia University Press, 1991), 96, 97, 190, 196,
234, and 257. Reprinted with the permission of the publisher.
    Poem on pages 83–84, by Suheir Hammad, is reprinted
with the permission of the author.

LIBRARY OF CONGRESS
CATALOGING-IN-PUBLICATION DATA

Hammer, Juliane.
Palestinians born in exile : diaspora and the search for a
homeland / Juliane Hammer. — 1st ed.
    p.   cm.
Includes bibliographical references and index.
ISBN 0-292-70295-7 (cloth : alk. paper) —
ISBN 0-292-70296-5 (pbk. : alk. paper)
1. Palestinian Arabs — Case studies.   2. National
characteristics, Palestinian.   3. Repatriation — Palestine.
1. Title.
DS113.6.H347   2005
305.892'74 — dc22   2004010011

Contents

Preface

*. . . the next day they sent me back to my
second home
but my spirit stayed and it flies in the stones.
Each burning tire carries the fire
of my love for the land and my deep desire
to return to the earth of my ancestors.
They can't stop me.*

—IRON SHEIK, "JUST TRYING TO GET HOME,"
CAMEL CLUTCH, 2003

This excerpt is from a rap song by the Palestinian American hip-hop artist Iron Sheik. The song tells the story of a young Palestinian American
who tried to go to Palestine but was detained by Israeli security forces
and subsequently banned from entering the country. This song, the existence of a Palestinian American rapper, his popularity with young Palestinian Americans, and my own involvement with the Palestinian community show me that the issue of return to Palestine has as much currency
today as when I first started researching this question.

This study of Palestinian return experiences is based on research and
fieldwork conducted between 1997 and 2000. It is a snapshot of a group of
young returnees to Palestine who had grown up in different corners of the
world as part of the Palestinian diaspora. Like a photograph, it has cap-
tured particular people at a particular moment in time. The years 1998–99,
during which I conducted my fieldwork in the West Bank, were a time
when the initial euphoric feelings about the "peace process," the partial
redeployment of the Israeli forces from the Occupied Territories, and the
establishment of the institutions of the Palestinian National Authority had
started to fade in the West Bank and Gaza. Palestinians around the world,
in the refugee camps and cities of the Arab world, and in the diaspora
communities elsewhere, were growing skeptical about the prospects for an
independent Palestinian state. The findings of this study must be viewed

in this light. Their value lies both in mapping out the range of return experiences in this particular context and time and in emphasizing the larger conclusions to be drawn about migration and return.

In September 2000 the Occupied Territories witnessed the outbreak of a second popular uprising of Palestinians against the Israeli occupation. This time the clashes with the Israeli forces were more intense, with the number of Palestinians killed and injured rising daily. This new uprising has been termed the Second Intifada (uprising). Since then, there have been a number of significant developments. Areas fully or partially controlled by the Palestinian Authority have been reinvaded and reoccupied by Israeli forces. Militant Palestinian groups have carried out suicide bombings in Israeli cities that have killed and injured many Israelis. The Israeli government has used a variety of "security" measures: targeted killings of suspected or potential suicide bombers and planners of such operations; home demolitions; rocket and helicopter attacks on Palestinian towns and villages; arrests of large numbers of young Palestinian men; curfews; and complete cutoff of the territories from economic, medical, and financial supplies.

All these developments have officially sealed the fate of the peace process as a failed project. The peoples of the Middle East, in particular Israelis and Palestinians, are more than ever in need of a solution to this conflict, a just solution that can reconcile the pain and distrust between them and allow for peace and stability in the region. As I write these words, new efforts are being made to reach an agreement on a proposal termed the "road map," initiated by the United States and debated among Israelis and Palestinians.

The events in the Middle East since I left Ramallah in the summer of 1999 have had a significant effect on the lives of the respondents to this study. Living conditions in the West Bank and Gaza have deteriorated enormously, and many Palestinians have left Palestine in search of a safe place to live. No figures are available regarding the number of Palestinians who have left since the beginning of the Second Intifada. The young returnees of this study might have been among those who left or among those who chose to stay in their homeland. The situation has made it impossible to stay in contact with all of them, and I can only assume what the effects on them might have been.

Palestinians in the West Bank, Gaza, and Israel are united in their struggle to survive and in their suffering and loss. Palestinians in the diaspora have intensified their activities and commitment to their homeland

and demand a voice in the search for a solution. While the future does not look bright for the Palestinians at home and in the diaspora, the difficult situation may breed a new generation of Palestinians who will not dissolve into post-national, postmodern identities before achieving justice and a homeland to which to return.

Acknowledgments

First of all I have to thank the young Palestinians around the world who agreed to share their stories and ideas with me. I have promised all of them anonymity, which makes it impossible to thank them by name. Without their willingness to work with me, and without their trust, this study would not have been possible. I hope that they find their experiences, hopes, and aspirations represented in this book.

Many other people have helped and supported me on my journey with this project, and my thanks go to all of them, whether mentioned by name or not. I am particularly grateful to my adviser, Peter Heine, at Humboldt University in Berlin. He supported my ideas and the ethnographic track that I chose early on, and encouraged me to follow my intuition. Over the years, several senior scholars have supported my endeavors and have been mentors to me: Gerhard Höpp at the Center for Modern Oriental Studies in Berlin, a source of knowledge on Palestinian history; Serif Mardin at Sabanci University in Istanbul; Hisham Sharabi at the Center for Policy Analysis on Palestine in Washington, D.C., a Palestinian and American intellectual with deep insights into the Palestinian fate; and Sharif Kanaana at Birzeit University.

John Esposito encouraged me to write this book and provided ideas and institutional support through the Center for Muslim-Christian Understanding (CMCU) at Georgetown University. Yvonne Haddad discussed my ideas at various stages of my writing and provided additional sources and angles. I thank Lesley Sebastian and Clare Merrill at CMCU for their cheerful presence and their patience with my requests. The faculty and staff of the Center for Contemporary Arab Studies at Georgetown were welcoming and helpful when I approached them in search of contacts in the Palestinian community in Washington, D.C. Zeina Seikaly deserves special thanks for opening the doors of many community members to me. Jim Fine and Carleta Baker at the Friends School in Ramallah provided access to their school and students and shared their experiences and insights with me.

For material support for this project, including writing and travel grants, I am grateful to the Municipality of Berlin for a two-year doctoral fellowship, the German Academic Exchange Service for supporting my fieldwork in the West Bank, the Fazit Foundation in Frankfurt for a writing grant that allowed me to finish on time, and the Ford Foundation in Cairo and New York for a conference travel grant.

My position as a researcher at SHAML—The Palestinian Refugee and Diaspora Center in Ramallah—provided material and institutional support, and insight into Palestinian civil society. I am grateful to my editor, Jim Burr, at the University of Texas Press for making this book possible and lending his support to it. I thank the reviewers for taking the time to read my manuscript carefully and provide detailed and helpful suggestions.

Many friends and colleagues have discussed this project with me along the way and have provided me with useful feedback: Allen McDuffee was my first editor and provided me with shelter, friendship, and support in Washington, D.C. Khaled Al-Khatib is my Palestinian connection in Berlin and has shared many of his stories and experiences with me. Ferida Jawad was a role model and source of inspiration as a scholar and a teacher. Franck Moroy sent energy from Beirut and showed me a different side of Jordan. Moataz Dajani opened my eyes to the situation of Palestinians in Lebanon and helped me discover the value of working with children and art. Awad Halabi was at times more excited about my research than I was. Vincent Ovaert made Berlin a friendlier place for me. Ejaz Akram introduced me to American academia, showed me Washington, D.C., and took the time to help in many steps of the research process. Jamila Bargach shared with me her experiences in writing a book and made difficult times seem less confusing and lonely. Her enthusiasm was a source of inspiration for me. Noha Bakr was there for me with advice, hospitality, and friendship.

Living in Washington, D.C., and working on this project was much more than a professional experience because of the warmth and hospitality of the Shami family: Dr. Jamil, Kamila, Jamilah, Muna, Mohammed, and Maha. Manal Omar has introduced me to many Palestinians and is my example for living political and personal engagement with enthusiasm, energy, and pride.

Scholars around the world shared their insights with me: Helga Baumgarten, Helena Lindholm Schulz, Philip Mattar, Fawaz Turki, Rosemary Sayigh, Dan Rabinowitz, Eyal Ben-Ari, and Elia Zureik took the time to meet with me and discuss my ideas.

Living in the West Bank would not have been the same without Carl

Dundas, who was always there with his friendship and a shoulder to cry on; Richard Clarke, the real anthropologist; Khaled Hmeid, a true Palestinian; and Sasha Evans, who shared discovering Palestine with me and was my roommate in Ramallah. My first memories in Palestine are forever connected to Sylva van Rosse, Magdalena Wernefeldt, and Annika Schabbauer.

My sister Susanne deserves special mention for her patience and encouragement while I was writing the first draft of this book. She put up with the constant state of emergency and my frequent absences. Her visit to Palestine helped me see the country from a new perspective.

Most important, I thank my husband, Cemil, for his unrelenting support and encouragement, for his love and patience, and for the fact that he believes in me and never ceases to see my potential. His optimism about life and his faith keep me going.

Palestinians Born in Exile

Introduction

CHAPTER 1

Palestinian Migration, Refugees, and Return

Migration in its various forms is a fact of the life of many people in our time. The last fifty years have seen particularly significant changes in numbers of migrants and patterns of migration. An integral part of the modern and postmodern migration debate concerns the relevance of national and local identities vis-à-vis powerful global forces and interests. Do we all live in a "world of movement"? What effect do migratory moves have on the formation and re-formation of groups and people and on their respective identities? Migration studies have analyzed different forms of voluntary and forced migration; economic, political, and social forces affecting emigration and immigration; migration strategies; the decision to migrate; and the influence of war, conflict, and social change. The ongoing globalization process has given an even newer dimension to migration, pushing the boundaries of the world to their extreme and providing the means for faster movement and communication.

Migration can be an enriching experience that introduces new ideas and concepts into a person's worldview and communal identities, opening up horizons and extending the borders of knowledge. At the same time it can lead to confrontation with others because of ethnic, cultural, and religious differences. It can also lead to a rethinking of ethnicity and therefore an interest in preserving this difference that creates boundaries and defines "otherness." Migration creates more-complex societies in which many people are not part of the nation in which they live, thus it partly accounts for the growing interest in finding one's roots and preserving family and cultural traditions (Gonzalez 1992, 27). For some migrants, movement implies transgressing the limits of their own culture and becoming comfortable with living in and between two worlds.

However, and more often, people do not move to other countries out of a desire to learn; migration is seldom a completely voluntary decision. One can identify different pressures that lead a person or family to leave their home or home country. The flight from actual dangers, such as wars, genocide, political persecution, or famine, is qualitatively distinct. However, other situations that are less threatening, if not less urgent, can thus also lead to the decision to migrate.

Migration has affected people around the globe in different ways. Many have a home and/or homeland and consider migration a choice and a blessing, not a burden. Diaspora communities and immigrants are a phenomenon concentrated in the Western world, while refugees are a problem that many Third World countries have to face on a much larger scale than does the West. The presence of others, strangers, in nation-states and societies challenges notions of national and cultural identities and questions the distribution of resources and wealth. More recently, postmodern theory has come to challenge the very notion of nationalism and national identity as historical constructions, while arguing for the relevance of localized and particular identities in the face of globalizing and unifying economic and political processes.

Palestinians look back at more than a century of migration history and more than five decades of displacement. They claim their right to an independent state and insist on their national identity. Where can they fit into this new world? Being at home or going home is something most people take for granted, but for many Palestinians having a homeland and feeling at home are not part of the daily experience. Moving, and living in places other than Palestine, has, throughout the last century, been an important feature of Palestinian life. There is not one Palestinian family that has been unaffected by this experience. Palestinians live in different corners of this world, in larger or smaller communities, but something and someone important is always missing from their lives. The longing for the absentees and communication through old and new means are an integral part of their life experiences. It is the sense of movement, the lack of stability and the quest for it, that this study attempts to capture.

This study describes the search for a homeland by a group of young Palestinians who were born and raised in the diaspora. They grew up outside Palestine and returned to their homeland as a direct or indirect result of the peace process initiated in the early 1990s. Their experiences of returning to Palestine are multifaceted and individual, and they form part of the larger Palestinian migration experience.

There is already a vast literature on Palestine and the Palestinians, so why write another book? While researching Palestinian diaspora communities and communicating with many Palestinians in different locations, I realized that Palestinians do have a sense of a shared national identity, but in reality the different groups of Palestinians know relatively little about each other. Such a situation can be an obstacle for relating to or understanding the problems of diaspora groups other than one's own. Living in different parts of the world, often out of touch with each other, has eliminated the shared daily experience. Living in different countries, cultures, and settings has produced particular lifestyles, value systems, and beliefs. Also, such factors as class, economic and legal status, and political affiliation influence every Palestinian's identity, although each has a self-perception that still pictures Palestine as one unified country with a language and cultural values, whether or not that is true of its present.

The idea for this project was born from my interaction with Palestinians over a period of almost ten years. Relations with the Palestinian community in Germany, and fieldwork in Jordan, the West Bank, and Gaza and in the United States gave me insight into different processes within Palestinian society. There are two striking features of Palestinian life, one being the diversity of stories and experiences of Palestinians and the other an overwhelming sense of belonging to one another as a people.

My Palestinian friends, mostly students at that time, were politically involved and always ready to talk about politics and Palestine. Their rooms were plastered with posters and pictures of the Dome of the Rock in Jerusalem, paintings by Palestinian artists, and old stamps and photographs of Palestine from the time of the British Mandate. Many of them had never been to Palestine themselves, but the images obviously meant something to them. I wondered what it was that tied them to a homeland they did not know. Why could they not integrate into and feel at home in any other place? Why was there this sense of bonding whenever they met a Palestinian, no matter where he or she had been raised? Why did they so often talk about loss, suffering, and feelings of homelessness and uncertainty about the future? For me, the pride they took in their material culture, such as music, poetry, dance, embroidery, and food, was unfamiliar and surprising.

Then, in the early 1990s, the peace process started, and many Palestinians abroad had high hopes for returning to their homeland sooner or later. So far, the return of the majority of the Palestinian refugees has not even been negotiated, and chances are that the issue of the right of return will pose the greatest obstacle to solving the Israeli-Palestinian conflict, for which the concerns of both the Palestinian and Israeli/Jewish diaspora will have to be taken into consideration.

Since 1993, approximately a hundred thousand Palestinians have returned to the West Bank and Gaza through a process that has disappointed most Palestinians with its premise and implementation.[1] There are different categories of returnees, but none of them includes a large number of

Palestinian refugees from the camps in Lebanon, Syria, Jordan, or Egypt. The returnees instead include Palestinians who were working for the PLO and applied to return and work for the Palestinian Authority and/or the police forces and their families; beneficiaries of family-reunification programs; returnees from Kuwait who were expelled in the wake of the Gulf War and could enter the Palestinian territories; and Palestinians with foreign passports who individually decided to resettle in Palestine.

Indeed, the situation of returnees in Palestine is very different from that of those who return to other countries, who are usually integrated into the existing structure of the society. They do not exactly resume the role they left before emigration, but bring in new ideas and worldviews, and, if they were successful migrants, also certain financial means for reintegration. The Palestinian case saw the influx of people with a history of service to the Palestinian national movement outside Palestine who gained much power in the newly established Palestinian National Authority (PA). The debate among Palestinians about the role of the returnees in Palestinian politics, society, and the peace process was clearly an extension of the older conflict between the inside (Palestinians in Palestine) and the outside (the PLO).

The term "returnees," or Aideen, needs explanation in this context. As will become clear throughout the text, there are different types of returnees. The Arabic term 'Aidin (colloquial Arabic for returnees) is, in the Palestinian context, applied only to people who returned to work for the PA. The connotation of the term is rather negative, or at least critical. Returnees as well as locals use the term either to convey this pejorative meaning or to debate it. For lack of a better word, I use the term "returnee" for all people of Palestinian origin (that is, having at least one Palestinian parent) who came back to Palestine with the intention of living there for a longer period of time. In the general understanding, the Arabic term does not apply to Palestinians who return from Western countries or from work in the Gulf.

Methodology and Sources

While studying Palestinian migration, I was startled by the fact that Palestinians all over the world have, to different degrees, managed to pass on a sense of Palestinian identity to their children since 1948. Because identity formation is a central feature of childhood and youth, I was especially interested in the experience of younger returnees. I decided to limit the scope of the study to those between sixteen and thirty-five. Another precondition for the sample group was that participants had to have been born outside Palestine.

For this group, using the word "return" is not literally accurate. Palestine is, or is considered, their homeland because one or both parents are Palestinian, but it is not a place to which they could in a physical sense "return," as they had never lived there. To them the very notion of return must be symbolic, and what they know about Palestine—how much attachment they feel to the country, the people, the nation, or the culture—is based on learning, on the transmission and re-creation of memories, images, and history.

Because it took place in other countries, not in Palestine, their youth was to a large extent defined by their migration experiences. Some were born and grew up in one place or one country, and others had a more diverse migration experience. For the former, it is the migration experience of their parents and the degree of integration, acculturation, or segregation that influence their lifestyle the most. They have had a cross-cultural upbringing and developed various degrees of cultural competence in more than one cultural setting. The other group had a migration experience that was their own, whether because their family moved during their lifetime or because they themselves made the decision to move from one place or country to another. In any case, they are distinct from people with a mono-cultural experience of childhood and adolescence in various host countries and from Palestinians in Palestine itself.

This is not a conventional study of refugees. Many Palestinians, even outside the refugee camps in the Arab world, consider themselves refugees, but the group studied here is privileged in a number of ways.[2] Unlike many of the Palestinians in the Arab world, they and their families did not live in refugee camps. And they had the privilege of returning, a fact that contributes to their "problems" with local Palestinians and explains some of the resentment toward them.

That I interviewed teenagers and young adults is also important. All my interviewees have experienced exile mainly as children, thus their stories reflect the experience of migration and living in exile from a child's perspective. The members of this group, now only young adults or adolescents, are still in a formative phase, a stage of development in which ideas, rules, and convictions are constantly being debated and life plans change quickly, largely depending on their parents and families.

It creates a very special type of oral history to interview people of this age group, precisely because of the floating nature of their identities and the various dependencies on family and environment.[3] They have a life ahead of them, with much more time to plan for and less that is already decided and fixed. Their oral history differs considerably from the life stories of older people who look back at a life and see their main task as making sense of what they have done and what happened to them. Younger people are able to be more flexible and to adjust to changing ideas and notions of identity. In older age the longing for stability replaces the young person's quest for change and challenge.

This study is an attempt to show the young faces of the Palestinian diaspora, those who had to create their Palestinian identity without having lived in Palestine. These young people are the generation that will decide the future of Palestine, that will implement or change the agreements and contracts made today, and that will determine whether or not the Palestinian nation as an imagined national community will survive.

I limited the scope of the study to the Ramallah/Jerusalem area for two main reasons. First, focusing on this area, where I was living at the time, provided the depth of observation necessary to evaluate and contextualize the personal interviews I conducted there. Though Palestine is a small geographical area (and the West Bank and Gaza are even smaller), the differences between towns and villages, north and south, the West Bank and Gaza are a fact and are ever-present in the minds of people living there. Second, returnees were concentrated in this area, along with Gaza, Nablus, Jericho, and Hebron, mainly because the offices and institutions of the PA were established in these areas. In addition, the presence of Birzeit University, the most prestigious Palestinian university, motivated some parents to bring their children to the Ramallah area. Many of the returnees with English-speaking children needed schools with English instruction, which existed only in the Ramallah area.

The interviews were half-structured, that is, they were designed to cover a number of topics that I would ask or try to ask about throughout all the interviews to get data that could, to some extent, be compared. The topics included the migration experience and origin of the returnee's family in Palestine; whether and how childhood was spent in one or more host countries and the involvement in a Palestinian community there; language, traditions, food, music, poetry, and fiction; Palestinian friends; the return decision; first impressions of Palestine; an evaluation of the level of integration and satisfaction with life in Palestine; and the returnee's plans for the future.

The interviews were conducted either in Arabic or in English, with the choice left entirely to the interviewees. Many of the interviews were taped, and individuals generally did not hesitate to be interviewed on the topics. Many of the interviews took place in my office in Ramallah, while some others were conducted in public places such as at the university or cafés in the area.[4] When interviews took place in my office, there was a clear hierarchy either created or reinforced by the setting, as it was considered my space, both familiar to me and to some extent official.

I also met with a number of individuals, researchers, political activists, teachers, and returnees of the older generation to gather more background information on the situation and Palestinians' perceptions of the returnees. Officially, returnees were not a topic; thus very little material could be found in newspapers or other Palestinian publications. Only one Palestinian journal had published one issue featuring reflections by returnees (*Al-Carmel* 55/56, 1998).

In preparation for my fieldwork I had collected what I could find about Palestinians around the world and the developments of Palestinian national identity and the national movement; I also gathered a selection of Palestinian literature, poetry, and music. The limited number of resources on Palestinian Americans inspired me to conduct a number of interviews with young Palestinian Americans in Chicago and Washington, D.C.

A special type of material, neither a secondary source nor an empirical one, came from the Internet. The growth and accessibility of online information and communication has provided Palestinians with the opportunity to post their opinions, information about their cause, and all types of discussions on the Web and has enabled members of the diaspora to communicate across large distances. However, the Internet is not available to everyone, insofar as it requires some technical equipment, computer skills, and a command of English.

No study has yet been conducted on Palestinian representation on the Internet, but observation shows that the Internet's importance as a source of non-scholarly information for both Palestinians and interested others is growing. The Internet turns an oral source into written material in a new and interesting way; one can find memory texts, poems, opinion pieces, and articles by nonprofessional writers. Especially since 1998, the fiftieth anniversary of the *Nakba,* Palestinian Web sites have provided much material that is printable, but not printed in the classical sense.[5] The Internet has also enabled Palestinians in the diaspora to track events in Palestine and to depend less on international news agencies and their selective coverage of non-domestic events, particularly in the United States.

Research of this type always creates hierarchies and involves imbalances of power. I chose the people for my study and had the power to drop them from my list. I decided what topics to talk about and how much to tell them about my research. At the same time, my potential interviewees could choose to talk to me or not. Palestinians are probably one of the best-studied national groups in contemporary area studies, and, as there are relatively few of them, many of them have experience with being interviewed or asked to participate in research. Palestinians tend to cooperate with researchers because many Palestinians know that research about their situation can help them gain the attention of the international public and thus influence political decisions in such arenas as the United Nations.[6]

I could not totally avoid the danger of "using" the stories I collected, and thus ultimately using the people I talked to, to make my arguments, to generalize, and to draw conclusions. My intention here is to let my interviewees speak for themselves, to give them a voice through my own discursive power.[7]

This study relates general themes and aspects of Palestinian migration to the particular and empirical material gathered during my field research. The empirical material is embedded in the larger picture of Palestinian history, with its political and social developments. It places individual experience in a larger context, thereby framing it, while the individual stories may serve as illustrations to explain more general developments. I describe individuals as actors who, as much as institutions and structures, determine what has happened and what will happen in the future, if not on the higher levels of Palestinian and Middle Eastern politics, at least in their own lives. I believe that social change has individual faces. From the individual's perspective, the objective is to survive — to cope with what happens and make sense of it. Within the framework of historical and political circumstances, subjectivity and awareness of a situation provide humans with the tools to understand and possibly change the situation in which people live. These tools may vary from culture to culture, region to region, and period to period, but they are accessible and comprehensible to others as essentially human experience. Consequently, individual stories can illustrate and help explain larger processes in a society.

From Exile and Diaspora to Palestine

The study revolves around the key terms — identity, migration, homeland, memory, history, diaspora, and return — that are vital to understanding Palestinian migration in the twentieth century, the formation of Palestinian identity, and the social as well as political implications of the Palestinian-Israeli conflict. Many of these terms will reappear throughout the text and will be discussed in relation to each other. The study connects these themes of Palestinian migration to the return experiences of a particular group of Palestinian migrants. Return is discussed in the larger context of Palestine and is linked to the individual narratives of my interviewees. These narratives are woven into the text. At times they seem to contradict the argument, at other times they clearly support the suggested line of thinking. They always represent the uniqueness and individuality of my respondents and their life stories. These stories are narratives told under particular circumstances, at a particular time, to a particular audience. And in the process of writing, I had to retell them in my own way. Not all stories could be told, although they all deserve attention. My hope is that the stories give the respondents a face and a personality so that the reader can look beyond the theoretical argument and data and recognize the experiences of other human beings.

Return of course requires departure, and the circumstances of departing from one's homeland, as well as the conditions of exile, determine the character of the return process. In order to place the particular experiences of my respondents into a larger framework, the remainder of this chapter presents information on Palestinian migration and the Palestinian refugee problem that is necessary for understanding the particular experiences of the respondents. The Palestinian exile and diaspora communities cannot be understood without an exploration of the historical development of Palestinian national identity, which in turn draws on memory and historiography as important sources (Chapter 2).

The dichotomy of diaspora and homeland, with its inherent tension, is explored in Chapter 3. It relates the discourse on the nature of diasporas in global migration and transnational movements to the notion of a Palestinian diaspora and links it to the image of a homeland as a defining factor for diaspora communities.

The particular return experience of my respondents has to be seen as part of a larger return movement, involving other generations and groups of Palestinian migrants with different experiences and migration histories. Also, the response to returnees by Palestinian society can be understood only by considering the political, economic, and social circumstances of return to Palestine in the period after 1993 (Chapter 4).

The return process in its different stages is described using Turner's concept of liminality, thus defining it as a process of rewriting identities. Chapter 5 compares the two main groups of returnees and their experiences within those stages. In an additional step, by breaking the lineal appearance of the process and linking return to the previous diaspora experience, different aspects of Palestinian identity—namely, political, cultural, and religious ones—are portrayed in the light of changing ideas of identity (Chapter 6). This study claims that the return process is characterized by rewriting these different aspects of identity to adjust to changing circumstances and new experiences.

The liminal character of identities of the Palestinian return migrants I interviewed never truly resolves into full integration, as they constantly have to renegotiate their sense of belonging, ideas of homeland, and definitions of being Palestinian. Thus plans for the future, whether personal, political, or professional, reflect upon their sense of identity and the options for integration into Palestinian society or into the larger frame of a transnational community in a world of global movement (Chapter 7).

Even if physical return to one's place of origin is possible, is it really "return," or is it rather the discovery of a new homeland? Will Palestinians continue to preserve "songs for a country no longer known," or is the question whether they can restore their "sense of self as a people"? How does a country that was "woven from memories, from songs, from stories of elders, from pictures, from old coins and stamps" appear upon return?[8]

The Palestinian Refugee Problem

Who is a refugee?
People who live in camps set up temporarily until they return to their homeland. (Ne'meh Shehadeh)
Someone who has been uprooted from his or her own land, and expelled to another place, and thus was destroyed emotionally and financially. (Taghrid Subhi Najim)
Someone who is lost, he doesn't know where he is. He is unsettled and unable to stay in one location. (Mahmoud Abdul Karim Abu Nahleh)

(QUOTES FROM INTERVIEWS WITH PALESTINIAN
REFUGEES TAKEN FROM YAHYA 1998, 19)

Emigration is a precondition for return. In order to understand how, when, and why people return to their home country, it is imperative to first understand the circumstances that led them to leave, the aspirations and plans they might have had, and the extent to which their emigration was voluntary. Palestinian migration is inextricably linked to the Israeli-Palestinian conflict. Without the war of 1948 and the creation of the state of Israel on the territory of historical Palestine, Palestinians might have become one of the Arab world's post–World War I and II nation-states.

The refugee problem, central to the Israeli-Palestinian conflict, has received the attention of politicians, scholars, and humanitarian organizations. On the humanitarian level, the United Nations and international organizations have attempted to assist the Palestinian refugees living in the Arab world. On the political level, the refugee question and the right of return have been called the core issues of a possible peace process and an end to the conflict.

For Palestinians, it is central to their collective memory, their political life, and their national identity. A solution that ignores Palestinians living in the diaspora is not an acceptable solution for Palestinians in Palestine. For Israelis, it is inconceivable to accept the right of return because it would in practice undermine the Jewish character of the state of Israel, thus they support the settlement of the refugees in the surrounding Arab countries only.

The causes of the Palestinian refugee problem have been well documented, especially in recent years. At the same time, historiography has become one expression of the conflict and is thus a subject of debate among scholars within the two camps.

According to the now commonly accepted version, Palestinians became refugees during the war of 1948 and in its aftermath as a result of pressure to leave their homes. Many were directly forced by the military to leave (these military forces later became the Israeli army); others left out of fear of military intervention. At least 726,000 Arab inhabitants of historical Palestine fled the country during the war, leaving behind their homes, property, and in many cases part of their extended family.[9]

Most of the refugees went to neighboring countries, namely, Jordan, Syria, Lebanon, and Egypt. In fact, even today, the majority (80 percent) of Palestinian refugees live within a hundred miles of the border of historical Palestine (Weighill 1999, 15).

Initially, the refugees expected to return as soon as the war was over. They received assistance from Arab host countries before a United Nations agency was established to provide for their initial needs. The United Nations Relief and Work Agency for Palestine Refugees (UNRWA), founded in 1949, operates in Lebanon, Syria, and Jordan, as well as in the West Bank and Gaza camps. The official UNRWA definition of Palestinian refugees reads: "persons whose normal residence was Palestine during the period of 1 June 1946 to 15 May 1948 and who lost both their homes and means of livelihood as a result of the 1948 conflict and took refuge in one of the countries or areas where UNRWA provides relief, and their descendants through the male line" (www.unrwa.org).[10] UNRWA started to register the refugee population and distribute food and basic equipment for their temporary settlement. Many of the refugees were grouped and settled in camps.

Because of ongoing migration and sometimes unstable conditions in the host countries, a large number of Palestinian refugees are not registered with UNRWA and thus cannot directly receive assistance. Among them are those who failed to register at the required time, those who obtained employment in host countries, those who did not need economic assistance (food, initial housing, health care, and education), and those who refused to register for political reasons. In 1967 only those who were already refugees could retain their status, while first-time refugees were defined as "displaced persons" (Gilen et al. 1994, 24). Palestinians who left Palestine and could not return because their residency permits (issued by Israel) had expired and those expelled for political reasons are also excluded from the official refugee statistics and thus from being recognized or receiving assistance.

UNRWA assistance does not affect the legal status of the refugees in host countries. Moreover, the operation of UNRWA is subject to separate agreements between the agency and each host government. UNRWA does not provide protection; rather, its activity is limited to material assistance, health care, and education.

Palestinian refugees in Arab host countries have been subjected to harsh living conditions. As they developed a distinct national identity and started organizing a national liberation movement, they were at times in direct conflict with host governments. The two main upheavals, "Black September" (1970) in Jordan and the intervention of Israel in the civil war in Lebanon in 1982 directly affected the situation of Palestinian refugees in these countries.[11]

Refugee situations can typically be solved in three ways: repatriation, permanent settlement in the (first) country of asylum, or resettlement in a third country willing to absorb the refugees (Rogge 1994, 16 and Van Hear 1997, 15).[12] In the case of the Palestinians, the Israeli expectation was that the refugees would easily integrate into the neighboring Arab countries, as they shared many features of cultural identity, including language. This assumption, for many reasons, has been proven wrong. One reason was, and is, the political unwillingness of host governments to integrate Palestinians into their societies, mainly based on the insistence of Arab countries on enforcing UN Resolution 194 calling for the return of the refugees to their homes, villages, and towns in Palestine. Full resettlement and citizenship rights, they argue, would jeopardize Palestinian political claims.

Lebanon has its own reasons for not permitting the permanent settlement of its refugee population, as the largely Muslim Palestinian community would threaten the fragile sectarian balance in the state; Palestinians are partly blamed for the fifteen years of civil war in Lebanon.[13]

Palestinians themselves have repeatedly refused resettlement and also insist on their right of return according to international law. Many authors have convincingly argued that the concentration of Palestinians in and around the refugee camps has been an important factor in the development of a Palestinian national identity (Sayigh 1977a, 1977b; Sayigh and Sayigh 1987).

Depending on the situation in each host country, the agreements with UNRWA, and changing political climates, Palestinians in various Arab countries experience various living conditions, legal statuses, and civil rights. Although they form one group of refugees, they are formally separated by the different laws and regulations of each host country. Many of them have been repeatedly evacuated from their places of residence because of war or other crises. A study in 1994 identified three main factors influencing the status of Palestinian refugees in host countries: the external character of legal definitions of them; the conflict of interest at the state level, involving the security and benefit of the host state, which can entail civil rights (such as in Jordan) or near-total exclusion (as in Lebanon); and the inherent contradiction between the Palestinians' interest in securing civil rights, and maintaining the refugee identity (Gilen et al. 1994, 40). It is important to stress that most Palestinians see themselves as refugees and victims, even if some of them have found economic stability, secured citizenship in other countries, or developed multiple identities and loyalties.

Patterns of Palestinian Migration

Over the last fifty years the focus on refugees has led to a neglect of other parts of the Palestinian diaspora and has lost sight of the fact that not all Palestinian migration has been a direct result of flight or expulsion. To portray Palestinian migration solely in terms of refugee waves during and after the wars with Israel would do an injustice to the complexity of Palestinian migratory patterns and would prevent a deeper understanding of the Palestinian migration experience.

In the framework of Palestinian migration, one has to consider not only migration from and to Palestine but also the various movements of Palestinians from first countries of refuge and exile to other countries, and subsequent movement among countries. Many Palestinians have experience with more than one migratory move, thus shaping their sense and longing for a place to call home. This also ties them in different ways to the Palestinian-imagined community as well as to different Palestinian diaspora and home communities.

Currently, four main groups of Palestinians can be distinguished on the territory of historical Palestine and in the diaspora: Palestinians in the West Bank and Gaza, Palestinians in Israel, Palestinians in Arab countries, and Palestinians in Western countries. They do express unity in their self-declaration as Palestinians, though it is for many of them a part of their multiple identities. Nevertheless, they feel that they are part of the Palestinian-imagined community. At the same time, their experiences over the last century have created diversity among them. Important to their maintaining and reproducing a sense of national identity in successive generations is their having knowledge about other groups of their own people.[14]

One cannot place Palestinians into just one or the other of the above-mentioned groups. Frequent movement between the groups continues to occur. Consequently, migration is an important aspect of Palestinian family life, and the reality of this migration is often a painful one. Palestinians have maintained networks all over the world, and modern means of transportation and communication have allowed them to keep in touch with each other. Of course, access to communication technology and travel is based on the ability to afford them, and there are still many Palestinians, especially refugees in the camps, that do not have the means. The problem is further complicated by the absence of a Palestinian state and the absence of travel documents. The stories about the treatment at borders and airports, the anxiety of traveling, and the denial of visas and travel permits are uncountable and are an indistinguishable feature of Palestinian existence. In the introduction to *Palestinian Identity*, Rashid Khalidi writes:

> The quintessential Palestinian experience, which illustrates some of the most basic issues raised by Palestinian identity, takes place at a border, an airport, a checkpoint: in short, at any of those many modern barriers where identities are checked and verified. What happens to Palestinians at these crossing points brings home to them how much they share in common as a people. For it is at these borders and barriers that the six million Palestinians are singled out for "special treatment," and are forcefully reminded of their identity: of who they are, and of why they are different from others. (R. KHALIDI 1997, 1)

Migration studies have shown that migration is often initially perceived as temporary, especially when it is involuntary. Very few migrants are willing or able to burn all bridges to the homeland, as this notion of the homeland includes family, culture, and everything familiar. Forced migration is neither planned nor wished for, thus it usually strengthens the ties to the homeland that one was forced to leave and creates a wish to return one day. In the Palestinian case, the desire to return was often combined with political activities to achieve this goal through military or political struggle. The aim was not only return but also the liberation of Palestine and the creation of an independent Palestinian state.

EMIGRATION FROM PALESTINE

The main causes of emigration for most Palestinians in the diaspora were the wars of 1948 and 1967. These wars prompted different forms of conflict migration, but are nevertheless characterized as forceful and involuntary in nature.

During these wars most Palestinians did not leave their villages and towns with the intention of leaving the country. Often they just moved to the next village, into the nearby hills, or to any place considered safe at that time. Consequently, flight involved several moves away from the place of origin (Abu-Sitta 1996; W. Khalidi 1992; Kanaana 1992b; Morris 1987, 1990). Recent studies show in much historical detail that, in the beginning, Palestinian villagers sent women and children from the villages to take refuge in safer places while the men stayed behind to defend the villages. Many people left their homes during the day and tried to return the following night. As a result of these moves, families were split and siblings separated, some of them never to meet again. During the 1967 war, Palestinians fled in a similar pattern. This time many of them became second-time refugees.

Besides during actual war times, Palestinian migration occurred because of political persecution, economic pressure, and the forcible eviction of political activists. With the evolution of the Palestinian national movement and the formation of a Palestinian national awareness, combined with resistance to the Israeli occupation, Israeli pressure to undermine and destroy Palestinian resistance increased. Some prominent community leaders were expelled, and political activists left Palestine after being subjected to torture, interrogation, and long prison terms in Israeli jails (without first being tried).

The economic deterioration of the West Bank and Gaza and the difficulty of making a living pushed many Palestinians to leave those areas.

High unemployment rates, economic underdevelopment by Israeli design, and Israeli confiscation of much Palestinian agricultural land left young Palestinians with few job options. Educational facilities were rather poor, and as a consequence many young Palestinians left Palestine to study abroad. Those who migrated for work or study often anticipated only a temporary migration.

The choice of country to which to migrate is related to the reasons that the migrant left Palestine in the first place. While having the financial means to get to a particular country was of course very important, the most important factor in determining to which country a migrant would go was legal access to that country. The absence of legal documents such as a passport or an identity card could make travel extremely complicated. Waiting for visas and travel permits is thus familiar to many Palestinians.

European countries, the United States, Canada, and Australia have accepted limited numbers of Palestinians as refugees or immigrants. Many Palestinian migrants have experience with illegal entry and the complicated ways of legalizing one's status in different countries.

Often, migration to Western countries and the oil-rich Gulf States was based on chain migration, that is, migrants followed relatives already living and working in those countries. Especially where the reasons for emigration were economic and educational, relatives would often help finance a new start by providing jobs and loans, or paying a student's tuition. In addition to the ability to enter a country legally, and the ability to afford going there, there was another consideration in choosing a country. This consideration relates to the migrant's images and knowledge of that country. More research is needed to determine how Palestinians have perceived different countries and how their images have influenced migration choices. Although Palestinians often judge other countries by their stand vis-à-vis the Palestinian problem, we know that many have made pragmatic choices about migration based on the economic and legal situation as much as on culture and politics.

(RELATIVE) SETTLEMENT ABROAD

Various factors influence the level of integration into a host society, among them the living conditions and place of residence, their legal status, and the reasons for emigrating. One especially important factor for Palestinians' situation in and integration into host societies has been the legal status to which they were entitled. Certainly the worst situation can be found in Lebanon where Palestinians are not entitled to passports but only to a refugee document that grants nothing but the right to residency, while

Palestinians are by law excluded from a long list of professions and the right to own real estate. Over the last several years, visa, travel, and re-entry regulations for Palestinians have been further tightened. Generally, Lebanon has refused to consider Palestinian refugees for naturalization and resettlement, mainly on political grounds.

In the past, Palestinian refugees have refused to settle in Arab host countries and have insisted on their right of return. Of course the Palestinian-camp situation of refugees is a negation of integration into the host country. It keeps the Palestinian community in confined spaces and reinforces the clear group boundaries. It makes the Palestinians, at least those in the camps, identifiable as an alien minority to themselves as well as to the host society.

The primary reason for emigration is directly linked to the chances and willingness of a Palestinian migrant to integrate or be integrated into a host country. As suggested above, eviction, flight, and deportation during times of conflict strengthen one's connection to the homeland and foster the strong wish to return, as well as the long-term identification with the place of origin.

In such a context, the political attachment of Palestinians to the Palestinian Liberation Organization (PLO) has proved influential in keeping a certain distance between migrants and the host societies. Palestinians involved in the national liberation movement, of which the PLO with its various political movements was a symbol for a long time, would often not get involved in the politics of the host society. And when they did, as in the cases of Jordan and Lebanon, the political power and influence of the PLO and its armed forces proved to have disruptive effects on the host country and ultimately led to conflicts.

Economic success, financial stability, and options for the future, as well as the existence of a family in the host country, can help temporary or long-term settlement and integration. In this context, intermarriage with locals or the birth of children in the host country facilitates integration. Here, gender is of particular interest. In Arab countries and other patriarchal societies, the national identity of the father determines that of the child. Palestinian men marrying women of other nationalities would thus have Palestinian children. In the case of Palestinian women marrying other nationals (which occurs less frequently) the children are not "properly" Palestinian. Nevertheless, the experience of the Palestinian people has created an awareness of national identity that connects children of Palestinian mothers to Palestine, even though they are, according to the laws in these Arab countries, not Palestinian.[15]

Another important factor lies in the generational differences of Palestinian migrants. The age of a migrant at the time that he or she left Palestine plays an important role, both for the possibilities and options of adjustment in the host society and for further migration. In the case of second or third generations of Palestinians in the diaspora, the grandparents or parents were refugees or migrants. These young Palestinians may be more integrated into the host societies, especially through intermarriage, while many other Palestinians still turn to Palestine to find a spouse, sometimes from the extended family or village.

For refugees, emigration was an uprooting. It entailed the loss of family members, land, and homes, and it implied fear and insecurity about the future. Their only consolation was in the hope that they might return soon and in the ability to share their traumatic experience with the Palestinian refugee community. Older people in particular struggled from day to day, trying to survive, to not despair totally, and to keep the family and the community together. For them the memory of life in Palestine was all that was left. The younger generation had to focus on daily life as well, but their eyes were also on Palestine. Out of this longing to go back grew a whole discourse of preserving memories of Palestine before the war, of keeping and passing on an eternal image of the country and its people.

Over the years, some groups of refugees were able to move out of the camps. At the same time, the refugee communities grew in size but became more differentiated according to status and economic situation. From the 1960s onward, political commitment to the PLO and its various organizations also differentiated Palestinian communities.

For Palestinians who were children when they became refugees, and even more for the generations born outside Palestine, the loss of the homeland was total, as they could remember little or nothing. Their actual socialization took place, and still takes place, in other countries and contexts. Depending on the country and situation of residence, the children are formed by the surrounding Palestinian community, if they are part of one, as much as by the society and situation in the respective host countries.

Young people who left in search of an education were more eager to take up the challenges involved in making a new life. They planned to get educational degrees that could help them in Palestine, and upon return they wanted to make a home and have a family in Palestine. Despite the fact that many of them did not plan on emigrating for good, a considerable number stayed abroad. The same is true for work migrants, who usually left because of economic depression and lack of employment and who sought jobs and higher wages in other countries.

For Palestinians who left Palestine to study, as well as for those who were born and grew up abroad, the host country's educational system played an important role in their socialization into the host society. Palestinian children who went to the camps' UNRWA schools, founded and maintained especially for Palestinian refugees, did not experience socialization that would facilitate their integration into a host society. Also, in some Arab countries, Palestinians were discriminated against in access to higher education. Others were marginalized by teachers and peers.

While most Palestinians who left Palestine were peasants, there was also a minority of Palestinians who were from the middle class. The distinction is important in studying their ability to participate in the host country's economy and thereby facilitate integration into the host country's society. Upon their flight, peasants lost their main source of livelihood — the land — and became refugees. The poorer of those refugees were a source of manual labor for the host economies or were unemployed. Over the years, some former peasants earned a living as small shopkeepers and city dwellers, catering to the needs of the growing camp community. Others found employment as seasonal agricultural workers. Between 1948 and 1966, the already difficult situation in the agricultural sector of the surrounding Arab countries condemned most of the refugees to a life of poverty (P. A. Smith 1986b, 93).

During this same time, Palestinians with a higher education moved to the oil-rich Arab countries, in whose economies their skills were valued. Also, urban Palestinians and members of the upper and middle classes were able to transfer some of their assets into exile, which helped them establish themselves economically abroad.

After the war of 1967, which created another wave of Palestinian refugees, the number of those depending on financial assistance from UNRWA again rose dramatically. But the following years witnessed a reverse trend: While in 1949 almost 77 percent of the Palestinian population was receiving relief, thirty years later this figure had declined to 41 percent (P. A. Smith 1986b, 99). Those who were able to achieve self-sufficiency often left the camps and thus the relief rolls. Small businesses in shantytowns and urban quarters provided some income, which was often combined with that of women doing sewing, laundry, and agricultural work, and children contributing as street vendors and messenger boys (P. A. Smith 1986b, 99).

At the other end of the social and economic scale, we find the economically successful exile bourgeoisie. Smith has remarked: "Palestinians, stateless and living by their wits, have been among the leading capitalists of the Middle East" (P. A. Smith 1986a, 23). They are affected by statelessness, although to a lesser degree than poor refugees, and have been major financial supporters of the PLO and Palestinian educational institutions.

The richer part of the Palestinian diaspora can be expected to contribute to the creation of an economically viable Palestinian state whether or not they return to Palestine themselves (see Mustafa 1996, 5).

That Palestinians left Palestine, and, in subsequent migrations, left neighboring Arab countries in search of education and economic opportunities invites a number of questions, most notably what effect their economic success and apparent integration had on their identity as Palestinians. On the one hand, many Palestinians have been naturalized elsewhere; on the other hand, many do not consider their country of citizenship to be their home.

As much as economic situation and legal status, the perception and treatment of the migrants by a host society influence integration. Ironically, while economic success can help integration and encourage acceptance by the host society, it can also cause envy on the part of the local population. In every case migrants are highly dependent on the image assigned to them by locals. Identities are developed in a process that entails being labeled, categorized, and named by others, a process equally important to self-perception and identification.

Economically successful Palestinians have to be considered to balance the picture of the impoverished Palestinian-camp refugees. Seeking economic success has been one driving factor for Palestinian migration and has influenced the level of integration into different host countries. It can be assumed that economic integration makes it more likely that the migrant will accept a host country as a more or less permanent settlement solution, while economic disenfranchisement in tandem with other factors supports a strong wish to return and a stronger attachment to the country of origin.

RETURN WISH

For Palestinians in the diaspora, the cycle of migration would not be complete without the wish or plan to return to Palestine one day.

The intensity of the desire (dream, plan, or "illusion") to return has much to do with the length of time one spends abroad, the degree of integration one achieves there, whether one has moved one or more times, and whether one has actually settled somewhere.[16] Palestinians who have moved many times had less chance to adjust and integrate, and instead developed a strong sense of Palestinian identity and a sense of being different from the people of the host societies.

With each year spent outside Palestine, the distance from the home society widens, and the familiarity with its details and developments and the intimate knowledge of it decreases. Some Palestinians were able to visit Palestine regularly, while others, especially the refugees, never saw their homeland. These issues play a role in the decision to return and in respondents' identification with Palestine as an actual place to live. There is a strong correlation between being prevented from visiting one's homeland and the intensity of the longing for return. Those who had no opportunity to see Palestine during their exile have higher expectations of that homeland than those who did get to visit.

Younger Palestinians often emphasize that the discussion of the right of return no longer means that all Palestinians around the world would actually return to Palestine to settle there. That demand seems unrealistic — the real issue for them revolves around having the right to choose where they want to live. Israel has made even visiting their homeland impossible for many Palestinians over the last fifty years.

To understand the situation that Palestinian returnees find upon arrival in Palestine, as well as the reactions of local Palestinians to them, one has to remember the disruptive effect that migration had on Palestinian family and societal structures. Of course, migration can also have the reverse effect of enriching a society. By bringing in new ideas and influences, migrants can help renew the society as well as bring about stability by challenging values, customs, and traditions, which can consequently produce a stronger conviction of one's own cultural system. Virtually every Palestinian family has experienced migration as separation from family members and the need for long-distance communication. Certainly, return migration is a new challenge to family ties, affection, and relations between people.

Migration not only changes the lives of those who migrate but it also questions those who stay behind about their aspirations in life and their relationship to the migrants. In the Palestinian case, the matter is further complicated by the conflict with Israel and the mutual perceptions of those who stayed behind and those who left — regardless of the reasons for and circumstances of their departure. These emigrants often have to deal with the tension between some Palestinians' image of them as cowards and traitors who left the country alone in difficult circumstances, and their self-image as both fighters and activists for the liberation of Palestine, working from the outside.

Local Palestinians face a similar tension between some diaspora Palestinians' image of them as collaborators who accepted Israeli rule and occupation, and their self-image as people exercising steadfastness, not giving up on the homeland under any circumstances. The events of the Intifada have raised Palestinian "inside" confidence and moved political activity from the outside back to Palestine. Many local Palestinians insist that they have had their share of casualties for initiating the peace process.

Either way, both self-perception and the image of the other as different make sense of one's life experience, but both also produce conflict. Of course these images are negotiable and can be adjusted over time, but they explain, to a certain extent, the clash that occurred when the diaspora Palestinians returned to Palestine.

CHAPTER 2

**Palestinian National Identity,
Memory, and History**

*Do we exist? What proof do we have?
The further we get from the Palestine of our past,
the more precarious our status, the more
disrupted our being, the more intermittent our
presence. When did we become "a people"?
When did we stop being one? Or are we in the
process of becoming one? What do those big
questions have to do with our intimate
relationships with each other and with others?
We frequently end our letters with the mottoes
"Palestinian love" and "Palestinian kisses." Are
there really such things as Palestinian intimacy
and embraces?* (SAID 1986B, 34)

National identity in different forms is something young Palestinians bring
back from their diaspora locations to Palestine when they return. They do
not have their own traumatic memories of 1948, but they know about the
Nakba as a part of the collective memory of their people. Their national
identity is framed and defined by how they were raised, by historiography, by political discourse, and by their experiences in various Palestinian
communities.

The emergence of a Palestinian national identity as a collective phenomenon has been a subject of debate on both the political and the scholarly levels. Denying Palestinians a national identity and character as a
people means delegitimizing their claims to a Palestinian state. Since 1948,
Israel has invested efforts in doing exactly that and has only recently acknowledged that Palestinians are a people, their neighbors, and that they
have a right to self-determination in a yet to be defined form. In the
dispute regarding national identities and self-perceptions on both sides,
Israelis and Palestinians have referred to their respective historiographies
to support their political claims.

Khalidi has argued that the Palestinian historical narrative is most often a counter-narrative to the Israelis' historiography. It works only in one direction: Israelis always have to be heard when a Palestinian voice is aired, while the reverse is not true (R. Khalidi 1997, 147).

Presenting Palestinians' narratives about their sense of national identity lends a voice to them and attempts to let them speak without the counter-narrative. One such voice is that of Tariq, who found his very own way of defining how he is Palestinian and what repercussions this fact has on his life.

Tariq's Story

If there were no Palestinian cause I would have to invent it.

Tariq was part of the foreign community in Ramallah/Jerusalem and worked at a joint Israeli/Palestinian nongovernmental organization (NGO) in Jerusalem. He was a voluntary returnee who came to Palestine to find out what being Palestinian meant for him. He was very committed to the Palestinian cause by virtue of his work, which focused on media activism and international information. At the same time, he was very critical of Palestinian politics and the peace process as it developed.

At the time of the interview, he had been in Palestine for almost two years and was beyond the initial period of finding out and adjusting to the realities of the country. Tariq was very outspoken, but it was easier to get him to talk about Palestine and the Palestinians, nationalism, philosophy, and struggle than about his family and other personal topics.

Tariq was born in Kuwait to a Palestinian father and an American mother. Both his parents were Christians. He called himself Palestinian American because of his parents' origins. Growing up in Kuwait, where his father worked, he knew of the existence of the Palestinian community there but did not feel a part of it. His father was born in Jaffa and his family had lived in Jerusalem before 1948. His grandfather had studied in Germany, and the family could be traced back to Syria, Lebanon, and different parts of Palestine. In 1948 the family left a few days before the end of the British Mandate, foreseeing the problems to come before the actual war broke out. They went to Syria where some relatives lived and later to Lebanon where they were granted citizenship.[1]

Tariq went to an international school in Kuwait where students learned Arabic but general instruction was in English. The students came from many different nations; a considerable part of the student body was Palestinian and many more of the students were Arabs. His father had never been politically involved; he focused on establishing himself economically in Kuwait and providing for his wife and five children. Tariq remembered the situation of Palestinians in Kuwait and the legal restrictions on foreigners in general as contrasted with that of the Kuwaitis, who had property but had little education and let foreigners work for them. Palestinians were in the middle of the social strata, doing the more skilled jobs (though some worked in garages, etc., as well), but they were never in the lowest ranks like Indians and Filipinos. He described his family as being in the upper-middle class. Through classmates and friends, he was connected to the Palestinian community, but he recalled that these were personal relations that did not create for him an image of the Palestinian people and their history.

The family would spend the school year in Kuwait and the summer in the United States with maternal relatives. His father was not only uninterested in political engagement but also hardly ever talked about Palestine, either in political or personal terms, though he had been ten years old when the family left Palestine, and most certainly remembered the country. Because of his work, he also spent little time with the family. In addition, there was relatively little contact with Palestinian relatives and, on the rare occasions when they met, their communication was limited because Tariq and his siblings spoke little Arabic. He described the family as very unemotional and was very factual about them. He tried to understand his father's motives in how he raised his children and made his life choices.

> I grew up unable to express my emotions in the house. I had a lot of problems with depression, but I realized that I could do college, I was a good student. I prided myself with how well I could adapt to situations, but it is so exhausting and so hurtful, there was a lot of pains . . . like I never said goodbye to anything, to Kuwait, it was as if emotions didn't count. The only thing was to concentrate on your work and see how much you could do.

Tariq's life changed overnight when the outbreak of the Gulf War prevented the family from returning to Kuwait after spending the summer in the United States. They not only had to decide about the children's schooling, but because they were cut off from their savings in Kuwait, they had to cut back on their lifestyle and lived in a small house with Tariq's grandparents. The parents decided to send the children to boarding schools and colleges. Later, when his father was able to go back to Kuwait (a rare exception, as many other Palestinians were unable), the family bought a house in the United States and settled there, with the father running the business in Kuwait. They spent all their savings on their children's education.

Tariq vividly described how the inability to return to Kuwait drastically changed his life. The media coverage of the Gulf War and his surprise about the ignorance of the American public, together with his personal experience of being different in school, made him aware of his identity.

> Imagine all of a sudden seeing your home on television, on CNN. It looks almost like a video game. It was really bizarre. I didn't know how to feel about a lot of things. There were a lot of unanswered questions. I knew I didn't fit in in Kuwait and obviously not in America. And Americans, they weren't accepting me so much. I mean all they had to do was ask my name and they would say, what is this name? I was different, especially because it was a discriminating society, a wealthy school, and kids who didn't know anything but American lifestyle. So, I didn't fit in so well. I tried to adapt and I realized I could do that very fast and I did it. I didn't care too much. I tried to hide my identity, I didn't like being a specimen, I didn't like being a refugee kid type of thing, I didn't like attention being brought to me.

His way of dealing with the disturbance he felt inside about his identity made him decide to study the Middle East in college. He learned about Palestinian history and Zionism and tried to integrate his knowledge into his personal life. This was made more challenging by the presence of pro-Israeli teachers. Thus, he not only learned "the facts" and how to evaluate them, but he was also radicalized by the experience, which implanted in him a strong sense that injustice was being done to him and his fellow Palestinians. His girlfriend encouraged him to start keeping a diary and writing articles on his reflections and ideas and to learn more about Palestine.

In a way, it was his discovery of philosophy as a tool for understanding the world and his "Palestinianness" that enabled him to distance himself enough to bear the dramatic inner changes taking place. Along the way, he lost his faith:

> I used to be religious as well. In Kuwait I used to go to church and there was a religious community there that was quite strong. And when we went to America I tried to keep it up, but I started losing faith, as we say. And philosophy began answering some of those questions, too. So it gave me tools of self-identity. . . . I started turning those questions on to who I was and why the hell I was in America and what it meant. I didn't

exist from nowhere; I was part of a historical continuum, I was a part of
the people. My father wasn't in Kuwait for nothing, I wasn't in America
for nothing, my father couldn't go back to Kuwait for nothing, my father
wasn't allowed a business in Kuwait for nothing. It all had meaning to it.

He put his energy into a project and scholarship application that became
the starting point of his commitment to Palestine and the quest for a Palestinian identity.

I wanted to study Palestinian identity in diaspora, compare the Palestinian diaspora. . . . I wrote a proposal; I just wanted to go to the different
communities. By that time I knew enough about Palestinians and what
it means to be Palestinian and the history. It is not a dry thing at all,
especially for me; it feels like a fire inside of me. Especially the identity
questions and especially if it invokes a sense of injustice. . . . I wanted
to study the communities in Syria, Lebanon, the West Bank, and inside
Israel and what it meant to be Palestinian, because by that time I had formulated a consciousness of "what does it mean to be Palestinian? What
does it really mean?" There is no essence to being Palestinian, and I was
combining philosophy and nationalism to begin with. There is no center
of being Palestinian; people who have never been in Palestine consider
themselves Palestinians—what the hell does that mean? And those whose
grandfathers died in that land and all that. I didn't know what it meant
and these questions were burning on my mind and that motivated me.

Although he did not get the scholarship, the project had developed his
passionate interest in these issues. At the end of college he decided to write
his thesis on a Palestinian topic:

So I did my thesis on nationalism, and my case was the Palestinians. I
did a philosophical study on what nationalism really means. And then
what it means in the Palestinian context. So I both wrote the Palestinian
history and I did a philosophical study on nationalism. . . . In the end it
was a strong support of nationalism, so it was called "Palestinianism: The
Making of the Palestinian National Movement."

In the introduction to the thesis he wrote:

Yes, I am part Palestinian, and try as I may to overcome the subjectivity
of my position, I inevitably fail. Yet my failure is perhaps not much more
than any other observer or critic. It may in fact be less. Knowing the
weaknesses of one's own position can only become a strength. . . . Occasionally my narrative may appear quite linear and rational. Other times, I

appear to be imbued with a passion that cannot necessarily be said to be rational. The fact is, aspects of identity and nationality exist in a parallel, tiered framework that is difficult to express without actually showing. It is possible for the multitude and polarity of emotions and attitudes to coexist in one individual, as well as in one community.[2]

After finishing college he decided to go to Palestine to find out for himself what it meant to be Palestinian. His trip was organized and supported by Jewish American contacts from college, a fact that he had difficulty reconciling with his Palestinian nationalist ideas. When he arrived in Palestine after having learned so much about Palestinian nationalism and Palestinian history, he was at first disappointed, because, he said:

> before I had an idealism about Palestinians especially; you believe in the trueness and the justice of their cause and then you come over here and there are bad Palestinians and they are not so straight and not so pure. And so when you come here you realize the grayness, as opposed to black and white. . . . There is Palestinian youth, in universities; they are richer kids and they don't really care that much about it. After the authority came, after Oslo, no one cares about these things so much. And it disturbed me. I didn't like the fact that people didn't care so much. Of course, I was coming as an outsider and everyone was telling me: Wait until you are here for a long time and you have to deal with all these things, you will become as complacent and as jaded as we are. In some sense it was motivating; I am much more motivated because I have seen how lazy many Palestinians are.

His experience working with and for Israeli and Palestinian academics was a deep disappointment and strengthened his belief in activism as opposed to academics. He was very outspoken about these academic encounters:

> And last year I wasn't doing activism, I was doing bullshit; I was writing papers for people who can never accomplish what they talk about, like cooperation and peace process, and a lot of phony stuff, just so that they can make money and make the news bigger and sell the right of the Palestinians for their own popularity, which is really disgusting.

It was the encounter with "normal people," refugees in a camp near Bethlehem where he lived with a family for some time, that gave him a sense of personal connection to Palestine.

> It was personal contact with these people who have suffered an incredible amount, but remained human throughout it, and I am not being

romantic here, remained throughout it honest, decent people who are just asking for simple rights, justice to their cause.

It was those people and their fate that personally affected him:

> I am getting comprehensive, when you look at the experience of millions of Palestinians getting by with some here and there, whatever they can make, and adapting to situations and just trying to make their malaise go by and politics is secondary here. They care about their family so much more, and if Palestinians would have ever had a chance, they wouldn't really be political. I mean, they weren't political to begin with. It is something forced upon them, and no one asked the Palestinians: They were kicked out. Even now the national movement is nothing of what it should be.

He felt that it was his responsibility to use his command of English and knowledge of the United States to benefit the Palestinians and their cause. He criticized the United States but, nevertheless, saw the need to address American audiences and fight for the Palestinian cause in the media, especially because in the past Palestinians had been weak and unsuccessful in this regard. The experience in Palestine, which is a combination of disappointments, new realities, and appreciation of him as a person, and his presence in Palestine and his work for Palestinians have given him more confidence.

> So I feel secure with where I am and . . . now the only struggle is to look forward to what I can do. . . . I know that I want to write books and poetry, I want to write fiction, I have to get into movies, I would really like to make movies.

For Tariq the future in terms of where to live was open, but it strongly pointed to a lifelong dedication to Palestine. In terms of material settlement, he was quite flexible about where and how to live.

Three main factors were responsible for distancing him from a strong Palestinian identity: his American mother, his Palestinian father (who was distant from Palestinian politics and the Palestinian community in Kuwait), and a sense of being different because he was Christian in a Muslim country (Kuwait). Yet Tariq had in a unique way developed such an identity. His idea of Palestine was clearly defined by what he called the Palestinian cause, the historical and political aspects of what has been done to the Palestinian people. His imagination was not romantic, not tied to personal or family memories, but was rather a rational or rationalized approach to what turned out to be the center of his life. His "unemotional" upbringing, the lack of emotional expression, was balanced by his practice of writing. His wish to write poetry and make movies especially points to a creative way of finding an outlet for his thoughts and emotions through artistic expression.

His future was not so much a matter of personal wishes, but of his concern for what happens to the Palestinians. At the same time, he was relatively independent in terms of personal relations, self-sufficient and able to adjust to new people and settings. He was involved in Palestinian society, but not socially integrated. That left him with more personal freedom, both because he was a man and because he was without a family in Palestine.

National Identity

Theoretical approaches to nations and nationalism are political theories developed in a European context, based on the development of nation-states in Europe. They emphasize territory, a shared economy, and sets of legal rights for the members of a nation on the one hand, and ethnic group identity and a shared myth of origin on the other. More recent approaches have pointed to the fact that these myths and identities are historical products and thus subject to creation, change, and dissolution (A. Smith 1991, 14–24). Markers of such national identities can be religion, language, customs, and institutions.

Anderson's influential term, the "imagined community" (Anderson 1994), is rooted in anthropology rather than political science. His idea of nationalism builds on language and the emergence of print media, specifically a vernacular print language that replaced the dominant dynastic languages of pre-modernity. He argues that imagined communities could only come into being through the existence of such sources of information as newspapers, which provide the members of a nation with a feeling of being linked by the same information (33). Anderson concentrates on "cultural roots," the origin of perceptions of people that lead them to see themselves as a nation, and the role of language, printing as a modern technology, and a changing market in early capitalist society. His model pays less attention to territorial or ethnic aspects of national identity. Thus, it emphasizes the invented nature of nations and nationalism.

The case of Palestinian nationalism is more complex, as Palestinians so far have no state, and the historical circumstances that led to the emergence of a Palestinian national movement are complicated and involve more players than just the Palestinians and a colonial power or dynastic ruler. Moreover, Palestinian claims of nationhood and the right to a nationalist movement have been contested since the early twentieth century, mainly by the Zionist movement and the state of Israel. Thus, all scholarship on the issue tends to be political and politicized.

If history is the basis for understanding national identity, then a study of Palestinian identity would be "an exploration of the interplay between different narratives that make up Palestinian history, meant to illuminate aspects of the identity of a people about which much has been written and said, but little understood" (R. Khalidi 1997, 11).

The Discourse on Palestinian Identity

In order to discuss "definitions" of Palestinian identity, it is useful to look first at the emergence of Palestinian identity as a scholarly concept. Parallel to the historical development of Palestinian national identities, we find reflections on the issue in several texts.

One of the early articles, published in 1975, is titled "Cultural Determinants of Palestinian Collective Identity: The Case of the Arabs in Israel." It argues that Israeli Arabs had acquired a sense of identity as part of the Palestinian people and that the "Arabs of Palestine" perceived themselves as people in a particular territory with a common "pattern of speech" and a, however brief, shared historical experience (K. Nakhleh 1975, 34). It was as a result of 1948 and the loss of territory that Palestinians became aware of the territorial component of their group identity and developed it into a symbol of "autonomy, stability, and return" (34). The author does not call Palestinians a nation, but emphasizes their being ethnically Arab, not Palestinian.

Two years later, Sayigh notes that Palestinians prior to 1948 had two ways of identifying themselves, as Arabs and as originating from a particular place, class, or sect. Following the dispersal of the Palestinians in 1948, it was the specificity of the Palestinian experience that made Palestinians different from other Arabs. In a study of Palestinian-camp refugees in Lebanon, Sayigh found that it was the second generation of refugees who identified with Palestinianism more than with Arabism, while until 1975 many had still identified with ideals of pan-Arabism. Palestinians were confronted with the actual experience of living in Arab host countries such as Lebanon, Syria, Jordan, and Egypt. The tense relationship with the host society and developments within the Palestinian communities enforced the development of Palestinian national consciousness (Sayigh 1977a, 3).

It was in 1977 that Edward Said published his path-breaking study of

Zionism and its impact on Palestine and the Palestinians. In *The Question of Palestine* he claims that Palestine became a "predominantly Arab and Islamic country by the end of the seventh century" (Said 1992, 10) and during the late nineteenth century developed a sense of belonging to the Arab nation, while their opposition to British rule and Jewish colonization together with their shared language and the sense of threat to the community defined them as Palestinians.

In a series of articles from 1979 to 1980, the author avoids the term "identity" altogether. He speaks of "the development of Palestinian entity-consciousness" and describes the Palestinian national independence movement, while attributing to the Palestinians of the Mandate period "both a sense of particularist identity and a link with the Arab world" (Shuaibi 1979/1980, 67). He argues that 1948 erased the concept of a Palestinian entity and that it was only revived by the emergence of Fatah (reverse acronym for *harakat al-tahrir al-filastiniyya*, Palestinian Resistance Movement) movement in the early 1960s.

Almost two decades later, a book with the title *Palestinian Identity* rejected the prevalent assumption that Palestinian national identity emerged in response to and as a result of the rise of Zionism and the creation of the State of Israel. Zionism only helped shape the specific form of this identity (R. Khalidi 1997, 20). Instead, the author argued that the formative years for Palestinian national identity were 1917–1923. Drawing from Anderson's imagined community, the author described the Palestinian urban elite's increasing inclination toward accepting a "growing national identification with Palestine, as the Arab residents of the country increasingly came to 'imagine' themselves as part of a single community" (149). And although he saw this identification as overlapping with other loyalties and identities, he identified it as both new and extremely powerful (150, 20).

These examples suggest how scholarship on Palestinian nationalism has evolved in parallel with larger theoretical developments and been influenced by political positions and challenges. Palestinian approaches to a national historical narrative have reflected a conscious attempt to achieve recognition as a people with legitimate claims to self-determination.

Palestinian National Identity: A Historical Overview

The emergence of a distinct Palestinian national identity is closely linked to key events in Palestine and the surrounding Middle Eastern countries. Migration itself is crucial for the development of the Palestinian national movement.[3]

If one agrees with the argument concerning the origins of Palestinian national identity, an overview would have to start by looking at two main developments in the Middle East at the turn of the century. There was, on the one hand, the rise of Arab nationalism, fueled by growing resistance to the weakening Ottoman rule in the region. On the other hand, Zionism as an ideology and settlement project increasingly affected Palestine. In fact, Palestinian peasants increasingly resisted Jewish immigration and the establishment of early Zionist settlements. And although during that period the Jewish settlers legally purchased land on which to build their new settlements, these land sales were met with opposition from the Palestinian peasants. The Jewish immigrants were considered strangers, and the peasant opposition, at times, resulted in clashes with the settlers. The *fallahin* (peasants) were, to some extent, supported by intellectuals and politicians and were vital in mobilizing public opinion in Palestine and the Arab world (R. Khalidi 1997, 114).

The second element in the development of a Palestinian identity in this early stage is closely linked to the development of the Arab print media, in particular, newspapers and journals. As Anderson has suggested, newspapers played a decisive role in the emergence of nationalist feelings. Khalidi shows how the Arab debate on Zionism was reflected in the media, especially in the intellectual and economic centers in Beirut and Cairo, but increasingly also in the urban centers of Palestine. At the same time, and despite censorship, the early Arab press reflected the rise of secular Arab nationalism in the region, a development that did not leave the Palestinian intellectual elite untouched (R. Khalidi 1997, 119–144).

It should be remembered that during this early period Palestinian identity presented a new element in the makeup of identities of the inhabitants of Palestine. Khalidi speaks of "the existence of overlapping senses of identity" and lists "transnational, religious, local and family loyalties" as some of the most important, not only for Palestinians, but for most inhabitants of the Arab Middle East (20). In the case of Palestine, he notes a strong religious attachment to the country for both Muslims and Christians, together with regional and local attachments—the urban population to towns and cities, the peasants to their villages and the land, and both urbanites and villagers to larger regions within Palestine. He describes all these as elements of Palestinian identity existent before 1948 and changing throughout the first half of the twentieth century.

The decades following World War I proved to be crucial to the emergence of different expressions of a strong Palestinian national identity. This historical development can be divided into three main stages:

1917–1948 — transformation from Syrians/Arabs to Palestinian Arabs
1948–1967 — transformation from Palestinian Arabs to Palestinian refugees
1967 onward — transformation from Palestinian refugees to Palestinians
(Peretz 1993; Kjorlien 1993, 1).

World War I ended for the Middle East with the partition of the former Ottoman provinces, which also led to the emergence of Arab nation-states. During the period from 1917 until 1948, the most crucial factor for Palestine was the British Mandate over Palestine. British rule in Palestine was perceived as colonial rule. In addition, Zionist immigration, supported by the British since the Balfour Declaration in 1917, caused considerable protest and resistance within the Palestinian population, especially the "urban, literate upper and middle class and highly politicized segments of the population" (R. Khalidi 1997, 173).

Religious (Islamic) discourse played a significant role in mobilizing nationalist protest. From the beginning of the British Mandate, the Islamic movement in Palestine adopted a nationalist discourse, and "secular nationalist" movements were often headed by prominent religious figures, thus creating a discourse that merged religious, nationalist, and pan-Arabist ideas (Budeiri 1997, 195).[4]

At the same time, the press and the educational system developed an Arab nationalist discourse that displayed distinctly Palestinian aspects in the frame of a larger Arab nationalism and facilitated the spread of these ideas beyond the cities and the literate population (R. Khalidi 1997, 172).

The Palestinian protest against Zionist settlements and British rule peaked during the revolt of 1936–1939, which was spurred by economic decline, large land sales to Jewish settlers and organizations, and shifts in the demographic and social structure of Palestine. The rebellion was carried out mainly by Palestinian peasants under the leadership of urban intellectual and political figures. Thus, the peasants became a "national signifier" for Palestinian historiography and nationalist discourse (Swedenburg 1990, 18).[5]

Despite the existence of a Palestinian-Arab national consciousness, a perceived link to Palestine as a territory, and overlapping loyalties and identities, Palestinians did not develop a strong enough national movement to prevent or resist the catastrophic events of 1948. The Nakba turned more than 726,000 Palestinian Arabs into refugees within a few months, expelling them from their houses and lands. As a result, not only did the Palestinian Arabs become Palestinian refugees, but the remaining Palestinian population was turned into a minority in their own homeland.

Egypt occupied the Gaza Strip, while the West Bank was declared part of Transjordan by the Jordanian king. These Arab moves could be interpreted as an expression of pan-Arab attempts to rescue as much as possible of Palestine.

The refugees were too shocked by the expulsion and the miserable economic and living conditions that they had to endure in the refugee camps in surrounding Arab countries to immediately develop a plan for national liberation. The Nakba destroyed the traditional social structure of Palestinian society and disconnected the rural population from their source of livelihood—the land—and their direct loyalty to it. As a result, the land and return to it became significant national symbols. The loss of the land increased its significance and supported cohesion within the group, while threats and opposition from the surrounding populations (both Israelis and other Arabs) reinforced their self-perception as a distinct group (K. Nakhleh 1975, 32; Kjorlien 1993, 1).

During the first years after the Nakba, Palestinians took the Arab people who had just achieved independence as a model. Thus, they consolidated their links with and support for the Arab nationalist cause by joining pan-Arab organizations and by contributing to the socioeconomic development of their host countries (Shuaibi 1979/1980, 67).

The dispersal of Palestinians also scattered their traditional leadership, and its failure to prevent the events discredited it in the eyes of Palestinians. Ultimately, it was the shared trauma of 1948 that "reinforced preexisting elements of identity, sustaining and strengthening a Palestinian self-definition that was already present. The shared events of 1948 thus brought the Palestinians closer together in terms of their collective consciousness, even as they were physically dispersed all over the Middle East and beyond" (R. Khalidi 1997, 22).

The war of 1967 aggravated this condition of dispersal. The development of the Palestinian national movement and its discourse of identity has taken place while parts of the Palestinian community have lived as a minority within Israel, under Israeli occupation in the West Bank and Gaza, and in Arab countries as well as others.

The Palestinian National Movement: Dispersal and Statelessness

Palestinian national identity cannot be understood separate from the emergence of the Palestinian national movement. Taking the national movement as the determining factor, historians have often assumed that a genuine Palestinian national identity did not emerge until the 1960s, thus declaring the years between 1948 and 1960 a time in which political activity was absorbed by other factors (R. Khalidi 1997, 180). The disempowerment and loss of credibility of the traditional Palestinian leadership elite because of the events of 1948, combined with the "failure" of the Palestinian resistance to prevent the creation of the State of Israel, were factors in the delayed formation of an effective political movement. It robbed the early Palestinian national movement of its political leadership. In the years that followed, a younger generation of educated Palestinians, often graduates of Arab universities and mostly from a lower- or middle-class background, emerged as new leaders (R. Khalidi 1997, 180).

Palestinians in Israel were actively prevented even from cultural expression of their identity and were completely repressed in terms of political activity. Jordan, which claimed the West Bank as part of its territory, gave Palestinians Jordanian citizenship and had an interest in actively preventing nationalist Palestinian expression or organization (Heacock 1999, 2).

Another powerful factor was the ideological influence of pan-Arabism. Consequently, the Palestinian liberation movement was Arab nationalist in character, and the logic of its appeal applied on two levels. The Arab national identity of the Palestinians was part of their set of overlapping identities at the time, and thus it made sense for Palestinians to attach themselves to this ideology. Second, the at least nominal commitment of the Arab states, as well as their participation in the war of 1948, had Palestinians hoping that the Arab states would support the Palestinians' aspirations of liberating Palestine from Israeli rule and expelling the Israelis (R. Khalidi 1997, 181). In addition, the condition of the Palestinian organizations and the complete destruction of institutions left Palestinians temporarily dependent on other Arab political institutions. Many Palestinian activists joined national pan-Arab parties and movements in the 1950s (Baumgarten 1991, 120). Many Palestinians joined the Movement of Arab Nationalists (R. Khalidi 1997, 182).

Meanwhile, the new Palestinian leadership began to form. Because the Arab states did not support the formation of nationalist organizations, Palestinians developed what has been termed a "culture of resistance" (Heacock 1999, 2), especially in Egypt, the Gulf States (which had already become a destination for Palestinian work migrants), and, later, Jordan. This development of a Palestinian culture of resistance outside Palestine planted the seed for the emergence of Palestinian identity as a diasporic identity or, at the least, for a deep rift in political identity between those Palestinians living "inside" and those living "outside." Mass organizations, such as the General Union of Palestinian Students, allowed the emergence of a Palestinian resistance movement on their fringes, while most Palestinians were challenged by the adjustment to life in the host country and the daily struggle for economic survival.

At the end of the 1960s, a new Palestinian organization appeared. First, a secret circle of political activists from different movements (notably the Muslim Brothers, Communists, and Baathists; see Shuaibi 1979/1980, 79), called Fatah (Palestinian Resistance Movement) was formally founded on January 1, 1960 (Baumgarten 1991, 133–215). It was to become "an entirely independent, wholly Palestinian, purely nationalist movement in the diaspora, dedicated to regaining Palestine (later on, part of Palestine) for the Palestinians through armed struggle (much later, diplomatic means)" (Heacock 1999, 3).

Fatah quickly gained support among Palestinians all over the Arab world and in parts of the diaspora in the West. Over the next decade or so it was to have more difficulty in recruiting Palestinians in Israel, as well as in the West Bank and Gaza. Thus, it came to be a nationalist movement of Palestinians outside Palestine and placed the center of political activity in the diaspora. In its main publication, *Filastinuna* (Our Palestine), Fatah called for the establishment of a Palestinian entity and for a detachment of Palestinian goals from wider Arab nationalism (Baumgarten 1991, 133–150; Shuaibi 1979, 80–84).

When, in 1964, the Palestinian Liberation Organization (PLO) was established, it was intended to be an instrument of Arab nationalist, especially Egyptian, policy (Heacock 1999, 2). And although it had wide Palestinian support, its primary achievement was legitimacy in the Arab world, particularly Jordan. Founding the PLO to represent the Palestinians in the absence of a state, and the start of wide-scale military activities, mainly carried out by Fatah cells since 1965, marked a new phase in the development of Palestinian national identity.

The failure of the Arab armies during the war of 1967 resulted in the Israeli occupation of the West Bank and Gaza, but it did not destroy Palestinian political structures. It reunited the Palestinians inside Palestine (as it reconnected the territory inside the Green Line with the albeit occupied West Bank and Gaza) and, through armed struggle, strengthened the base of support of the Palestinian resistance movement. This marked the third phase in the formation of the Palestinians: going from being Palestinian refugees to being Palestinians.

Between 1967 and 1969, the PLO radically changed its political profile. With the election of Yasir Arafat, the leader of Fatah, to the post of chairman of the PLO in 1969, the organization was transformed into the legitimate and accepted representative of the Palestinian people and became the leader of the struggle for an independent Palestine (Baumgarten 1991, 217).

Many authors agree that the battle of Al-Karama in March 1968 was significant for Palestinian identity building because the event was quickly mythologized by nationalists. Even today the battle has a symbolic meaning for Palestinians because it demonstrated that defeat (if only temporary) of the Israeli army by Palestinian fighters was possible. Despite the Palestinian casualties, the battle was an ideological success and shows how important events in history, as a shared collective memory, can be used for identity building. In a more critical way, Khalidi calls Al-Karama, which means "dignity," "a case of a failure against overwhelming odds brilliantly narrated as heroic triumph" (R. Khalidi 1997, 197).

In the following two decades the gap between inside and outside stayed one of the dominant features of Palestinian identity. Inside, the Communist Party (CP), an indigenous political organization, developed its grassroots activities against the occupation. The disadvantages of the CP were its secular orientation, the support from the Soviet Union, and the advocacy of a two-state solution at a time when the PLO was calling for the military liberation of the entire Palestinian homeland. Gradually, the PLO gained more ideological influence on the inside (Heacock 1999, 5).

Meanwhile, the Palestinian national movement faced severe crises in 1970, when Jordan rejected the presence of a Palestinian pseudo-state on its territory, and in 1982, when, as a result of the Israeli invasion of Lebanon, and the Lebanese civil war, the PLO's institutions and cadres had to move to Tunisia. Both events were a blow to Palestinian institution building in the diaspora, and the move to Tunis geographically disconnected parts of the Palestinian diaspora from Palestine. In both Jordan and Lebanon, Palestine had always been a neighboring country and homeland, literally visible and at close proximity. At the same time, the hostility of the host states reinforced Palestinian in-group cohesion and reminded them of their unique, vulnerable status.

The events of 1982 had a direct effect on the relations between inside and outside and on the growing domination of the PLO and especially Fatah over the inside leadership. The PLO lost its bases on the Israeli border, and Palestinian forces were removed to distant locations in North Africa and Yemen. The PLO wanted to concentrate on the West Bank and Gaza but did not want to lose its authority to the inside leadership (Heacock 1999, 6). The PLO leadership could not travel between inside and outside, but it was not willing to share its power or delegate responsibilities. At the same time, a growing sense of disillusionment became apparent, with Palestinians asking critical questions about why they had not achieved any major change in their situation, instead being "defeated" and expelled time and again.

The connotation of "inside" and "outside" was also changing. Until the late seventies, being from the inside implied a kind of unspoken suspicion toward those Palestinians who lived under Israeli rule, first only inside Israel, but since 1967 in the West Bank and Gaza as well. Later, these Palestinians were considered privileged, because they were already there, in Palestine and were thus entitled "to a kind of grace denied the rest of us" (Said 1986a, 51). Said explains this change in the perception of the Palestinians who stayed as resulting from the political "failure" of the Palestinians in exile. This new attitude reflects the mood of exiled Palestinians before the outbreak of the Intifada (the Palestinian uprising in the Occupied Territories) and the power shift from the outside to the inside.

The start of the Intifada in December 1987 took the PLO leadership by surprise. The uprising itself boosted Palestinian self-confidence and called for new strategies in the national struggle, thereby moving the center of Palestinian activity back to Palestine (R. Khalidi 1997, 200). In Palestinian collective memory, the events of the Intifada shifted their identity from that of victim to that of proud Palestinian. For Palestinians in the diaspora, the youth of the Intifada became a source of pride and thus reinforced Palestinian national identity. And although the outside leadership quickly gained influence on the United National Leadership of the Uprising by constant communication, the declaration of independence (November 15, 1988) in Tunis and the start of the Madrid negotiations can be attributed to the growing weight of the inside movement.

The return of parts of the PLO leadership to Palestine, and the joined although not unproblematic construction of Palestinian institutions in the West Bank and Gaza saw the development of Palestinian national identity come full circle. Palestinians have been accepted as negotiation partners by Israel and the United States, have signed agreements, and were hoping to achieve statehood through agreements yet to be implemented. Most recently, these negotiation partners have challenged the same Palestinian leadership—namely, President Arafat—and the Palestinians have been called upon to replace their leadership with a more democratic one.

It is the absence of a Palestinian state that makes the history of Palestinian national identity different from those of the surrounding Arab states, in which people have lived for more than half a century in independent nation-states that provided them with a national narrative and domestic as well as international legitimacy.

Palestinians as a nation did not have the tools to develop a national narrative based on education, museums, memorials, media, coins, and stamps, but rather were confined to telling bits of the story, developing many narratives, but still lacking one Palestinian history. Because a shared set of memories is a vital basis for national identity, we will now discuss the role of memory for identity building and look at two distinct forms of collective memory for the Palestinians: scholarly historiography and oral history.

Memory and Identity

Palestine exists because Palestinians have chosen to remember it. But memories fade and people die, and some are better at remembering than others. Memory is no longer enough. It is time to write history and time for each of us to become a historian.   (ABUNIMAH 1998, 4)

A shared history or historical memory is one of the factors determining whether a group can be called a nation. This indicates that history is not a report on the past, but rather a set of fixed memories, collected, preserved, and transmitted by people and thus constructed or even "invented" (Hobsbawm and Ranger 1983). Therefore, collective memory and recorded historiography depend on particular parts of the group, power relations within that group, and a need to serve the interests of the group.

Memory and identity are connected: Both are bound to historical contexts and have to be seen as constructions, intended and developed for particular purposes. They are subjective phenomena, changed over time, shared and contested. Group identity is based on "a sense of sameness over time and space, is sustained by remembering; and what is remembered is defined by the assumed identity" (Gillis 1994, 3).

Both memory and identity can be individual and collective, and identities are changing and subject to negotiation, with individuals as well as groups able to have multiple identities. "Memories help us make sense of the world we live in" and "identity has taken on the status of a sacred object, an 'ultimate concern,' worth fighting and dying for" (Gillis 1994, 3).

It was postmodern theory that set out to deconstruct meta-narratives and grand theory and allowed the recording of alternative histories, helping "discover" histories of oppressed and disenfranchised members of societies and generally raising awareness of the constructed nature of what was previously considered historical fact. At the same time, national narratives have a political function, for example, for people striving for independence or international recognition as a nation. In such a political context it is an ethical question for a scholar to argue for or against an ideology or narrative that supports and justifies the claims of an oppressed and exiled people. No matter how invented or constructed, many aspects of contemporary politics are legitimized and justified by the same ideas of identity, memory, history, and nation.

It has been argued that Palestinian historiography has emerged in response to the powerful and dominating Israeli historical narrative. This Israeli version of history has not only dominated the media, scholarship, and curricula in Israel, but has also been accepted internationally. In addition, Palestinian resistance on all levels has been branded anti-Jewish and anti-Semitic, not just anti-Zionist. The powerful association between the victimization of Jews in the Holocaust and the existence of the State of Israel as a safe haven for Jews has made offering a counter-narrative to the Israeli view of the Palestinian-Israeli conflict impossible for decades.

Yet, research and publications by Palestinian scholars as early as the 1950s challenged the Israeli narrative (see, for example, W. Khalidi 1959). The following decades saw well-founded studies by and about Palestinians, reflecting a different historical narrative (for example, Hadawi 1988, 1990; W. Khalidi 1992) and attempting to break the Israeli domination of "history." Ironically, what has most helped break the dominant Israeli national narrative was the emergence of the "New Historians" in Israel.[6]

Concerning the Palestinian narrative and the representation of Palestinians, Edward Said has repeatedly argued that Palestinians are represented in wrong and negative images in the Western media as terrorists and as "the other" and that this representation is in sharp contrast to that of Israel and the Israelis (Said 1986a, 134). He concludes that the war of words, fought in the space of international public opinion and public policy, might prove decisive for the fate of the Palestinians. This assessment has not lost any of its validity since 1986.

Others see the Palestinian national narrative as a direct response to Zionism, which is defined as "an exclusivist and settler variant of colonialism, which aimed at the establishment of a strictly Jewish state" (Swedenburg 1991, 157). The construction of a historical identity as Palestinians and canonization of their collective memory is then described as "defensive nationalism," namely, "the effort to sustain the sentiment that all the Palestinian people share a national past is a significant part of their battle for an independent state" (157). Israel has implemented strategies to ensure the repression of a Palestinian national narrative, namely, by censoring Palestinian publications in areas under Israeli control; by promulgating a curriculum teaching Palestinian children nothing about their people's history; and by harassing scholars, journalists, and teachers who attempt to provide a different picture. In addition, the political climate of fear can even affect personal memory, as with Palestinians' memories of the Arab Revolt of 1936–1939 (160).

At the same time, the development of a national narrative, so crucial for identity building, has been hindered by the absence of a state with the institutions and instruments to support such a narrative.

As a result, Palestinians have developed a variety of narratives, born from different life circumstances, in different places of exile and within Palestine, rewritten and adjusted to new events and experiences. Said has called for a unified Palestinian history and for maintaining the diversity of these Palestinian narratives, acknowledging the fundamental differences in the identity of Palestinians in different communities and parts of the world (Said 1992, 121). Thus, his advocacy for "a definite masterwork, an institutionalized narrative of Palestinian history" (Rushdie and Said 1991, 179) should be interpreted as an attempt to prevent the Palestinian narrative from disappearing.

A study of narratives of the 1936–1939 revolt concludes that history is "a restaging of a national past" and that "the national past serves as one of the fundamental discursive producers of identity" (Swedenburg 1991, 155). The PLO is identified as the main antagonist of Israel in "the battle over memory" (165), and it is through PLO institutions that a narrative of the past has been developed as a "framework that teaches Palestinians to remember their successes as a unified people and to be aware of the danger of fragmentation" (166).

This approach stresses the importance of deriving orientation and guidance from the leadership of the present, that is, the PLO. The study points out that the leadership of the revolt (members of the upper class) is depicted in the narrative of this historical event in much more detail than are the peasants carrying out the actions. In addition, the revolt is used as an inspirational symbol, rather than studied in detail.

Israeli censorship has forced the Palestinian narrative of the past to develop rather symbolic evocations of history. The same peasants become the central "symbolic representative(s) of the cultural and historical continuity of the Palestinian people" by symbolizing the attachment to and love for the land. In order to confront fragmentation and destruction in Palestinian society, the Palestinian national movement has developed "an ideology of timeless rural tradition" (168).

What is the role of the historical national narrative for "building" national identity in the younger generations of Palestinians? The oral traditions, stories, and memories of the Palestinian past play a crucial role in educating them, inside as well as outside Palestine. For young Palestinians in Palestine, they provide the missing pieces in the picture depicted by schools and curricula under Israeli occupation and for the longest time presenting a history bereft of Palestinian elements. For those Palestinians who were born and raised in exile, these memories are their connection to Palestine—their source of knowledge, attachment, and national identity. Of special importance in this context is the memory of 1948, the decisive event in Palestinian history and a collective trauma for the Palestinian people.

Memories of 1948: Historiography and Oral History

Early examples of scholarly Palestinian historiography on 1948 can be found as early as 1959. In response to the dominant Israeli narrative, Walid Khalidi researched Arab, British, and Israeli radio sources to counter the allegation that the Palestinians fled their towns and villages following the calls of Arab and Palestinian leaders to vacate the country temporarily in order to make space for the military battles. His study "Why Did the Palestinians Leave?" concludes that no evidence could be found in radio broadcasts of the time to substantiate the claims of an evacuation order by Arab leaders. He writes, "The Zionists themselves admitted this before they had thought of inventing the order version" (W. Khalidi 1959, 35).

The last two decades have witnessed an increasing variety in the field of 1948 historiography, and the emergence of the new historians has played an important role. Some of their books have become a central source for young diaspora Palestinians to learn about Palestine and the history of their people. Important examples for these years are Khalidi's *All That Remains* (1992) and the research conducted by Abu-Sitta on the history of the villages and towns destroyed and depopulated in 1948. Abu-Sitta has produced a map with all Palestinian villages, indicating the direction of flight and the destinations of many of the refugees, along with numbers and events during the war.[7]

My interviews show that some of these works were central for acquiring knowledge about Palestinian history, especially for those Palestinians living in Western countries. Examples are Said's *The Question of Palestine* (1992)and *After the Last Sky* (1986a), Hadawi's *Bitter Harvest* (1990), Farsoun's *Palestine and the Palestinians* (1997), Turki's *The Disinherited* (1974a) and *Soul in Exile* (1988), and many others. These are nonfiction works, written and published mostly in English, so they appeal to Palestinian Americans and those with little or no knowledge of Arabic.

My research also indicates that young Palestinians in Arab countries were not dependent on sources of this type. For this much larger group of Palestinians in exile, life within Palestinian communities provided knowledge in a different form and reinforced it daily. For them the sources for oral history, namely, the stories of the older generations—their memories and narratives of the past—prove to be an important factor in building a Palestinian identity. It is difficult to evaluate how much of this storytelling happens within families and communities, as research about this would turn them into oral history and thus change the audience and, with it, the stories. Certainly, these narratives have, over time, been adjusted to one another, and, depending on who is telling them, always contain the background of that person's decisions and experiences in life. Consequently, they form part of the collective memory of the Palestinians.

Kamila told me that she did not speak with her grandparents about Palestine because she did not live with them, but that she learned from other old people and from documentaries:

> I used to go with my dad to Sabra and Shatila in Beirut, and old people always talked about that, but you never really listen to them. I do love to listen to that now; I definitely can understand it a lot better. I am thinking about doing a television report about this. It intrigues me that you have two brothers from the same family: One of them left Palestine, and one of them stayed, and how different the experiences have made them.

Basma had thought about the same question before and had found the answers very dissatisfying:

> I always asked that question. Why am I Palestinian? Why I am not Syrian, especially because I was in a Syrian school. They used to tell me that they moved from Palestine during 1948 because there was war between Palestinians and Jews and it was horrifying, and I asked my grandfather: Did you see someone killing or killed? And he would tell me, no, it was only that we were horrified and we heard rumors that the Jews are coming to kill us and rape our daughters and wives, so we were really frightened of that. And we moved thinking that we will move for

about two or three months and then come back to our homes, but that didn't happen; it lasted fifty years. That's what I always heard, but I was never convinced, because I think people who believe in rumors will continue their life believing in rumors and they keep on making the same mistakes; they never learn. Especially in Jaffa there are people that stayed in their homes and they didn't leave, so I hate what they did. You know I am not proud of them at all.

Ghada Karmi, in her memoirs of childhood and youth after 1948, described how her parents never talked about Palestine, at least not in the presence of their children, and especially not about the events that led them to leave Jerusalem and go to Damascus and later London. She assumed that it was too painful for them, especially for her mother (Karmi 1994, 39, and 1999, 55).

The year 1998, marking the fiftieth anniversary of the Nakba for the Palestinians and the creation of the State of Israel, saw a dramatic increase in Palestinian historiographic texts, particularly materials that can be considered oral history. Oral history literature is not a new phenomenon in Palestinian historiography. The anthropologist Rosemary Sayigh started interviewing Palestinians in a refugee camp in Lebanon as early as the 1970s. Her book on this research (*Palestinians: From Peasants to Revolutionaries,* 1979) became the foundation of a Palestinian oral-history tradition. She recalls how difficult it was at that time to convince respondents that their stories were important and mattered. In the following decades, she recorded the life stories of Palestinians in the camps, always focusing on those without a voice—the poor, the illiterate, and in particular women. About collecting the memories of 1948, she said in an interview in 1995:

> The best time for it has gone, but there are still some older Palestinians left. One can still record through third parties: people were often told a great deal by parents and grandparents. This can be a very interesting form of recording oral history: recollections of what one was told in childhood. . . . On the other hand, if you don't record with the older people from *Jeel Filastin* who can't read and write, they'll be gone. And what they know is so rich.
>
> (ARAB RESOURCE CENTER FOR POPULAR ARTS 1998B, 9)

Many Palestinian intellectuals felt compelled to write memoirs and books of the type that she mentions.[8] Sayigh quotes Palestinians remembering the events of 1948, with interviewees often focusing on fear and suffering:

My father, brother, wife and children stayed with me on the outskirts of the village of Farradiya, southwest of our village. My mother, sister, cousin and nephew remained in Safsaf. We stayed there until the Jews bombed the village of 'Ailaboon, forcing its people to flee north . . . there we learned that the Jews had also bombed Safsaf. My mother, sister, and other relatives were amongst those killed there.   (R. SAYIGH 1979, 85)

In a later essay she emphasizes the role of women living in the camps as preservers of stories of Palestine, and demonstrates the centrality of the meaning of 1948 in the narratives of these women:

A striking feature of the life stories is the primordiality of the exodus from Palestine as "beginning," displacing the more usual starting points such as birth, place of origin, or first memories. Most speakers already adult in 1948 began with it, as did many of the "generation of the Disaster," too young in 1948 to have personal recollections. . . . The degree of detail of that terrible journey preserved in memory over four and a half decades signals not only the significance assigned to it retrospectively—as historic mistake, rupture from Palestine and beginning of exile, precursor of other tragedies—but also suggests processes of collective memory formation as individual stories were told and retold in refugee gatherings.   (R. SAYIGH 1998, 45)

The quote points to the transformation process from individual memory to collective memory, in which the narratives of the individuals are adjusted to fit the unified version of Palestinian collective history and to serve different audiences. This makes clear that there is no simple recording of oral history without considering the effect of a particular researcher and the fact of the interview's being recorded.

When, in preparation for the fiftieth anniversary of the Nakba, various activities and projects to collect narratives of 1948 started, and first publications were available, the attempt was to make Palestinians' voices heard, to collect the narratives of the Nakba generation that was slowly dying away, and to prepare a body of knowledge to pass on to younger generations.

Many of these narratives emphasized the victimization of the Palestinians, the memories of suffering, loss, and fear. The production of "memorial books" on a number of the destroyed villages was the central goal of a project conducted over several years at Birzeit University. These books not only collect all available information about the villages, and their history, geographical setting, and inhabitants, they also attempt to present a unified collective version of the village past (see Slyomovics 1994, 1995, and 1998). The introduction to one of the memorial books published at Birzeit University explains their methodology:

> Each study will attempt, to the extent possible, to describe the life of the people in that village such that the reader is able to picture it as living, inhabited and cultivated as it was in 1948 before it was destroyed. This portrayal will allow Palestinians, especially those who had left these villages at an early age or were born outside of them after 1948 to feel tied and connected to the villages, society and real country as if they had lived in it, rather than it just being a name on a map.
>
> (KANAANA 1989, QUOTED IN SLYOMOVICS 1995, 42)

A study of the village of ʿAyn Hud and its collective narrative also suggests the possibility of discovering "narrative discontinuity," class differences, political diversity, and poverty in a narrative of a past that is "discontinuous with the present" (Slyomovics 1995, 42). The author interviewed many of the former inhabitants of ʿAyn Hud and their descendants who settled nearby after the village was turned into an Israeli settlement and later an artist village; other former villagers became part of the diaspora.

Another, somewhat similar, project studies the history and the memory of the destroyed village Lubya, and maps out the connections between families and descendants of village inhabitants in different migration countries.

> Lubya . . . was totally demolished, and its inhabitants uprooted and dispersed to as many as 23 countries: Within, nearby, and far from Palestine. Before its demolition, however, this village once had its own historical, cultural and social narrative. Fifty years' displacement did not succeed in abolishing its history in the minds of its inhabitants, nor in the minds of those who uprooted them. The stream of past memories is still fresh in the minds of the older generation. Men and women in their sixties, seventies and eighties are still discussing and recollecting their past, for their own sake and for the children's; and the latter were transmitting, more or less accurately, the same histories and traditions to their sons and daughters. (ISSA 1998, 2)

In addition to scholarly studies, memorial books, and other printed materials, recent years have witnessed the rise of a new medium of communication, information, and collective memory. In the wake of the anniversary in 1998, a number of Internet sites have been created, most notably a site called www.alnakba.org. Among the sources posted there one finds

"Testimonies of Survivors." The memories of the witnesses draw a terrifying picture:

> I cannot forget the three horror-filled days in July of 1948. The pain sears my memory, and I cannot rid myself of it no matter how hard I try. . . . Outside the gate the soldiers stopped us and ordered everyone to throw all valuables onto a blanket. One young man and his wife of six weeks, friends of our family, stood near me. He refused to give up his money. Almost casually, the soldier pulled up his rifle and shot the man. He fell, bleeding and dying while his bride screamed and cried. I felt nauseated and sick, my whole body numbed by shock waves. That night I cried, too, as I tried to sleep alongside thousands on the ground. Would I ever see my home again? Would the soldiers kill my loved ones, too?
>
> (WWW.ALNAKBA.ORG, TESTIMONY NO. 3 BY
> FATHER AUDEH RANTISI FROM LYDDA)

But as important as the postings on the site is the response and popularity of such sites among young Palestinians who can learn about Palestine and Palestinians and also make their own voices heard. Some of the comments read:

> The Palestinian story must be told, the memories must not be forgotten, the testimonies must never die. Pass your history down to your children for that is the only way they shall know the truth. I applaud this site. "One day . . . we shall be free men." (TAREK JALLAD)

> Brilliant site. . . . Another reminder for Palestinians everywhere that we are truly alone in our loss. . . . This section should be academic and not full of propaganda or hysteria. We have an honest and noble cause. We should advertise it. (RAMZI NAHAS)

> To all of you out there, I do hope one day to go back to Palestine and settle down in the land left to me by my grandfather. This piece of land is the most important aspect of my life. Without it, I would die. The hope lives on. (AHMED KHAWAJA)

In 1998 I learned about a group of young Palestinians in Lebanon who worked on an oral history project in Beirut. During a visit to the Arab Resource Center for Popular Arts in Beirut I could see with how much enthusiasm and interest these members of the third or fourth generation in exile discovered the narratives of the old people in the camps and how the experience had transformed them. The project was inspired by the realization that many Palestinian children in the camps knew shockingly little about the events of 1948 beyond the symbolic realm. The young researchers assessed their experience in this way:

> The older generation lived Palestine and its history; even if it is now only a dream to them, they did live it. But if we were to continue this way, and nothing of Palestine were to reach the new generation, we might not last even another twenty years. . . . Rights in history are a general concept; they can be falsified or counterfeited. But people's emotions, when they are spoken truthfully and emotionally to you, and when you are told the same story over and over from so many different sources, lead you to a different conclusion. Then you feel a real difference between oral history and standard history.
>
> (ARAB RESOURCE CENTER FOR POPULAR ARTS 1998B, 43)

There is an intersection between the memory of life in Palestine prior to 1948 (and exile) and Palestinian national and cultural identity. At this intersection the expectations and images of Palestine and the Palestinians are formed. These images have to meet reality upon return to the homeland. Palestinian national identity, largely based on collective memory and historiography, is a defining aspect of being Palestinian. For Palestinians in the diaspora they constitute the missing link to their homeland. What do exile and diaspora mean for Palestinians, and what images of Palestine do they have?

CHAPTER 3 **The Country of My Dreams**

Departure, eternal departure
when will exiles sit
around one table
and a family rejoice
knowing
that despite sorrow
it is our homeland!

(ALI AL-KHALILI, IN JAYYUSI 1992, 196)

Exile and diaspora are the antithesis of home and homeland. The traumatic loss of the homeland strengthens the connection of refugees and exiles to the homeland, and it continues to play an important role in their individual and collective imagination, constituting a central aspect of their self-definition.

Where do the notions of being refugees, exiles, and members of a diaspora intersect? Can Palestinians be described as a diaspora, based on the larger theoretical application of the term to different types of modern migration? And if, as modern diaspora studies claim, the "myth of the homeland" plays such an important role in the definition of diaspora communities, how is Palestine "imagined" and how is the process of developing images of Palestine as a homeland linked to literature, poetry, and visual arts?

During the early stages of my research I frequently encountered images of Palestine, stories of the sweetest grapes and figs, the most beautiful orange and lemon trees, the amazing seashores, and the friendliest and most educated people in the Middle East. Similar images can be found in Palestinian poetry and literature. They raised the question of how relevant these images were for the young generation of Palestinians that I was interviewing. Did they subscribe to the same idealized image of their homeland? What happened to that image when they actually arrived there?

With all these questions in my mind, I was relieved when the first interview partner told me exactly what I had expected. I am telling his story here to show his individual way of connecting image and reality. It is a narrative about his images of Palestine as much as about his return, as the two are inseparable to him.

Majid's Story

Majid was twenty-seven at the time of the interview and returned to Palestine in March 1998. His parents were refugees from a village near Ramleh, "from 1948," as he said. They fled to Bethlehem in 1948 and became second-time refugees in 1967 when they left the West Bank for Jordan in the wake of the war. Majid grew up in Jordan, in Aqaba and Amman, where most members of his family still lived. He left Jordan in 1987 to study and work in Tunisia. The memories of his childhood reflected two main points of reference for his feeling Palestinian: the stories he heard from his mother about Palestine and the Palestinians, and the treatment of Palestinians in Jordan.

> The life of a Palestinian in Jordan is hard for him, because the opportunities are limited, unlike for a Jordanian. A Jordanian is in his country, but the Palestinian doesn't interact with Jordan as his country, because it is not his. There are a lot of small things where they always let you know this is not your country, especially in government activities or such things as the military. The Palestinian does not participate in that, has never been responsible for a country. He is always loyal to Palestine. Because of that, he has to work in special factories, in special businesses. It is the only way to make a living. That is why his situation is not very safe or stable in Jordan. One cannot rely on anything one achieves and have continuity in it, even for two or three years. There are always dangers ahead of him; his life can be turned upside down at any moment.

Although this is clearly his own experience of living in Jordan, he chose to speak in the third person, thereby projecting the frustration, anxiety, and uncertainty onto the Palestinian per se instead of speaking about himself. This strategy of expression points to his feeling of belonging to the Palestinians as a group, community, and people. Personal experience is translated into more general expressions in order to strengthen the group feeling. His image of Palestine and his feeling of not belonging in Jordan were born out of being "the other" in the Jordanian context, his being non-Jordanian in turn defines him as Palestinian. Balancing this negative side of identity, the stories about Palestine that he heard as a child provided a positive image as he developed his own identity. The stories, told by his mother, father, and other Palestinians, focused on Palestine as a special place and the Palestinians as special people. His mother was an especially important source of these stories.

> I remember a lot of beautiful things, but I haven't seen them, all the things that were so beautiful and that I had heard about. . . . For example, they would tell me first of all how beautiful the place is, how good the people are. I remember hearing that, at the house of my grandfather in Bayt Sahur, there is a very large tree; when you walk under it you smell something special, a very sweet odor. The odor of jasmine or something like that. . . . When I first entered the bridge, my mum had told me how the entrance was, a lot of details. She said that on the bridge the car would start making this ticking noise. She always told us that.

Majid chose not to tell me everything he wanted to say while I was taping the interview, but said more only after I had turned the tape recorder off. He told me that his mother always told him and his siblings with much pride about the glorious and brave Fida'iyin (freedom fighters), and that he grew up proud of being Palestinian. They did not dream of becoming teachers, doctors, or engineers, but fighters like those in the stories of his mother.

Phrased in many different ways, he repeated his connection to Palestine and his feeling of its being his homeland, even if it was not what he had imagined before he returned.

> Because it is my country and I had to come back. . . . The Palestinian who lived outside had a dream in his life, to return. Not even return to live here, but just return to see what that country is all about. . . . Other than that I have the feeling that the national feelings for the homeland were weaker outside than here. Maybe not all of them: Some have more, some have less; you can't say generally. It can be less because they are far, but it can also be more love for the place because of that, that the memories of the place make it strong. As I told you, the memories of my parents were passed on to me, I love this country, because that is what I learned from my father. . . . I mean, I had a lot of problems in life because of Palestine; I don't say that to get sympathy from people or compliments. But I feel that I am a Palestinian; my father was born here and my mother was born here. I am a son of this land.

What became clear during the interview, despite this attachment, was his deep frustration and disappointment with what he had found upon his return. He told me that the place where the house of his grandfather and this tree were supposed to be was not nearly as beautiful as the images, but just a place full of sun, cold, dust, and dirt. He expressed his anger about the way people treated each other, how mothers hit their children on the streets and people did not even smile on holidays. He blamed his parents and their generation for telling lies about Palestine and raising their children with a fake dream of a Palestine that did not exist and would never exist, neither as a place to live nor as a state. He added that he never felt like a stranger in any of the places in which he lived, but in Palestine he did feel like a stranger. An explanation could be that when his dreams and expectations were not fulfilled upon arrival in Palestine, a place associated with home, warmth, and security, the place appeared cold and strange. The sense of being a stranger becomes most acute when it is linked to the place closest to one's heart. It was and was not his country, and he was not sure anymore if he wanted to stay. The love for Palestine was there, but he often questioned it, creating a picture of intense contradiction and frustration:

> But when I came here I stopped loving it, to be honest. It was my wish to come here, but now I am arguing with myself, saying, oh Allah, I wish I had waited longer and not come here yet. Why did I hurry and come here so soon? When I tell people that, they say that a country is never what you expect it to be. I didn't want to come to a country that is like that. I don't want to live in a country in which all is wrong, nothing is right here. They have stolen the dream of our children. We are mocking our children; what are we leaving for them? Yes, all our lives we talk about these children, the children of the stones; we make a festival of that, but that is all just an image. How many were injured during the Intifada? What did we do with those? We didn't achieve anything; we just made fun of ourselves and those children.

And yet, when I asked him about the future, he replied by simply saying, "Yes, I will stay here, this is my country." And there again, developing a picture of the future and listing what needed to be done to change the country, he switched from "I" to "we," placing himself in the Palestinian community. At the same time, this expression depersonalized his essentially personal experience and thus allowed him to distance his feelings from his statement:

> I would change the minds of people first, their way of thinking. There is something like looking ahead, because it doesn't help you to look back all the time. There is a life and it is beautiful. . . . This land is not going to

change; the land itself is beautiful, but we don't understand the country. We don't know what it needs to work with it and develop it. But the freedom you have is the freedom of the others too. . . . This is my country and I am free in it, but I know that my freedom is built on the freedom of the others and has to cooperate with it. If all people would live according to that rule, we could have the best life.

His own conclusion in this interview was not optimistic. He told me that he thought the Palestinians would not survive as a people, because they had lived for a false dream for the last fifty years, and now after so much disappointment everyone was just trying to survive, to live a life. He did not explicitly say that he wanted to leave again; he fought his lonely daily fight against the conditions and survived only with the help of friends who thought like him. His work with a prominent Palestinian filmmaker gave his everyday life meaning and provided him with an income.

Majid's story challenged my assumptions about images of Palestine. It also proved the importance of those images for his generation of Palestinians outside Palestine. This gives the title of this chapter, "The Country of My Dreams," a rather ironic shade; it could have a question mark at the end. But is an image of something—especially that of a homeland—not doomed to be an illusion, an imagined landscape, better and more beautiful than the reality in order to survive as a dream in the minds of people? Does living in exile or diaspora require that one have a dream to hold on to? What do the terms "diaspora" and "exile" mean to people?

Notions of Diaspora and Exile

Numerous discussions and publications have appeared in recent decades, reflecting a new interest in the phenomenon commonly called diaspora. The reemergence of the classical term as applied to the Jewish diaspora can be located in the late 1960s, and it "is now used as a synonym for related phenomena until recently covered by distinct terms like expatriate, exile, ethnic minority, refugee, migrant, sojourner and overseas community" (Tölölyan 1996, 10).

Traditionally applied only to the Jewish diaspora, but later also to Greeks and Armenians, the word itself is Greek, derived from the verb *speiro* (to sow) and the preposition *dia* (over) (R. Cohen 1997, xi).[1] The Greek term *diaspeirein* means "an abrupt but natural process, the fruitful scattering away of seeds from the parent body that both dispersed and reproduced the organism" (Tölölyan 1996, 10). The term diaspora brings together the ambiguity of traumatic destruction and the successful reformation of economically affluent communities outside the homeland. Only the Jewish encounters with the Romans, the destruction of Judea, and the complete loss of the homeland inscribed a painful meaning onto the term.

In modern discourse, notions of diaspora are discussed in relation to ideas of postmodern mobility—concepts of nation and nation-states, identity, and migrancy. Definitions range from "that part of a people living apart from the homeland" to distinct criteria such as origin from one particular center or homeland, collective memory of that homeland, return wish, commitment to restoration of the homeland, and definition of the community as being connected through common origin (Safran 1991, 83).

Drawing more on the classical Jewish notion of diaspora, scholars have emphasized key features such as the traumatic loss of the homeland, collective memory and group identity, community boundaries from without and within, connected diaspora communities, and perception of kin (this reminds one of Anderson's definition of a nation), as well as ties to the actual homeland or an idea of it combined with an actual or symbolic return wish (Tölölyan 1996, 12–15).

By broadening the criteria beyond victims, Cohen, in the most systematic approach, has included different forms of work, trade, and colonial migration to define different categories of diaspora communities, namely: victim diasporas, such as the Africans and the Armenians (he mentions the Palestinians as well);[2] labor and imperial diasporas, such as the Indians (labor diaspora) and the British (imperial diaspora);[3] trade diasporas, such as the Chinese and Lebanese; and cultural diasporas, exemplified by the Caribbean experience (R. Cohen 1997, 26–29).

Postmodern definitions of diasporas focus more on the metaphorical use of the term "diaspora," as a literal application implies hegemonic claims to a territory, often oppressing the claims of others to the same territory. This approach calls for an emphasis on the diversity and hybridity that diasporas can produce and with which they can confront societies. Diaspora identities are defined as "constantly producing and reproducing themselves anew, through transformation and difference" (Hall 1990, 235). In this view, diaspora as a phenomenon is connected to globalization, a crisis of the nation-state as a point of reference for identity, and a new dimension of global migration.

In his influential essay "Diasporas" (1994), James Clifford distinguishes diaspora from another commonly used term, "border/borderland," and emphasizes the longer distance and separation from the homeland, a taboo or impossibility of return, and the connection of multiple communities of dispersed people that diaspora implies. In the context of homeland as a focus of diaspora identity, he remarks that "the transnational connections linking diasporas need not be articulated primarily through a real or symbolic homeland. . . . Decentered, lateral connections may be as important as those formed around a teleology of origin/return. And a shared, ongoing history of displacement, suffering, adaptation, or resistance may be as important as the projection of a specific origin" (Clifford 1994, 306).

Clifford attempts to define diasporas by positioning them in relation to other phenomena. He sees diasporas as distinct from the nation-state on the one hand and indigenous claims by local, "tribal" peoples on the other (307). At the same time, diaspora is different from travel, in that it is not intended as temporary, though travel is a precondition for the formation of a diaspora. Also, diaspora is based upon the formation of collective homes, and life in distinct communities. Diaspora is different from exile in this respect, as exile is more individualistic in focus (308). In his argument, the currently emerging value of diaspora and the claims that various minorities are diasporic are a result of new strategies in minority discourses that allow them to move away from the duality of minority/majority conflicts. This new definition of diaspora also distinguishes immigrants from people collectively uprooted from their homeland and dispersed among various host countries, stating, "People whose sense of identity is centrally defined by collective histories of displacement and violent loss cannot be "cured" by merging into a new national community" (307).

Based on these different notions, one can ask whether the discourses on diaspora can and should be applied to the situation of Palestinians. Is the idea of the constructed and constantly reconstructed nature of diasporic identities productive for the achievement of a political goal, such as the creation of a Palestinian state?

A Palestinian Diaspora?

The term "Palestinian diaspora" is widely used in the literature in the West. Looking at the various definitions of the term, and going beyond the casual use of the word to mean the phenomenon of scattering and separation from something, can the communities of Palestinians around the world be described as a diaspora?

Cohen clearly identifies the Palestinians as a victim diaspora, even though he does not go into detail about its history or structure (R. Cohen 1997, 31). A more critical approach is represented by the idea of hybridity as a strategy for minorities, exiles, diasporas, and other marginal groups to reject the notion of difference from the Eurocenter as a new way of excluding them from any relevant discourse. Lavie and Swedenburg counter the postmodernist celebration of fragmented, floating, and changing identities with an approach that calls for the acknowledgment of the history of oppression of the margins by the center. Instead of essentializing non-Eurocentric identities and exoticizing cultures while making them available for the entertainment of the Eurocenter, they suggest that it is through migration that the margins have become a part of the center. Marginal groups are present in the center and can thus deploy themselves to be heard in exactly that center. The acknowledging of hybrid identities can in fact help minority groups recognize shared histories and ideas, while not overlooking the differences. This recognition can cause minority groups to forge temporary alliances in order to be heard (Lavie and Swedenburg 1996, 7–10).

On the other hand, the authors propose to rethink cultural essence, and argue that although essence is a social construction, under certain circumstances it can have an important function for minorities and national liberation movements in authenticating their experience as an act of resistance. They explain, "Hybridity therefore does not appear to be a viable strategy in the struggle for Palestine — a case of exilic identity demanding to return to its historic territory" (12).

If one chooses to stress those aspects of diaspora identity that focus on the connections between diaspora communities not primarily through their attachment to a symbolic and mythical homeland, but through their kinship ties among communities outside the homeland, then calling the Palestinians a diaspora could well help deny their claim to their homeland. Diasporas can develop an ideology of nationalism as a counter-narrative to the nationalistic narrative of the host country. While "positive articulations of diaspora identity reach outside the normative territory and temporality (myth/history) of the nation-state" (Clifford 1994, 307), even the establishment of a nation-state does not necessarily dissolve the diaspora community, as nation and nation-state are not identical. A case in point would be the State of Israel, and it is quite possible that a similar development would occur if a Palestinian state were established.

Another author argues that the Palestinian fate resembles that of the Jews and Armenians in the displacement, preservation of a collective memory of the homeland, desire to return, and connected communities in the Middle East, Western Europe, and North America, and that they can thus be called a diaspora. But he points out that those Palestinians who live in Arab countries are not altogether strangers there, as they share a language and many aspects of culture and religion with the host societies. They may not have full political rights in these countries, but many of them enjoy economic prosperity. Moreover, in his view the Palestinians lacked community consciousness before uprooting and cannot now agree how to define the physical boundaries of their homeland. Dismissing Palestinian claims to Palestine on political grounds, he then surprisingly concludes that Palestinian refugees and expellees show a strongly perpetuated "collective diaspora consciousness," although it is more diluted in the case of Palestinians who are well integrated into Western countries (Safran 1991, 88).

Coming from the opposite political direction, Kodmani-Darwish states: "The creation of the State acknowledges the diaspora as a permanent state, the transition from a psychology of the provisional towards one of permanence" (cited in Harlow 1998, 81). And although the Palestinian state has not so far been established, the existence of the Palestinian National Authority and its limited control over part of the Palestinian homeland has already initiated this transformation, challenging long-held notions of the homeland and questioning the viability of the return wish or myth.

Although her book is called *The Palestinian Diaspora*, the text itself states that "to identify the Palestinians as refugees is to recognize that there is a problem requiring a solution. To label them a diaspora is to eliminate by the very language the need to change their situation" (cited in Harlow 1998, 81). This argument is convincing and invites the question of how Palestinians themselves describe the status of their communities and whether or not they use the term "diaspora."

In a conversation with Salman Rushdie, Edward Said argues against calling the dispersed Palestinians a diaspora because he is weary of the notion of homeland:

Salman Rushdie: You say you don't like calling it a Palestinian diaspora. Why is that?

Edward Said: I suppose there is a sense in which, as one man wrote to me from Jerusalem, we are "the Jews of the Arab world." But I think our experience is really quite different and beyond such attempts to draw parallels. Perhaps its dimension is much more modest. In any case the idea that there is a kind of redemptive homeland doesn't answer to my view of things. (RUSHDIE AND SAID 1991, 173)

His statement can be interpreted as a rejection of comparisons between Jewish and Palestinian fates, which, at any rate, is difficult, as it seems impossible to compare the dimensions of human suffering, pain, and loss to each other. But it also forsakes the chance to relate the Palestinian experience to that of other dispersed and marginalized people. The question here is not only whether or not Palestinians can and should be defined as a diaspora, but whether, if they are a diaspora, other notions, such as exile, refugee, and migrant, can be brought into the picture.

In his essay "The Mind of Winter: Reflections on Life in Exile," Said calls for a differentiation of exiles and refugees, because refugees are "politically disenfranchised groups of innocent and bewildered people." Exile is, in his view, a more individual condition, because the exile knows that "in a secular and contingent world, homes are always provisional. Borders and barriers, which enclose us within the safety of familiar territory, can also become prisons, and are often defended beyond reason and necessity. Exiles cross borders, break barriers of thought and experience" (Said 1984, 54).

This view of the exile stresses the individual as opposed to groups of refugees and migrants. It might be produced or at least reinforced by the fact that exiles are often heard as such only when they express themselves in literary, journalistic, or poetic forms, which by the very nature of these expressions makes them individual. Indeed, it is often a leadership elite of the diaspora community, a minority within the minority, that voices specific diasporic concerns on behalf of the majority of the silent community members lobbying both for the diaspora community and the homeland. Another group of diasporic individuals is not engaged in the political and institutional struggles of and for the community, but consists of "loosely connected scholars and intellectuals who produce a diasporic discourse, and above all the writers, musicians and other artists who produce high and low cultural commodities that underpin diasporic identity" (Tölölyan 1996, 19).

In which ways do Palestinians and others speaking for them describe Palestinians in competing terminologies as refugees, exiles, and/or migrants? Concerning the Palestinian refugee problem, the right of return, and its implications for Palestinians and the peace process, the political discourse is dominated by the term "refugee." Palestinian politicians, as well as scholars and individuals, insist on using the term refugees because it expresses their political claims, their right to return to their homeland and to have sovereignty as a people. The UN definition of a Palestinian refugee provides the narrowest basis for such claims, while the current demographic situation implies a more complicated picture. The political claims are important; nevertheless, there is a variety of expressions and notions related to the Palestinian situation of diaspora and exile.

To highlight the fact that there is an ongoing debate about these issues among Palestinians, one example shall be mentioned. The founders of SHAML—the Palestinian Refugee and Diaspora Center, established in 1995—chose to incorporate both "refugees" and "diaspora" in the name, indicating that they recognize the difference between the two.[4] The Arabic name of the center, *Markaz dirasat al-laji'in wa-l-shatat,* refers us to a notion that is used in Arabic, *al-shatat,* which literally means to be scattered, dispersed, or separated. I am unable to tell for how long it has been used. It might well be an adaptation of the English term "diaspora." Clearly, the Greek notion of being scattered and separated from the homeland or parent is semantically present here. In possible reference to this meaning, a Palestinian American writer chose to title his first novel *Scattered Like Seeds.* In an interview, Shaw Dallal related that Thafer Allam, the hero of the story,

> is an Arab American who replicates and symbolizes the Palestinian who has one foot in the United States and the other in the homeland. He is a divided soul caught in the ambiguities of history. This is the antagonizing reality of many Palestinian Americans, who will undoubtedly identify with him.   (DALLAL IN THE SYRACUSE UNIVERSITY PRESS CATALOG)

The Arabic term that has been in use much longer and is richer in meaning is *al-ghurba.* The Arabic-English dictionary translates *al-ghurba* as "the absence from the homeland; separation from one's native country, banishment, exile; life, or place, away from home" (Wehr 1994, 783).

Arabic is a language that is closely linked to the Qur'an and thus to Islam. Therefore one should go beyond the "modern" meaning of the word and look for deeper and more religious and philosophical explanations. The root of *ghurba,* the verb *gharaba,* is in a lexical/philosophical sense linked to its opposite *sharaqa. Al-sharq* is related to the rising sun; it is the East or Orient. Even in European languages, to be oriented literally means to face the sun. The sun as the source of light is, in Islamic philosophy, a symbol for God, who is the One from whom all light originates. The West, as the opposite, implies being away from the sun, in the darkness. Thus, the term *ghurba* means religiously and philosophically barred from the light.[5] The Arabic terms discussed here carry some of these philosophical meanings, even if their contemporary use is not always conscious of the philosophical associations.

Edward Said translates *ghurba* as estrangement, and uses the term *manfa* for exile. Indeed, *manfa* is exile in a more literal sense, as the verb *nafa* means to banish or expel. In Palestinian literature and poetry, it is *ghurba,* where the Palestinian is a stranger, that carries all the notions of suffering, cold, winter, estrangement, and dislocation.

One of the most eloquent Palestinian writers and intellectuals frequently uses the term *ghourba* (a different spelling of *ghurba*) for the desperate and hopeless situation of the Palestinian refugees, especially in Lebanon (Turki 1974a, 4 and Turki 1975/1976, 82). In an early attempt to describe the transformation of Palestinian consciousness from total hopelessness to a sense of national pride and a project of national liberation, he writes:

> The myth of the feda'i is the myth of the Refugee transformed. . . . It is the ethos of Palestine Returned. We Returned. To Palestine. Its liberation became in a sense the liberation of men and women. Regaining it became, in another, the regaining by its people of their sense of worth. Before we Returned, a whole generation of Palestinians had been born, had lived, grown up and acquired a consciousness without a homeland. The *ghourba,* with all its pain, its fantasies and sense of disconnectedness became in a sense *the* homeland. (TURKI 1974A, 16)

In later works he also deploys the term diaspora for describing the Palestinian experience:

> And we, the children of the Palestinian diaspora, coming as we did in 1948, had to fight for our way there . . . pending our return to Palestine, our homes and homeland. In the meantime, ours would remain a reality scorched by alienation. We were destined to wander the face of the earth, creating a ceremony of shadows that was to become our homeland in exile. (TURKI 1988, 26)[6]

The experience of exile, and its poetic and literary description, emphasize suffering and loss and feeling uprooted, unprotected, and without a home. It impersonates one side of the duality of exile and homeland. In his poem "In the Deserts of Exile," Jabra Ibrahim Jabra juxtaposes the images of homeland and exile:

> Spring after spring,
> In the desert of exile,
> What are we doing with our love,
> When our eyes are full of frost and dust?
>
> .   .   .   .
>
> O land of ours where our childhood passed
> Like dreams in the shade of the orange-grove,

Among the almond-trees in the valley—
Remember us now wandering
Among the thorns of the desert,
Wandering in the rocky mountains;
Remember us now
In the tumult of cities beyond deserts and seas.
Remember us
With our eyes full of dust
That never clears in our ceaseless wandering
They crushed the flowers on the hills around us,
Destroyed the houses over our heads,
Scattered our torn remains,
Then unfolded the desert before us,
With valleys writhing in hunger
And blue shadows shattered into red thorns.

(JABRA, IN KHOURI AND ALGAR 1974, 225)

In one of his "Love Poems," Samih Al-Qasim recalls the pain of waiting to return and the hopeless present of the Palestinians in exile:

Your hand in mine
Your eyes in mine . . .
The motherland is a train
disappearing behind the collapsed horizon of time
leaving behind a whirlpool of dust
and newspaper shreds
leaving behind a returning man and woman
surrounded by stacked suitcases
of sorrow and waiting.   (AL-QASIM, IN JAYYUSI 1992, 257)

Poetry immediately after 1948 and until 1967 reflects the shock of the up-rooting and the years of disorientation, dispersal, and hopelessness. The developments after 1967, with the emergence of the Palestinian national movement and the formation of political and military resistance inside as well as outside Palestine, show a more self-confident and nationalistic tone. What remains is the longing for the homeland, its recreation, imagi-nation, and description in Palestinian poetry as well as art. It forms in all its aspects the antithesis to exile, encompassing safety, rootedness, peace, and comfort. This supports our earlier point that the collective conser-vation of the image of the homeland is one vital factor for a diasporic community to survive as a community. It passes the connection to and the longing for return to that homeland from the first generations to the descendants born in exile.

Clearly, the notions of diaspora, exile, refugees, minorities, and homeland at times overlap and at other times contradict each other and differ in their specific use by scholars and writers, Western as well as Palestinian. Given the polysemic nature of the very definition of diaspora as discussed above, the only strategy is to contextualize the implication of each of its uses while bearing in mind that the notions and their meanings are contested and ambivalent.

Homeland Palestine: The Image in Poetry and Arts

For the generation of the Nakba, those who lost their homeland in the catastrophe of 1948, memories of the homeland were all they could hold on to immediately after their uprooting. The traumatic experience of the flight and the battles, together with the devastating situation in the refugee camps, made them turn to the past, a past that was preserved as peaceful and safe, in a country that was their homeland. This image of the past is closely linked to a sense of national Palestinian identity or to considering Palestine "a place called home." It also engenders the complex process of constructing a collective memory in order to build a collective identity on it. Different types of memory—official (Palestinian) historiography, oral history, and the arts—were vital in this process. Poetry more than prose, and literature more than visual arts, had an effect on the construction of this collective memory.

Our concern here is which images of the homeland emerged in Palestinian literature (especially poetry, but to an extent visual arts) and what influence these images had on the following generations of Palestinians, those who were born and grew up without their own memory of the place and its people. It will become clear that these images coincide with those constructed in popular memory. This can imply one of two things: that poetry and arts reflect popular memory adequately, or, that these artistic productions had a considerable influence on popular memory. Without doubt, poetry plays its role in popular Arab culture, and spending time with Palestinians in Palestine and abroad, I frequently encountered their fascination with reciting poetry. Many Palestinians can recite their favorite poems by Mahmud Darwish, probably the most outstanding Palestinian poet. Some famous poems have been turned into lyrics for popular songs and are thus sung on many occasions.

Many of Darwish's love poems can be interpreted as symbolic addresses to the homeland, speaking to a woman but at the same time, in a symbolic subtext, referring to Palestine, imagined not only as the beloved, but also as the mother to whom Palestinians are longing to return.[7]

To imagine the homeland as a caring mother is of course no invention of Palestinian poetry. Still, Darwish's poem "To My Mother" (*Ila ummi*) deserves mentioning, not least because it was turned into a song by the Lebanese musician and singer Marcel Khalifeh and became very popular beyond the borders of Palestine. Khalifeh has often used Darwish's poetry for his songs and by doing so has helped popularize it among Palestinians and others around the world.

TO MY MOTHER

I long for the bread of my mother
The coffee of my mother
The touch of my mother
Childhood memories grow up in me
Day after day
And I love my life because
If I died
I would be shamed by the tears of my mother!

(DARWISH 1997, 93; MY TRANSLATION)

The beauty of Palestinian landscape is often evoked in poems, with a sad and dramatic undertone expressing the loss of the beauty and the security it embodied. Salem Jubran describes a scene in his town of origin, Tulkarem, while at the end of the poem pointing to the pain associated with the fact that he cannot reach this place anymore, that he would be endangered if attempting to cross the borders that bar him from returning there. Despite the occupation and the presence of Israeli soldiers and settlers, the nature of Palestine remains peaceful.

REFUGEE

The sun crosses borders
without any soldier shooting at it
the nightingale sings in Tulkarem
of an evening,
eats and roosts peacefully
with kibbutzim birds.
A stray donkey grazes

across the firing line
in peace
and no one aims.
But I, your son made refugee
-Oh my native land-
between me and your horizons
the frontier wall stands.   (JUBRAN, IN JAYYUSI 1992, 190)[8]

In a competing vision, Abu Salma, a poet whom Palestinians often called "The Olive Tree of Palestine" because of his rootedness in the land and his unceasing love for it (Jayyusi 1992, 19), assumes that the displacement of his people and the occupation have even affected the nature of Palestine, suggesting that the loyalty of the homeland would hinder its blossoming without its native inhabitants.

Has the lemon tree been nurtured by our tears?
No more do birds flutter among the high pines,
or stars gaze vigilantly over Mt. Carmel.
The little orchards weep for us, gardens grow desolate,
the vines are forever saddened.   (ABU SALMA, IN JAYYUSI 1992, 97)

In his famous short story "Land of the Sad Oranges," Ghassan Kanafani has described the same "sympathy of nature with the Palestinians" (Bardenstein 1999, 152). The hero of the story, a boy experiencing the flight of his family to Lebanon and observing the actions of the adults around him, remembers how a peasant back in Palestine told him that the orange trees would shrivel and die when left to the care of strangers. The story ends with the boy's discovery of a dried and shriveled orange next to a handgun at the bedside of his uncle who had been contemplating suicide over the loss of the homeland (Bardenstein 1999, 153).

Trees, especially olive, almond, and orange trees, symbolize the rootedness of the Palestinians in their homeland and speak of the fertility and beauty of the country. They also remind the Palestinians of a peaceful past as peasants. The tree as a symbol evolved as a central feature in the Palestinian collective memory of an idealized past. Trees figure prominently in Palestinian poetry and fiction, showing the Palestinian himself as a tree, rooted in the soil, having a long history, and unwilling to give up his homeland (Bardenstein 1999).

Many poems focus on Jerusalem as an emblem of Palestine, encompassing both the notions of Palestinians' deep rootedness in history, and their being endowed with a heritage of special significance to the foundations of Western civilization. In the complex symbol of Jerusalem, Palestinians find both the national importance of the place as their capital and the religious significance of the Holy City as the crossroads of numerous religious and historical encounters. To be rooted in a country that is not simply a "place on earth" but that has been contested over many centuries evokes pride but also exacerbates the pain of loss for the Palestinians.[9]

Palestinian visual arts have contributed to the development of an idealized and highly symbolic image of Palestine. It employs the same markers of beauty, peace, and rootedness, as reflected in a number of Palestinian paintings produced during the last fifty years. As an outstanding Palestinian painter, Sulaiman Mansur, expressed it in an interview:

> The Nakba greatly affected Palestinian art. Even now when we want to document the history of Palestinian art, we start with the Nakba. . . . After 1948, Palestinian painting had for subject, naturally, refugees, the dispossessed living in a tent or in the open air. At the end of the 1950s, another trend took place: artists started to paint nostalgic subjects, such as the good life they had led in the villages prior to the Nakba, the homeland, working the fields, wedding scenes. Later, the hero of Palestinian painting became the fighter, the proud Palestinian. . . . Speaking of all these stages, I noticed that the young artists in the 1970s and 1980s went through all the above-mentioned stages in their paintings, all in the span of two years. Then these artists moved on to their own personal experimentation, but the political influence was always there.
>
> (MANSUR 1998, 91)[10]

Some examples may illustrate the power of the symbolism developed in poetry and used in paintings as well. In 1973 Sulaiman Mansur painted a canvas entitled "Carry On." It shows an old man in poor clothes, carrying the city of Jerusalem with the Dome of the Rock wrapped in a sack on his back. He looks tired, yet his strong hands hold the rope of the sack with a tight grip. The picture unites the notion of Jerusalem, both as a national and universal religious emblem, with the theme of being a refugee carrying all his remaining belongings on his back, declaring the memory of Jerusalem particularly precious. I have seen reproductions of this painting in several Palestinian homes.

Another painting by Sulaiman Mansur, titled "Salma," shows a Palestinian woman wearing a traditional embroidered dress and holding oranges in her arms. A scarf partly covers her black hair, and her appearance is proud. Again we see strong hands, able to clasp and protect the things that are precious to her: oranges—recalling the lost groves of Jaffa as a symbol of the fertility and the beauty of the land of Palestine. The background of the painting shows other women picking oranges from trees. The woman's name, Salma — meaning peace (*salam*) — and the scene itself, evoke the vision of a peaceful pre-Nakba time in Palestine.

The Palestinian artist Fathi Ghabin created a series of paintings called *Folk Design* (*Min al-turath* 1983).[11] The pictures show men and women dancing *dabkah* (a Palestinian folk dance) together. Women in traditional embroidered dresses and white scarves are making bread under an old olive tree.

Nabil Anani's "Memories of 'Amwas" (*Dhikrayat 'Amwas* 1981) is one example of a series of "Palestinian village" paintings.[12] It shows a woman with a white scarf, this time accompanied by two children, under an olive tree in a Palestinian village. On one of the houses we find a map of Palestine — a reminder of the intersection between political and emotional perceptions of space.

How then have these images of Palestine as the lost and beautiful homeland been passed on to the younger generations of Palestinians in exile? Answers to this question can be found in the interviews conducted with young returnees. They recalled their upbringing in different diaspora countries and provided personal recollections of how they developed an image of Palestine. How did they relate to the memories of their parents and grandparents, and what other sources of learning about Palestine did they have? What images of Palestine did they have before they returned?

Cultural and Imagined Homelands

The young Palestinians interviewed for this study are all part of the second or even third generation in exile. Some have experienced migration themselves; others grew up as children of Palestinians in only one host country. One line divides them clearly. Throughout their childhoods, a number of them had the opportunity to visit Palestine, some every summer, others just once during their childhood and teenage years. The other group, because of their passports, legal situation, parents' professions, or the Israeli occupation, never got to see the country that they and their parents call their homeland. For those who had opportunities to visit Palestine, it is a cultural homeland more than a national one. It is not imagined the way it is for the second group, because those who have visited are familiar with its nature, geography, and people. For those who grew up in exile, without ever seeing Palestine, the country is an imagined homeland. Their image of Palestine is more idealized, influenced by memories, pictures, stories, and the media. Not surprisingly, these different perceptions of Palestine as a homeland directly influenced their coping strategies upon return.

This study distinguishes two groups of young returnees: those who returned from Arab countries (the Aideen) and those who returned from the United States and Western Europe (the Amrikan) (see Chapter 4 for more detail). For the purpose of this study, it would have been convenient if all the Aideen saw Palestine as an imagined homeland and all the Amrikan were connected to Palestine as a cultural homeland. The complex realities of Palestinian migration did not do us that favor, so the differentiation is more complicated. In both groups there are people who never visited Palestine and others who did. Generally the division could be made, with the necessary caution, between political emigrants — the refugees and exiles, and economic emigrants — those who went to some other country for work.[13]

Most Palestinian refugees in Arab countries, such as Lebanon, Egypt, and Iraq, could not return to Palestine for visits. Refugees in Jordan could not visit Palestine anymore after 1967. Work migrants in the Gulf countries, if they came directly from Palestine, often had the necessary documents for visits or permanent return. Of those who migrated to Western countries, the group that migrated directly from Palestine, especially in the sixties and seventies, either kept the required status and papers, or were naturalized in their country of residence and could visit with foreign passports. Those Palestinians in Western countries who came from other exile countries in the Arab world, to continue studies or escape persecution for political activities, most often could not or chose not to visit or return, for fear of persecution.

AL-WATAN: THE IMAGINED NATIONAL HOMELAND

For the second and third generation of exiled Palestinians in the Arab countries, Palestine was part of their childhood, as was the fact that they were Palestinians, living in al-ghurba. Their sense of being part of a distinct group was enhanced by living within a Palestinian minority community (even if not always in a refugee camp), where Palestine was present in stories, pictures, and memories. With similar sources for images of Palestine, but less integrated into a Palestinian community, those who grew up in Western countries had to find different ways of knowing Palestine.

From the interviews, three main sources for these images evolve: memories of the parents and grandparents, represented in stories, political discussions, and pictures; Palestinian poetry and fiction, as well as visual arts and books on Palestine; and media coverage of events in Palestine.

The memories of the older generations entailed descriptions of childhood in Palestine, the beauty of places, especially homes of the family before emigration, less often the traumatic events surrounding the flight. Memories of the parents resemble in a rather striking way the images described in poetry and visual arts, recalling the peaceful village life, the olive, almond, fig, and orange trees, and the most beautiful landscape.

In Hanadi's recollection of what her father told her, we find exactly these images:

> He certainly said that life was simple, my father is old, fifty-four, and of course it was different in the way people lived from agriculture. Not as it is now; they would plant and then they would harvest the wheat; they would all leave their houses and live in tents on the land. They had sheep and camels—it was a totally Bedouin life. So the whole summer they would live with the crops, far from the village, and just work there. And also, that they had really big families: We are seven, but they had more. How they married and then lived in the same house.

> They always say that there is nothing tastier than the fruits of the village at that time: When I was a child I could smell the cucumbers from afar; when I eat cucumbers now, they don't have any taste! In the past I could find the cucumbers by smelling them, and I loved them so much. And the melons and all that, everything was better for him in the past, he says. And also the way they exchanged goods—you could pay with wheat, I give wheat and you give me something else.

In Sandy's story the images were developed through her mother, who herself had never seen Palestine. Sandy often talked to me about how these things evolved in her mind, and ever since she came to Palestine, she has tried to find out how she grew up feeling or becoming more Palestinian:

> I was actually trying to work this out the other day, and I was trying to remember, and I am sure we did. Because I don't know where else I could have got it, you know, the idea that it is the most beautiful country in the world, and it's got everything you need in a country, and it's got the tallest mountains and the bluest sea and the most velvety grass and blah, blah, blah. And fertile. And everybody is the most educated, it is the most educated Arab country in the Middle East, and they are the best, most honorable, most noble people.

In a surprisingly different interpretation, her brother Nigel described the much less positive image that his mother had of Palestine and that she subsequently passed on to her children:

I think that as far as she is concerned, she felt that she didn't feel a great amount of pride about being Palestinian as such because she didn't know what Palestinian people were like, the society, and she assumed that they would all be full of hatred, from being oppressed. And she was pleasantly surprised with the fact that this was only a minor point of society and, in fact, she found a lot of other really positive and genuine aspects to Palestinian society which she discovered.

In Marwan's memory, the things his father told him about Palestine when he was a child were even more precious, because his father was killed in an Israeli attack in Tunis. The village of 'Amwas, where he was born, was destroyed in 1967. Its inhabitants had been expelled in 1948 but returned to 'Amwas and lived there until 1967, when they were forced to settle in the nearby village of Abu Ghosh. Marwan's father became a fighter and left Palestine for Jordan. Marwan recalled many details of his father's narrative:

> My father always talked about 'Amwas and the green, the almond trees; there were lots of them and it is true—when I went there I saw them. A lot of green plants, the land is good, the weather is wonderful, the area has very beautiful places, and the village of Abu Ghosh was very beautiful. He always talked about the village itself, but then also about Palestine in general. That it had fruits you couldn't find anywhere else. That it had different kinds of landscapes, like deserts and plains, and snow on the top of Jabal al-Shaykh, and about 'Akka and Yafa, and at the same time Gaza. That it was a small country but that it had a lot of interesting things and features you could visit. Of course, there was a certain degree of exaggeration; he would say that as soon as you entered the territory of Palestine, the air would have a different smell.

Nimr, who was the son of a prominent Palestinian politician, carried both beautiful images of Palestine's natural environment and images of Palestine as a historically and religiously important place. He told me about the lemon trees on his family's land and about his father's insistence that he go and see them. He also made his son read books on Palestinian history and would often test him on what he had learned. Nimr developed pride in his homeland by realizing how important it was to others, namely, the believers in the three monotheistic religions. He emphasized the importance of Palestine in history and the holy books.

Visual images of Palestine most often originated from pictures and paintings decorating the houses of Palestinian families in the diaspora.

The most prominent image is the Dome of the Rock, a symbol for both Jerusalem and Palestine. Dalia recalled the prominence of that image in her childhood. Later, she developed a deep interest in Islamic architecture and called the Dome of the Rock her favorite Islamic building.

> Somehow, to me, my homeland is Jerusalem, it is the Dome of the Rock, it has just been engraved right in here [her heart], maybe because that is the picture I have seen all around. Although the Holy Land is not just where the Dome of the Rock is, it is the whole city. I used to draw it a lot, I remember when we were in Cairo we went for a trip with my family to a beach. And someone had a competition on the beach; we were supposed to build things from sand. And I remember I made a sketch of the Dome of the Rock. That day my dad was so proud, and he said that above all the things in the world, that is the thing you were thinking of. I was a kid, I was about eleven or twelve; obviously I hadn't seen the Dome of the Rock for real, but all the pictures and everything were just engraved right there, and so until now I am so related to that place.

Palestinian poetry, fiction, and nationalistic songs played a role only in the lives of those young Palestinians who lived in Arab countries, partly because of their command of Arabic (which many of those in Western countries did not have) and partly because they were part of Palestinian community life. However, the stories and memories of the elders were not always met with a positive attitude. Several interviewees recalled feeling distant from what their parents talked about, not so much because they rejected the idea of a national homeland, but because they wanted to distance themselves from the older generations.

As all the respondents in this study were relatively young, the outbreak of the First Intifada had a great impact on their image of Palestine. Because of TV and newspaper coverage, videos, and discussions, their focus shifted from the natural beauty of the Palestinian homeland to images of the brave, stone-throwing Palestinian youth. The pride in the courage and achievements of these fellow Palestinians was often accompanied by shock and anger about their suffering, and intense wishes to be in Palestine, struggling with their people. Images of Israeli soldiers beating up Palestinian children, and the news about martyrs—jailed, tortured, and injured Palestinians—connected the exile community to the homeland. In some cases, especially for young Palestinians in the West who had not been exposed as much to Palestinian national discourse and politics, the pictures of the Intifada were remembered as a turning point in their identity building and national consciousness.

Amina recalled that her mother did not talk much about Palestine, possibly because her father was in jail, and talking about him, as well as about Palestine and politics, was painful for her. Amina learned much more in school and through the media, and she connected her pride in the Palestinian youth to her longing to be there.

> The school and TV and all that created a beautiful picture. I had this idea that I would come to Palestine once and then I could die. Once with the school we went on an excursion to a place close to the border in Jordan. After I came back I kept some soil from that place because I was convinced that some of it would be from my country. Possibly these ideas seem exaggerated now, but we were very connected to Palestine. It is enough to remember that my dad sacrificed his lifetime for Palestine. I was very proud to say that I am Palestinian; that is how I saw myself. I always wished that I could have been here during the Intifada, to throw stones and see the Jews; I wanted to be here during events to participate in them. I would see people here on TV, and I felt that they were very connected with each other; the young people were very aware. They had a message, they had something they lived for and it was no problem to die for it. Whatever blood the Jews would shed, with guns and tanks, they would not be afraid: They only wanted their land back. That is the picture I had.

For Allen and Tariq, as for others, the pictures in the Western media, which led to their first forays into activism during the Intifada and the Gulf War, not only raised their consciousness as Palestinians and inspired them to inquire about their Palestinian identity but also influenced their images of Palestine. I myself remember the postcards, posters, and videos about the Intifada—strong images of Palestinians with *kufiyya* (the Palestinian black and white headdress), Palestinian flags, and stones; children holding stones in both hands; women and children demonstrating in the streets; and Israeli soldiers firing at the demonstrators. These materials could be found anywhere there were Palestinians.

The interviews show that the images of the homeland were beautified, emphasizing the connection to Palestine and the positive sides of the country and its people, thus helping diaspora Palestinians identify with their homeland. For those who had never seen the country themselves, Palestine was almost mythical, being the best of all places, a place where Palestinians feel at home. Most of those who could not visit Palestine before their eventual return were involved directly or indirectly in Palestinian issues. For them, it was the whole country, not a particular place, that they imagined. If their town or village of origin was considered, it was only as a symbol of all of Palestine. Jerusalem was also taken as a symbol for Palestine and appreciated for its religious and historical importance. For these young Palestinians, Palestine was *al-watan*—their fatherland or national homeland.

AL-BALAD: THE CULTURAL HOMELAND

The second group of respondents comprised young Palestinians who were born abroad but had the opportunity to visit—some just once or twice, others every summer of their childhood. The accessibility of the homeland, and the economic reasons for emigration from Palestine coincided for most of them and led to the emergence of a dramatically different image of Palestine.

The summer visits were a feature of their childhoods and were the highlight of the year because they would meet relatives, especially cousins of the same age, with whom to play and socialize. Aunts, uncles, and grandparents spoiled the visiting children, and the family reunions often had the character of extended summer parties. Parents also seemed to be more lenient in Palestine, allowing their children to play outside, discover the place, and socialize with children of the same age. Parents spoke about relatives and society in positive terms. For Rami, it was a combination of media images and parents' descriptions:

> Before I came? I thought it was like a desert, you know, something like Walt Disney's *Aladdin;* I pictured it like that, very Egyptian, desert and all that. . . . See, they wanted us to come here, so they would tell us a lot about all the good things—oh, it is nice, it is beautiful over there, you have a lot of land to go and play around over there—I was still a little kid; you play around all day and you get to know a lot of people. They told me we have a really big house, which we do, a sort of villa, and I can stay out long. And those are the things that attracted me most, so I wanted to come. That is pretty much how they explained it to me.

For some, the first visit to Palestine would have the character of return as well, as Rayda remembered. The whole family went to visit Palestine and her father's village. She described this visit as leaving her with only a superficial image of Palestine, mostly related to her meeting relatives and her being uncomfortable about not speaking enough Arabic. However, she recalled very emotional moments, such as when they all went to her father's village in Israel and to the camp near Jericho where her mother was born.

So we went to al-'Abasiyya and we went to Jericho and saw their refugee camp. So it was really intense, the building; the small house that my mum had lived in still had my grandmother's needles stuck in the wall, because she used to stick her needles from sewing in the wall. I remember it being an intensely emotional trip, it was the first time I saw my father cry.

Generally, these respondents referred to Palestine as *al-balad*, the place, community, village, or town. In the plural form, *al-bilad* also means the "country" or "homeland." Both are commonly used to describe the place of origin, whether to mean the actual town or village, or the country. Those interviewees who spoke English as their first language often used only a few Arabic words and phrases. "The *balad*" or "the *bilad*," English article and Arabic word, were words they used frequently.

Concluding from these observations and interviews, it is argued that those of the returnees who could visit Palestine had an image of the country that was deeply influenced mostly by pleasant holiday memories, meeting relatives, and having unusual freedom. Those who recalled such images in the interviews also responded to questions about their identity and Palestinianness with examples from their cultural and social life, telling me that language, family, bloodline, religion, customs, and traditions, rather than the struggle for a national homeland, made them Palestinian.

The image of Palestine had different sources for the two groups. Both found the images to be different from what they would experience as the realities of Palestine when they returned. Such a gap between image and reality is not entirely unexpected, yet often comes as a surprise and challenge to returnees. For Palestinians living in diaspora communities, the myth of a shared homeland, a place of ancestry as well as a place of symbolic or real belonging, is one of the founding pillars of their relative stability as a community and of the Palestinians as a nation.

CHAPTER 4 **Return to Palestine:**
Dreams and Realities

*I'm here to find out what dreams or nightmares
are all about, to touch a country woven from
memories, from songs, from stories of elders,
from pictures, from old coins and stamps, from
dreams that refuse to come to terms with an
unfair reality.* (N. KANAFANI 1995, 40)

Return, *al-ʿawda,* is one of the central concepts of Palestinian ideology and
life. It includes the dream of return, in political expression and literature,
and the right of return. The right to return is a subject of international
law, Palestinian demands, and Israeli rejections. There is the dream of return, never abandoned but incorporated into daily life in diverse ways.
And there are the realities of those who have been able to return since
the signing of the Oslo agreements. The conditions and circumstances for
their return as well as the reflections of those who wrote about their experiences are discussed here. I encountered the most moving narrative of
return in both its aspects of dream and reality when Nimr told me the
story of his and his father's return.

Nimr's Story

Nimr was born in 1971 and grew up in Lebanon. His father was Palestinian
and his mother Lebanese. He returned to Palestine in 1995, after earning
a degree in political science in Beirut, where he also worked on behalf of
Palestinian refugees in Lebanon.

Nimr's life is synonymous with Palestinian politics. During the interview he responded to each of my questions with information about political events, political leaders, and movements, while relating personal information. His interview reads like a historical introduction into the politics
of Palestinians in Lebanon. He did not differentiate between his own life

and political events, as they were an integral part of what he perceived as his personal history.

Unlike most of the other interviewees, Nimr is the son of a high-ranking Palestinian official who became a freedom fighter in 1948 and spent a lifetime in the Palestinian national movement. Consequently, Nimr grew up hearing about politics, important political figures, and what it meant to have a clear sense of Palestinian national identity. He described himself as both Palestinian and Lebanese, with a connection to both countries, but with more attachment to Palestine "because it is threatened, under occupation." For that very reason the civil war in Lebanon caused much tension in his life, though he was very young when it started.

His childhood was spent in school and summer camps. At camp he learned to feel Palestinian and proud of it. In school, however, he was always reminded that he was different, Palestinian and not Lebanese. Since 1982, when the Palestinian fighters were forced to leave Lebanon and move to Tunisia, he was constantly afraid that someone would kill his father and that the "struggle" would destroy his family. He felt isolated because the Lebanese part of his family was distant and his father did not have any close relatives in Lebanon. Even more, he feared that if his father died, he would lose all the family safety he had.

> I didn't leave my father at all. Although I was small, I went anywhere with him; I stood beside him. I felt and feared that my family would be destroyed too. I didn't have a family in the way my friends did.

Nimr's father talked about Palestine, about his upbringing in a village in the north of the West Bank, about the land the family once owned, and about how it was his greatest wish to return to Palestine and die there. He had left Palestine in 1957 in fear for his life, wanted by Jordanians and Israelis alike. The beginning of the Oslo process turned the dream of going back to Palestine into more realistic plans of return. Nimr realized that the peace process was not what Palestinians had desired and fought for, but he could explain why it was necessary. He praised Arafat's visionary leadership and his realization that after the Gulf War the PLO was running out of support and money and thus had to choose the road to "peace."

He recalled that after the Intifada started in 1987 his father spoke more about return and also encouraged him to read more about Palestinian history. His father would talk about the beauty and uniqueness of Palestine, and Nimr developed an image of Palestine that made him feel proud and long for return.

Sometimes when we would walk around, in an area north of Tripoli where we used to play as children, he would look at it and say, You know, Palestine is more beautiful. I started imagining Palestine as something very special. . . . The Jews are in Palestine, the Christians are in Palestine, and Islam is in Palestine; the prophet Jesus was born in Palestine, all the cultures of the world are present in Palestine. It is not just some country. . . . We are talking about a homeland we have here, a home to live in.

His father knew Palestine, which only increased his wish to return there. On the one hand he found it hard to accept that Palestine would only be the West Bank and Gaza (a third of original Palestine), and on the other, it was what Nimr called the "bitterness of Palestinian exile" that made his father and many others of his generation turn their hopes to Palestine. In the process, they were forced to accept the political realities of Oslo. Nimr agreed with his father on all these questions; his father was his role model and the most important person in his life.

A combination of political and personal circumstances led to his father's return to Palestine:

Then my father started saying that he wanted to return. In 1994 he was diagnosed with cancer. He was so afraid that he wouldn't die in Palestine, that he would die in Lebanon. . . . So he started saying, There is no good in this country, I want to go to Palestine and be buried there, next to my father and mother, I want to die there. He called Abu 'Ammar (Yasir Arafat) and told him, I am about to die, maybe another month and I will die. Quickly get me an ID so that I can return and die next to my father; I don't want anything else from you. Abu 'Ammar showed his kindness and understanding and got the ID for him as fast as possible. He entered Palestine in 1995, on the 18th of June.

Nimr accompanied his father to the Allenby Bridge but could not enter Palestine at that time. He got his permit two days later and followed his father to see his homeland for the first time. His father, very ill already, tried to connect his son to the country. Nimr tells his own story here:

I entered Palestine on June 20, 1995.

The first thing that happened was that the people, inhabitants of Qalqiliya, the older generation who remembered him came and greeted him, and the younger ones who had only heard about him also came to greet him. With them he started remembering the days of his childhood, the school, and how he fled and all that. I was just sitting and listening. But every day I could feel more that he became increasingly tired. He started telling me that I had to go and see the land, where the lemon trees are, the land he had always told me about. My father wanted to connect me to Palestine and connect me to the lemon trees.

And I think that he insisted to die in Palestine so that even if I decided in the future to sell the land or even accept compensation (because in the final phase the Israelis will compensate for these lands), if I sold the land and went to America or Denmark, or returned to Lebanon, he wanted to connect me to Palestine by force, by creating a grave there, the grave of my father. My father is in Palestine. Every time I come back from Amman, I go and I read the *Fatiha* (first verse of the Qur'an) at his grave. He wanted to connect me to this place by force. He also told me that on the land that we still own there is the grave of the prophet Benjamin and the prophet Suraqa. Have you heard of them? They are buried in the middle of the land that belongs to us. But the Jews came and built something on the graves, to make them Jewish graves, and they come and pray there. He said to me, Go and see the land; it is beautiful land next to Kfar Sab'a. I started going there. . . . Then when I told him afterward that I saw this and went there he started crying. In the end he couldn't walk anymore, not even sit, so he couldn't go and see the land himself.

The last day, it was a Friday, the last three days he didn't eat anymore; I would make him milk and dip some bread in the milk and feed him that so that he would eat something. When I got up in the morning I kissed him and I wanted to go; I brought him his medicine and also fed him a lot of food. He started joking with me. The last three days he had stopped talking to me. His throat was so dry, you couldn't understand him anymore. The last days when he could still walk, he walked with a stick. This stick was next to his bed, and once he grabbed it and waved it and kept on saying, I want to kill them, all of them. Gaza and Jericho only, Palestine and Qalqiliya, why not? Why don't they give us that too? In 1995 the Israeli army was still there. The last day I kissed him and I told him, Today I want to go to the Al-Aqsa Mosque in Jerusalem, and I will pray for you there. He hugged and kissed me and said, May Allah be with you. So I prepared myself and left for Jerusalem. When we reached the checkpoint in Ram, they didn't let us enter. So we turned back, and I said to my cousin, Let's call; I want to ask about my father. So I called and his wife Maha said, Come back here quickly. Oh, and I didn't tell you on the way my cousin said, Oh, Allah, we couldn't go to Jerusalem, and I said, No, don't be sorry, because "Don't get upset about something negative; there could be good for you in it." There was Allah's plan in that; He didn't want me to go and leave my father alone. So I told him to hurry because Maha said that we should hurry. So we went and when we got there I sat with him and I felt that he was about to die. I knew it was almost over. I was very sad and started crying. After a little while he died.

I wanted to talk to someone, inform someone, so I took the phone and called Abu M. (a close friend of my father) in Amman. I told him, see, Abu M., my father just died. And he told me, Really, I am glad. I said, Why? And he said, Do you remember how much your father wanted to die in Palestine? Allah fulfilled his dream; your father left this country in 1957 and came back in 1995. So it was almost forty years that he was away from the land, and then he was allowed to die in the same place, the place he loves. You don't have to be sad; it was his dream.

The next day, the first of July, he was buried. The procession for him was something amazing; everybody came. People, not that I know many people, but even my cousins didn't know many of them. But after we put the condolence in the newspaper, so many people came. I was also happy because all the groups of the PLO, PFLP, DFLP, Fatah, even Hamas, they were marching and they had the coffin wrapped in the Palestinian flag. They showed so much respect for him. When he was carried out of the mosque, on the way to the cemetery Israeli soldiers passed by on the highway. I was walking and crying, and I looked at them, thinking that my father died and the Israelis are still here; they didn't go. We went and buried him.

After his father's death, Nimr went back to Lebanon to see his mother. He returned to Palestine because friends of his father pushed him to work for the PA. But it was only after a personal meeting with Arafat that he received the necessary permission to stay and work with the PA, together with a post at one of the ministries. Nimr held Arafat in high regard and even connected his feeling of being at home in Palestine to him:

After I left him I could feel that I have a place in this state, in this country. My only place is here, in this homeland, because it is there for me. When my mother is sick they pay; when I need to see her, they help me, even though it seems simple things.

Four years after his father passed away, Nimr worked within the PA and also tried to organize a political party that could connect the Palestinians inside to the refugees who were not able to return, a party that could speak for the right of return and its implications. His political ideas, his pride in being Palestinian, and his life plan were the legacy of his father's life:

> My father taught me something that I find very important: A father can leave a villa, land, a company for you, but I inherited from my father that: *karama* (dignity). I have dignity and I can wear it proudly; my father didn't steal anything from Palestine, or from the PLO, the opposite, he gave what he had. I can prove that; we don't have a palace, but whenever I enter a gathering and say I am the son of so-and-so, they know me.

The Dream of Return: Politics and Poetry

As represented in Nimr's narrative, return to Palestine has, ever since 1948, played an important role in both Palestinian politics and the personal and collective imagination of the Palestinians.

Al-ʿawda, the Arabic term for return, has a highly symbolic and almost mythical meaning for Palestinians. It relates their exile, suffering, and homelessness to the place in which they have their roots, and it concentrates their life's efforts on returning to that place of origin, thus finding the stability and context missing in their diaspora experiences. For Palestinians inside Palestine, it relates to reunification with family members and the end of decades of longing to see close relatives in person again.

The Palestinian Liberation Organization, founded in 1964, was from its very beginning focused on liberating the occupied homeland, thus laying the ground for the return of the uprooted Palestinian refugees who led miserable lives in the surrounding Arab countries. In the years following its foundation, the PLO also became the political representative of Palestinians both inside and outside the occupied homeland. It became a network of institutions in different countries and an umbrella for various Palestinian political parties and organizations, even as the return to Palestine remained the ultimate goal.

This is reflected in the PLO charter, adopted by the Palestinian National Council in July 1968, which states:

> Article 3: The Palestinian Arab people possess the legal right to their homeland and to self-determination after the completion of the libera-

tion of their country in accordance with their wishes and entirely of their own accord and will.

Article 4: The Palestinian identity is a genuine, essential, and inherent characteristic; it is transmitted from fathers to children. The Zionist occupation and the dispersal of the Palestinian Arab people, through the disasters which befell them, do not make them lose their Palestinian identity and their membership in the Palestinian community, nor do they negate them.

Article 5: The Palestinians are those Arab nationals who, until 1947, normally resided in Palestine regardless of whether they were evicted from it or stayed there. Anyone born, after that date, of a Palestinian father— whether in Palestine or outside it—is also a Palestinian.

(PERMANENT OBSERVER MISSION OF PALESTINE
TO THE UN, WWW.PALESTINE-UN.ORG)

There is a close connection between a people's political aspirations and the themes chosen by its poets and writers. Thus, the dream of return would have to be an important topic in Palestinian poetry and fiction.[1] Indeed, we find numerous examples of poems speaking about the longing to return, and short stories expressing the same sentiment.

Famous examples of fiction include Ghassan Kanafani's novel *Return to Haifa* and the short stories "Land of the Sad Oranges" and "Until We Return." In *Return to Haifa,* Kanafani describes the journey of a Palestinian couple from the West Bank back to Haifa after 1967. There, they search for the son they had to leave behind in 1948 and find that he was rescued and raised by a Jewish couple. Neither Haifa nor their child is what they expected; both have changed in unanticipated and traumatic ways.[2] In "Until We Return" a Palestinian peasant struggles to cross the desert in an attempt to return to his village and destroy the irrigation system that the Israelis have built to better exploit the land that was once tilled by him. He knows that his land and village have changed, and his plan is to reverse those changes even if he cannot take back the land. The story also reflects on the countless attempts of Palestinian refugees after 1948 to cross back into the territory that became Israel.

Palestinian poetry clearly expresses the dream and intention to return to Palestine one day. In his poem "Reverse Journey," Taha 'Abd al-Ghani Mustafa reflects on the hardships of exile, but also describes how a new generation of Palestinians will overcome the humiliation of being only helpless refugees and form a resistance movement to return to and live in

Palestine as their homeland. In his imagination they will march back by the millions and sing:

> To our land we return
> to sit beside our own hearth
> toasting bread and remembering
> We'll renew old times when life was radiant
> and listen to the old relating ancient tales,
> of the brave who rejected humiliation.
>
> Return to Galilee, to Hebron
> to Gaza, to Jericho!
> Ride the impossible, return to stay
> your country calls on you, don't look away.
> ('ABD AL-GHANI, IN JAYYUSI 1992, 234)

In his poem "We Shall Return," Abu Salma speaks of Palestine's calling him home, but expresses doubts about whether or not Palestinians will ever be able to return. His poem concludes:

> Beloved Palestine, how can I sleep
> when phantoms torture my eyes?
> In your name I greet the wide world,
> But caravans of days pass,
> ravaged by conspiracies of enemies and friends.
> Beloved Palestine, how can I live
> away from your plains and hills?
> The valleys call me and the shores
> cry out, echoing in the ears of time!
> Even fountains weep as they trickle, estranged.
> Your cities and villages echo the cries.
> Will there be a return, my comrades ask,
> a return after such long absence?
> Yes, we'll return and kiss the moist ground,
> love flowering on our lips.
> We'll return some day while generations listen
> to the echoes of our feet.
> We'll return with raging storms,
> holy lightning and fire,
> winged hope and songs,
> soaring eagles,
> the dawn smiling on the deserts.

Some morning we'll return riding the crest of the tide,
our bloodied banners fluttering
above the glitter of spears.   (ABU SALMA, IN JAYYUSI 1992, 96)

These examples of Palestinian poetry date back to the decades after 1948
when the first generation of Palestinian refugees could still remember the
homeland, a time when Palestinian national identity was transformed into
the foundation of the struggle for liberation.

More than thirty years after the establishment of the PLO, in a different
part of the world and under dramatically different conditions, Palestinian
American poet Suheir Hammad still speaks of return to Palestine. In her
poem "Dedication" she describes the life of her uncle, a refugee child in
Jordan, growing up in the misery of the camp, his mind full of longing for
Palestine and rage over the Israeli occupation. His only aim in life is to go
back to the homeland, a land close enough to see and yet unreachable for
him. When he finally does reach it, he is killed by Israeli soldiers.

his name could've been
ahmad   mustafa   jihad
could've been
mohammad   yousef   hatem
his name was hammad

standing on a mountaintop in jordan
looking over the vast sea
saw the land his people had come from
land of figs and olive trees
what should've been his *phalesteen*

it was close   god it was
so close and
forbidden to him
him the son of the land

. . .

he'd prove them wrong
his warm human blood would
fertilize the soil of *phalesteen*

his heart transcending his body
he vowed to return to *phalesteen*
bil roh   *bil dem*
with his life   with his blood

three years later   he was shot
and killed by israeli soldiers
his blood never reached the soil of no palestine
his body never reached home

five years later
his niece travels far
to sit on that same mountaintop
sees palestine over the sea
feels her uncle's heart join hers
thinks of exchanging her books and pencils
for a knife   a small pistol

she vows she'd return to *phalesteen*
ib rohi   *ib demi*
with my life   with my blood

i close my eyes
and smell the ripe olives   (HAMMAD 1996A, 3–6)

Hammad related to the story of her uncle, and in writing this poem she dedicated her poetry as a whole to him and his dreams. But there is distance in her perception, and doubt if dying without reaching the homeland is worth the loss of life. A few years after this poem was written, in 1998, Hammad did visit Palestine and discovered like so many other returnees that the real country was different from the dreams (Clarke 1999). Poems about return remain to be written. Possibly, the frustrating realities of return do not inspire poetry.

Recently, and in response to the failing peace process, a new worldwide movement for the return of the Palestinian refugees to Palestine has emerged. Palestinian intellectuals, mainly in the diaspora, initiated a petition for the right of return and established an Internet site, where supporters could sign the following petition:

> I affirm that every Palestinian has a legitimate, individual right to return to his or her original home and to absolute restitution of his or her property.

A network of activists was developed to organize a series of rallies to promote the right of return of the Palestinian refugees. The nonprofit organization founded for this purpose is called Coalition for the Palestinian Right of Return (CPRR). The board of advisers and the list of prominent signatories of the petition is a "who's who" of Palestinian intellectual and grassroots activism.[3]

After the petition was posted on the Web site (www.rightofreturn.org), a network of committees, called "Al-Awda," was developed to rally for the Palestinians' right of return. This network has an Internet site, a number of e-mail lists that include both local and international recipients, and committees specializing in various grassroots activities. Al-Awda has organized public rallies in London, Beirut, and Washington, D.C., in an attempt to capture media and public attention for the situation of Palestinian refugees. Their main goal is to educate the public, especially in the United States and Europe, about the fifty-year-old Israeli bias in historiography and the resulting injustice and inferior negotiating position of Palestinians. These networks operate without PA support and attempt to influence the PA's negotiations by giving a voice to Palestinians marginalized by the political process.

One rally in Washington, D.C., on September 16, 2000, united approximately four thousand people in a march through the city center. Posters centered around the will to return, displaying the symbolic keys to houses lost in 1948, and affirming that young Palestinians in the diaspora are not ready to give up on the right of return. One important feature of the rally was that the statements used were only those with which every Palestinian would agree. The organization is trying hard to overcome political schisms among different groups of Palestinians, which are symptomatic of the problems of many grassroots organizations over the last decades. Instead, the statements emphasized the feelings about injustice and suffering, thereby presenting a unified Palestinian voice whose strength might garner public and international support (www.al-awda.org).

This event and the organization supporting it demonstrate that the dream of returning to Palestine is still alive, even if, in reality, Palestinians remain divided on many issues. The different political positions on the right to return, whether international, Israeli, or Palestinian, official or unofficial, are vital to understanding the framework of the issue of return.

The Right of Return

The right of return, or, more precisely, the right of Palestinian refugees to return to their places of origin, is often cited as the core issue of the Palestinian refugee problem. Many analysts point out that this is the greatest obstacle to peace and may prove to be the most difficult to overcome as it involves a range of moral, economic, political, and emotional—not to mention logistical—issues. In addition, more than any other issue, it is linked to the self-definition of both Israelis and Palestinians (Hallaj 1994).

The largest part of the Palestinian diaspora community consists of the refugees in Lebanon and Jordan, many of whom still live in camps. For them, physical return to Palestine and the building of a stable existence within the boundaries of their homeland, together with the establishment of a Palestinian state, would free them from difficult living conditions, legal discrimination, and the lack of a viable future for their children. A smaller segment of Palestinian society, namely, Palestinian exiles and refugees in other countries, live under more settled conditions. They and the younger generations of Palestinians in the diaspora emphasize that granting them the *right* to return would reaffirm their national identity and give them the choice of living in the country they continue to call their homeland.

The history and causes of the Palestinian refugee problem and its implications for the demographic situation of the Palestinian people were discussed earlier. Most discussions of the right of return in the relevant literature start with legal questions, but the problem cannot and should not be reduced to a legal question, as the solution to the problem will most likely not be a legal one. Much has been written on the topic, and this is no attempt to reflect the width or depth of these discussions. The following paragraphs summarize basic positions, as far as they are of concern to the question of return and the returnees (see Zureik 1996; Akram 2000; R. Khalidi 1994 and 1999; Kossaifi 1996).

THE RIGHT OF RETURN IN INTERNATIONAL LAW

The international community's attempts to deal with war, crisis, and other causes for forced migration, codified in international law, as promoted and upheld by the United Nations, has defined the rights of refugees and strategies for their protection. The Universal Declaration of Human Rights of 1948 states in article 13 that "everyone has the right to leave any country, including his own, and to return to his country" (Zureik 1994, 9).

Zureik points out that "since international law is premised on state sovereignty, there seems to be a problem in successfully applying these criteria to the Palestinian case" (Zureik 1994, 9). Clearly, the 1951 Geneva Convention Relating to the Status of Refugees (Refugee Convention) and its 1967 Refugee Protocol, intend to protect refugees and assist them in various ways. In his analysis of the position of Palestinian refugees vis-à-vis international law, Zureik emphasizes that the focus in international refugee law has been to provide places and opportunities for resettlement and to protect refugees from persecution. Palestinian refugees are not seeking to resettle anywhere besides their country of origin; they demand to be allowed to return to their homeland. This is, according to Zureik, the reason that they were excluded from protection by the UNHCR and other international bodies (Zureik 1994, 8).

In a dramatically different interpretation of the same documents and laws, Akram argues that UNRWA was established to provide a heightened protection regime. She assigns the weak position of Palestinian refugees not only to incorrect interpretations of the law but also, and more significantly, to the weakness of the law itself. The UN as a body is actually more a platform for the United States and Israel to dictate conditions, rather than for the United Nations to promote refugee protection. As a consequence, UNRWA has been concentrating its efforts on assisting Palestinian refugees, not protecting them, though the latter was intended by the UN resolutions (Akram 2000, 8–10).

The central resolution, affirming the right of return, is the often-quoted Resolution No. 194 of the United Nations General Assembly of December 1948. Among other things, it "resolves that the refugees wishing to return to their homes and live at peace with their neighbors should be permitted to do so at the earliest practicable date, and that compensation should be paid for the property of those choosing not to return and for loss of or damage to property" (Kossaifi 1996, 10).

The second central resolution for affirming the right of return is concerned with those displaced in 1967, the second wave of Palestinian refugees. Resolution No. 237, adopted in June 1967, "calls upon the government of Israel to ensure the safety, welfare and security of the inhabitants of the areas where military operations have taken place and to facilitate the return of those inhabitants who have fled the areas since the outbreak of hostilities." (Kossaifi 1996, 10).

In 1974 the General Assembly adopted Resolution No. 338 and reaffirmed not only the right of the Palestinian people in Palestine to self-determination, national independence, and sovereignty, but also "the inalienable right of the Palestinians to return to their homes and property from which they have been displaced and uprooted," and called for their return (Kossaifi 1996, 11). These points have been reaffirmed numerous times by follow-up resolutions without causing a qualitative change in their implementation. Also, every year, the United Nations Organization calls for the implementation of Resolution No. 194, concerning the 1948 refugees, and Resolution No. 237, concerning the displaced Palestinians of 1967 (Kossaifi 1996, 18).

I agree with Akram that it is not the status of Palestinian refugees and their right of return in international law that is problematic or weak, but rather the fact that it cannot be implemented because the UN has been excluded from solving the conflict.[4] Scenarios for the return of Palestinian refugees are always based on the UN resolutions, and Palestinians have been calling for their implementation for decades, but they do not expect the UN to play a major role. The international community's weak stance weakens the Palestinian position, while empowering Israel. Human rights activists point out that "the very fact that refugee rights, which international law defines as individual, inalienable and non-negotiable, are being subjected to negotiation, illustrates the weakness of the Palestinian position" (Susskind 2000, 8).

It is somewhat confusing to speak here of the Palestinian position and the Israeli position, as one has to distinguish between official political discourse and other opinions and suggestions from groups and individuals in both camps.

THE RIGHT OF RETURN: PALESTINIAN AND ISRAELI APPROACHES

The Palestinian leadership position on the right of return is based on the UN resolutions and calls for the right of Palestinian refugees — displaced and expelled Palestinians — to return to their homes and be compensated for their losses (Zureik 1996; Susskind 2000; Kossaifi 1996; R. Khalidi 1994 and 1999). As Haidar Abdul Shafi, speaking on behalf of the Palestinian delegation to the Madrid Conference in 1991, put it: "As we speak, the eyes of thousands of Palestinian refugees, deportees, and displaced persons since 1967 are haunting us, for exile is a cruel fate: bring them home. They have the right to return" (Zureik 1996, 91).

In the years since the start of the peace process, Palestinian ideas of how to solve the refugee problem have ideally insisted on a literal right of return and compensation. However, within the Palestinian political scene, more "realistic" approaches have emerged, attempting to find a durable and implementable solution without eroding the right of return as a principle.

These ideas call on Israel to recognize the right of return as a principle while offering negotiations on the modalities of its implementation. In addition, the right of return is offered to be interpreted as return to a future Palestinian state rather than return to the refugees' former homes and villages inside Israel. Only "several thousand" of 1948 refugees could be permitted to return to Israel and become Israeli citizens through a family reunification program.

Over the last decade, Rashid Khalidi, a Palestinian historian and former adviser to the Palestinian negotiation team (and the author of *Palestinian Identity*), has developed what he calls "elements of a solution" to the Palestinian refugee issue (R. Khalidi 1994, 1999; Zureik 1996, 95-97).[5] These suggestions are based on the idea of attainable as opposed to absolute justice, as Khalidi argues that absolute justice will never be achieved for Palestinians, adding that for the Palestinian refugees in the camps a practical improvement of their situation would count more than the insistence on a principle that could never be implemented (R. Khalidi 1999). These elements, calling for truth, justice, and reconciliation, include:

1. Formal recognition of Israel's primary responsibility for the creation of the Palestinian refugee problem, expressed in the formation of a truth and justice commission;

2. Acceptance of the right of Palestinian refugees and their descendants to return to their homes as a principle, with actual return of as many refugees as possible without upsetting the demographic balance or challenging the Jewish character of the Israeli state;

3. Provision of reparations for all those who choose not to return, and compensation for all those who lost property in 1948;

4. The right of all Palestinians to live in a future Palestinian state and carry a Palestinian passport, entailing a right of return to Palestine, not subject to Israeli decision or control, but the right of an independent state, only limited by its absorptive capacities;

5. A viable solution to the particular problems of Palestinians in Jordan and Lebanon, with acceptable status of Palestinians in Jordan as either Palestinian or Jordanian citizens, and a groundbreaking change in the situation of Palestinians in Lebanon, based on bilateral negotiations between Palestine and Jordan, and Palestine and Lebanon.   (R. KHALIDI 1999, 232–237; R. KHALIDI 1994, 24–25)

These elements require steps from both the Israeli and the Palestinian sides, and require both to swallow bitter pills.

The Israeli approach to the refugee problem and the right of return has traditionally been one of rejecting historical responsibility for the creation of the refugee problem, thus refusing any attempts to be involved in its solution. Israel has called on the Arab states to implement the necessary measures for permanent settlement of Palestinian refugees in their host countries. Israel would "offer" financial assistance for resettlement without acknowledging any historical responsibility. As a gesture, a controlled number of refugees could return under a program of family reunification, with Israel controlling conditions and modalities of such return. Israel would allow restricted return of Palestinians to the territories under Palestinian control; in exchange, the PA would be expected to sign a document declaring the end of the refugee crisis and any further Palestinian claims (Susskind 2000; Zureik 1996, 65–77; Kossaifi 1996, 17).

In 1998 a group of Israeli and Palestinian researchers held a discussion on the future of the refugee question and formulated a report that reflects how far both sides would go in a compromise on critical issues. The report is not an official document, but the participants were considered to be speaking on behalf of their sides. It suggests that Palestinians would go as far as accepting that despite the right of return there will be no en masse return of refugees, but that Israel would allow a small number to return, and the Palestinian state would absorb a higher number of refugees in accordance with its capacity. Collective compensation would be paid to the Palestinian state and used for integration projects, with Israel responsible for providing or finding the funds for compensation. The report says that UNRWA should be dissolved after resettling the remaining refugees in their host countries.

Israel would, on its side, share the practical responsibility for the refugee problem, but not acknowledge moral or sole responsibility. It would demand control over the numbers and modalities of returning refugees to the Palestinian state. Compensation of Palestinian refugees would have to be linked to that of Jews who left Arab states in 1948 and after. Through the compensation funds, Israel would have the opportunity to control and alter the return flow if considered necessary (Badil 1998a, 3).

Political and media discussions in 2000 reflected the various Israeli positions at the time. On January 2, 2001, a group of Israeli left-wing intellectuals published a declaration of their opinion on the right of return in the Israeli newspaper Ha'aretz. Its key statement reads: "We want to clarify that we shall never be able to agree to the return of the refugees to within the borders of Israel, for the meaning of such a return would be the elimination of the state of Israel" (Ha'aretz, January 2, 2001). Among the signatories were well-known Israeli authors such as Amos Oz and David Grossman. Needless to say, the Israeli government position went even further in rejecting Palestinian claims.

In October 2001 the new PA representative for East Jerusalem in a speech at Hebrew University called for the Palestinians to take a more realistic position toward the right of return, and declared that a solution could entail return to a Palestinian state, not homes and places of origin, and compensation in exchange for offering the Israelis lasting peace. His ideas were met with harsh Palestinian criticism. The discussions following his statements demonstrated the variety of opinions on the issue within Palestinian circles. (Greenberg in *New York Times,* October 17, 2001).

RETURN VS. COMPENSATION

The compensation of Palestinian refugees for losses in 1948 was mentioned earlier, for example in discussions about UN Resolution 194. Restitution of property or compensation for loss are a part of recognized international law and have been practiced in and after other political and military conflicts, for example, in Yugoslavia, Kuwait, and South Africa.

In the Palestinian case, there are many obstacles to practical compensation. First of all, if Israel does not recognize its responsibility for the refugee problem, what reason would it have to pay compensation? Consequently, wherever discussion about compensation appears, it is depicted as a compromise on Israel's part to either find necessary international funds and/or provide the necessary amounts from its own sources.

An additional problem lies in individual versus collective compensation, with the PA favoring collective compensation to facilitate integration and resettlement of refugees. That still leaves the question of how lost property can and should be measured in numbers that both sides can agree upon. Numerous attempts have been made to estimate Palestinian losses (Hadawi 1988; Kubursi 1996; Peretz 1994). Compensation can only be part of a larger settlement of the refugee question and will face problems such as the measurement and adequate registration of property before 1948, the consideration of international aid to Palestine as part of compensation, and the question of lost Jewish property in Arab countries. Concerning this question, Palestinians rightly claim that if compensation had to be paid to these Jews, it would have to come from the Arab governments in question, not the Palestinians. A recent study provides an overview of the history and current state of the land and property records before 1948, which would have to be the basis for any assessment of losses and compensation (Fischbach 2003).

On the Palestinian side, the question may be asked as to whether it is possible to compensate the refugees and their descendants not only for lost property but for suffering and loss of life as well. In any case, collective compensation (proven by German reparation payments to Israel), hardly reaches those who experienced the loss. Thus, it is hard to believe that monetary compensation could be a step toward reconciliation between Israelis and Palestinians.

Return and the Oslo Process

During the Madrid talks and in preparing the Declaration of Principles (DOP), signed in September 1993 between Israel and the PLO, it became clear that, among other questions, the refugee problem was too thorny an issue to be dealt with in these negotiations.

Two different types of committees were set up to discuss matters related to Palestinians living outside Palestine. The main division was between "1948 refugees" and those who became "displaced persons" in 1967. The functions, meetings, and discussions of the committees were never very clear, and none has made major progress in implementing any durable solution (Badil 1998b, 2; Tamari 1996, 9; Kossaifi 1996, 14).

The Refugee Working Group (RWG) was established as a result of the Madrid Conference in 1991. This multinational body held several meetings, each meeting making it clearer that the negotiations of these multilateral working groups would focus on humanitarian issues and avoid the political question of right of return and compensation (Kossaifi 1996, 44).

Limited progress was made on the issue of family reunification, with Israel conceding the processing of two thousand cases each year, which would allow return of up to six thousand Palestinians under this particular program. Israel insisted that these Palestinians could only "return" to the West Bank and Gaza, not to its own territory. Even these limited numbers of cases were delayed, and the procedures made extremely complicated. Additional work of the RWG focused on community development and refugee living conditions; family reunification was the only issue related to the question of return. Most of the suggestions and reports issued by the RWG link refugee aid to creating options for integrating refugees into Arab host countries, thus working against the right of return and its implementation. In 1995 the debate over refugees shifted from the RWG and the 1948 refugees to the question of persons displaced in 1967.

The establishment of the Quadripartite Committee on the Right of Return of Displaced Persons (sometimes also called the Continuing Committee on the 1967 Displaced Persons) is based on Arab-Israeli agreements, such as those signed at Camp David; the Israeli-Jordanian peace treaty; and the agreements signed in Madrid and Oslo. The committee consists of Jordan, Egypt, Israel, and the Palestinians. Article XII of the Oslo accords stipulates that the committee would "decide by agreement on the modalities of admission of persons displaced from the West Bank and Gaza Strip in 1967, together with the necessary measures to prevent disruption and disorder" (Tamari 1996, 17).

In several meetings, more specific guidelines for the definition of displaced persons were discussed. Israel only agreed to the most restricted definition of "citizens of the West Bank and Gaza who were displaced during or in the aftermath of the war." Jordan and the Palestinians wanted to include those who were outside the West Bank and Gaza on the eve of the war and who were prevented from return by the Israeli occupation, as well as those who left the Occupied Territories after the 1967 census and were prevented from returning (Tamari 1996, 18).

The main point for the inner-Palestinian discussion on the right of return and the hope of return of refugees as a result of the Oslo process is clearly the fact that in the decade since the signing of the DOP, the process itself has failed, in part due to its failure to address the refugee issue. Many Palestinian refugees, especially those living under the most difficult of conditions in Lebanon, felt forgotten from the very start. Within the Palestinian territories, the sentiment toward returnees was influenced by the fact that their return was viewed as a trade-in for the return of all refugees. The modalities of return remain a confusing and unreliable labyrinth of legal definitions and procedures.

Realities of Return: Politics and Economy

A review of the literature on return and returnees reveals that the term "returnee" has been applied to different types and waves of Palestinians returning to Palestine. While the Oslo process raised hopes for Palestinians, both inside and outside, for economic prosperity, freedom, a state, and the opportunity to return, the Palestinian leadership tended to paint a rosy picture of the process in order to gain political support for it. The term "*Aidin*" was coined to imply that the return of some people, mainly those who would work for the PA and police, would be only a first step meant to open the door on a solution to the refugee problem.[6]

Three distinct categories of "returnees" can be identified: those who returned after the Gulf War of 1991 from Kuwait, the PLO returnees, and returnees from the United States.[7] They can be clearly distinguished chronologically, but also show different return and adaptation patterns.

The first wave of returnees, coming from Kuwait, were Palestinians driven out of the work and life they had there by the turn of public opinion against them after the Iraqi invasion of Kuwait. As the Palestinian leadership chose to support Saddam Hussein, mainly for his threats toward Israel, an estimated three hundred thousand Palestinians left the Gulf region, following their dismissal from work, deprivation of public service, arrest, torture, and their mounting fear of loss of life and property. Despite the high numerical presence of Palestinians in the Gulf region, they had "remained marginalized, politically disenfranchised and economically underprivileged as compared to Arab Gulf nationals" (Palestine Human Rights Information Center [PHRIC] 1993, 1). Of those who left, thirty to forty thousand returned to the Occupied Territories. Many others, those who had lost residency there and did not have the necessary documents, were absorbed, and settled into a difficult life in Jordan. Others migrated to the United States and Canada. A majority of them lost all their savings and property due to the circumstances of their departure.

A study of their living conditions, reasons for emigration, and settlement patterns reveals that Gulf migrants have kept close family ties to the West Bank and Gaza and express considerable desire to return (Hovdenak 1997). The sudden nature of their departure from the Gulf, a second uprooting for them, turned their return and adaptation process in Palestine into a frustrating and disillusioning experience. The main problem turned out to be the already depressed economic situation in the Occupied Territories, which was incapable of absorbing such a large number of potential workers.

A number of corresponding features appear in the available studies (Nour 1993; Le Troquer and al-Oudat 1999), listing, for example, a dramatic drop in the standard of living relative to life in Kuwait and a sense of emotional loss and estrangement from the general population. In addition, the studies identified uncertainty about the future, isolation within the community, limited employment opportunities, and curtailed opportunities for advancement as causes for their feeling of having reached a dead end. On the positive side, they became more conscious of Palestinian nationalism and had an increased sense of homeland (PHRIC 1993, 3). The same study concludes that the experiences with the return of Palestinians from the Gulf should be taken as reminders of what problems other Palestinians might encounter on return, and it therefore recommends programs to generate employment and financial as well as infrastructural assistance to facilitate returnees' adaptation.

Conversely, Palestinian Americans returning to Palestine cannot be said to have returned in a "wave." Their migration patterns were "oscillating" and were characterized by relatively frequent migrations and regular visits. More people within this group held the necessary legal documents to allow return and resettlement. Family networks functioned over long distances and kept relations between relatives current. Nevertheless, the number of "returnees" from the United States and Canada had dramatically decreased because of the unstable situation during the First Intifada and the closure of schools and universities. An increase can be assumed since the signing of the Oslo agreements. No reliable statistics were available, but estimates reported approximately thirty thousand Palestinian Americans living in the West Bank and Gaza (Associated Press 1999). Based on their migration patterns, more Palestinian Americans lived in the West Bank, concentrated around Ramallah, and a high number of them were either minors or mothers of minor children, whereas the fathers often stayed in the United States to attend to businesses and secure an income.

The third category of returnees, the real 'Aidin, were those who returned to the West Bank and Gaza after the DOP signing in 1993. Many of them worked for the Palestinian Authority directly, or the police; others were dependent family members, or came with the wave of returning PLO officials. The estimated numbers of these returnees range between sixty and a hundred thousand people, with no reliable data available. Most of them came from Tunisia, but there were offices to facilitate their return in other countries, such as Egypt and Yemen. While no comprehensive study on these 'Aidin has been published yet, a number of sources touch upon the political implications of the returnees, focusing on the continuation of the historical conflict between "inside" and "outside."

The arrival of the outside leadership in Palestine considerably changed that situation. The PLO leadership in Jordan, Lebanon, and Tunisia dominated the political discourse and directed political activity prior to the Intifada. The start of the Intifada in 1987 temporarily shifted leadership to the Occupied Territories. This development was partly reversed by the start of the Oslo process (Hilal 1993; Schiff 1995; Brynen 1995). Since 1994 the center of Palestinian activity has moved from Tunisia to parts of the West Bank and Gaza.

An analysis of the establishment of the PA since 1993 shows that the PLO leaders used the agreement as a way to expand their authority from "the political periphery to the center" by geographically moving from Tunisia to the Occupied Territories and by expanding their activities from political representation to other activities such as economics, health, tourism, and education. The conflict over the division of power between inside and outside was one of the major challenges for the leadership. Dominated by Yasir Arafat's personal (or autocratic) rule, the establishment of PA institutions appears as a careful balancing of these arising tensions and dilemmas (Klein 1997, 386).

Members of the PA were almost evenly divided into locals and return-ees. However, observers have pointed out that the returnees received more of the key posts and that locals were concentrated in the medium and lower levels of the administration.

> The most notable instance of quarreling over patronage and pie-dividing in the area of international aid moneys and programs has taken place at the top. . . . It is always Arafat who makes the crucial decisions in his "neo-patrimonial" style, aimed at maintaining a "healthy" level of competition among his followers, while avoiding an explosion.
>
> (HEACOCK 1999, 5)

Personalities of the inside leadership had less political experience and a different social background than the outside PLO cadres, but they were important actors during the Intifada and the peace talks (Klein 1997, 386). However, they lacked the close personal ties to Arafat that were vital for "real" political influence. As a result, some of them, such as Hanan Ash-rawi and Haidar Abul Shafi, resigned from PA positions, while others, in-cluding the late Faisal Husseini, tried to change the power balance from within.

A list of cabinet members from 1996 shows that out of twenty-one members, ten were returnees and eleven were residents, with returnees occupying the two central resorts of finance and planning/international cooperation (*Palestine Report,* June 21, 1996; Brynen 1995, 39).

In a similar way, posts and positions within Fatah, the movement Yasir Arafat built and led, as well as within the police force, have been distrib-uted. Especially within the police force, the conflict is "inside" versus "out-side" as well as older versus younger. Arafat resolved the growing tension by building a system of security apparatuses that are so complicated that, as Klein has observed, "there is neither a clear definition of authority nor a distinct picture of who is subjected to whom in the security establishment" (Klein 1997, 390). This led to clashes and conflicts between the different security units, but these did not take place along the lines of "inside" and "outside."

Nevertheless, the returnees had a considerable effect on the texture of Palestinian politics, and while the inside elite focused on institution building and civil society, the outside elite had a different vision of political practice. The Oslo process brought the outside elite to power. In response to the conflict arising between those who "created" the Intifada and those who "ended" it by initiating the peace process, the outside elite chose to neutralize the inside elite by co-opting them into the bureaucracy, but only on lower and medium levels. A part of the inside elite chose to retreat into civil institutions, which the PA has tried to dominate and control through laws (Robinson 2000). The role of the new Palestinian prime minister Mahmud Abbas in the "road map" negotiations of 2003 point to a decrease in Arafat's control and power over the PA.

Beyond politics, another important aspect of integration of returnees is their economic situation. While no data on investment and economic status in a statistical sense could be obtained (because such data seems not to exist or because Palestinian officials are reluctant to provide such information), a small-scale study, conducted in 1996, interviewed approximately four hundred returnees working within various ranks of the PA (Abdelhaqq 1997).[8] In summarizing the findings, a number of issues are worth mentioning.

The survey was met with little cooperation from the PA; the higher ranks typically did not respond to the questionnaires sent to them. The age structure of the sample shows that the majority of the returnees (77 percent) were less than fifty years old. Sixty-two percent of the returnees were born in the West Bank and Gaza, which facilitated reintegration into Palestinian society. Seventy-seven percent brought their families back to Palestine, an additional factor helping the integration process. Statistically, the level of education among returnees was higher than that of the local population, which would partly explain or justify their higher positions in the ranks of the bureaucracy of the PA. The salaries of returnees were higher than the average income of local Palestinians. Concerning the issue of privileges for returnees, such as mobile phones and cars or subsidized housing, the survey found that 10 percent of the returnees had a car provided by the PA, 8 percent had a mobile phone from that source, and 6 percent benefited from assistance in finding housing. Seventy-eight percent stated that finding appropriate housing for themselves and their families had been a major problem and an obstacle to settlement in Palestine. Main reasons for discontent were the lack of services available, the poor state of many buildings, and increased rents. Many returnees would prefer to buy property to feel more settled and secure.

These findings point to one of the major material problems that the returnees faced upon their return. The PA has never developed any programs to assist in reintegration, based on the assumption that locals and returnees are all Palestinians, and return to the homeland could not possibly be a problem. Many have proposed approaching the integration problem more actively, for example, by establishing a Ministry of Absorption for returnees that would facilitate their social and economic integration (Tamari 1996, 46).

Returnees were often accused of having economic advantages. Local Palestinians pointed to returnees' opportunity to import a car, furniture, and other items tax-free upon return, as well as their getting higher salaries with positions in the PA. Returnees, in turn, argued that most of them did not lead a life of luxury or have much saved from their life in exile, and thus the few privileges were crucial for their economic settlement.

Many returnees, from both Arab countries and the United States, were economically successful because they brought capital and skills that proved useful for them and the Palestinian economy. One can call it a "reversal of the brain-drain, but has to point to the fact that the construction of smaller and private businesses is not a solid basis for long-term economic growth. Unemployment rates did not rise or drop considerably because of the returnees" (Sayre and Olmstedt 1999, 3). The closure of the territories, their reoccupation, and other Israeli measures during the Second Intifada have reversed the slow economic growth that the West Bank and Gaza had experienced, and have virtually destroyed the Palestinian economy, affecting local Palestinians and returnees alike.

Reflections on Return

At first, the return of exiled Palestinians to Palestine was considered one of the positive aspects of the peace process. Hamzeh-Muhaisen described the feelings of many Palestinians at the time:

> In the increasingly bleak tunnel in which the Palestinians find themselves today there is perhaps one thing they can be cheerful about. Peace made it possible for tens of thousands of Palestinians to return to Palestine after years, and even a lifetime, of living in exile. . . . All brought with them their intricately diverse backgrounds, cultures and varied experiences in life. Their return, even to a small chunk of their homeland, meant that Palestine was no longer a picture of the Dome of the Rock hung on their living room walls but a real place where they live, work and raise their children. . . . To Palestinians in the West Bank and Gaza

Strip, the return of loved ones was a heartfelt joy. Relatives were reunited and friends met after long years of separation. The influx of returnees between 1994–1996 gave everyone hope that there just might be justice in this world after all. (HAMZEH-MUHAISEN 1998C, 6)

A number of Palestinian writers and intellectuals have chosen to write about their return experience and to reflect on their expectations and the realities and difficulties of return. These published accounts are interesting because they touch upon many of the topics discussed in the interviews, while viewing the situation from a somewhat different perspective. Two differences are especially important. The return experience of these intellectuals is different in that they were all born in Palestine. Most of them remember Palestine from their early childhood, so they do not rely entirely on the memories and stories of their parents.

Another interesting aspect of these texts is that not all of them are by "returnees," in the common understanding of the word. Some of them were written by people who came to visit Palestine after a very long time, often decades, to somehow rediscover the homeland, without choosing to stay for good. These return visits can be seen as a clear statement to claim Palestine as their homeland, logically tying in with a transnational yet Palestinian identity.

The texts available in English, written by Palestinian intellectuals in the United States and Europe, are most often return-visit narratives, while a number of texts in Arabic were written by intellectuals who returned to Palestine from Arab countries and stayed.[9] In their narratives, there are recurring themes, such as their images and memories of Palestine, anxiety about what they would find upon return, and disillusionment with the realities of the homeland. These themes resemble those found in the personal return stories collected for this study. But they differ in that they were not reflections induced by the questions of an interviewer, but careful and sometimes poetic accounts of emotions and observations put into words by experienced writers. And they are as much reflections and memories of exile as they are accounts of return, because the challenge of return makes them rethink and remember. It is their memories of exile that distinguish them from their relatives and friends in Palestine. In the words of one writer:

One of the hazards of exile is that, over the years, the physical reality of a place begins to recede and gradually enters the realm of the imagination. In the imagination of Palestinian exiles, Palestine was an idyllic place of orange, olive, fig groves and hillsides covered with varieties of grape vines. The fruits and the vegetables were, of course, the biggest and the most delicious in the entire world. We remember the taste of pure olive oil, *za'atar,* and *tabun* bread. . . . We recall Palestinians as a wonderful and caring people who have suffered great injustice at the hands of foreign invaders and occupiers.   (MOUGHRABI 1997, 5)

While a large number of exiled Palestinians with foreign passports could have returned earlier, at least for a visit, many feared that what they would find might destroy their cherished memories of the homeland.

My father, who had a British passport, could have returned to West Jerusalem as a tourist. He never chose to exercise this option and both he and my mother preferred to preserve the memory of their home as it had been before they left, intact, like a photograph. Seeing the place altered in alien custody would tarnish the image.

But the day came when I decided to return. In August 1991, after forty-three years, I took a journey to Jerusalem to face the monster I had been hiding from all my life.   (KARMI 1994, 39)

As she went to see the house of her family in West Jerusalem, she found that new buildings had replaced all the houses in the street. She concluded her return story:

I stayed for a long time, trying somehow to absorb what remnants of my history still lingered there, but no use. The place for me was desecrated and spoiled.   (KARMI 1994, 40)

Other stories speak of the anxiety before arrival and, not seldom, of the fear of crossing the border, of being faced with the Israelis, and of expecting some "homeland" feeling with different smells, lights, and sounds.

Kanafani recalls how at the airport in Tel Aviv he observed the nervous waiting and fear of fellow Palestinians before being questioned by the border police, and concludes that he never thought that he would return to his "country in such an uncelebrated and undignified manner" (N. Kanafani 1995, 40). He describes his expectations and first feelings:

I'm here to find out what dreams or nightmares are all about, to touch a country woven from memories, from songs, from stories of elders, from pictures, from old coins and stamps, from dreams that refuse to come to terms with an unfair reality. Never mind how and why, never mind justice and rights. Palestine is about to transform from the visionary to the concrete. Oh, if my father was with me. I have no memories to come back to, only his memories. No properties to look for, only his properties. But I have a homeland to find.

There was nothing special in the smell. I always thought that a homeland smelled differently. Nor did I feel the landscape as part of my body, though I thought it would be. It is not like any other landscape, yet I do not feel at one with it. (N. KANAFANI 1995, 40)

Abunimah (a Palestinian American whose parents had been born in Palestine) begins his account of return with a comparable sensual experience and relates his own return to Palestine to the experience of his father, a year later, and to the role that memory plays in preserving Palestinian identity:

I don't know if I had expected to hear an appropriately evocative soundtrack of the sort that accompanies dramatic moments in movies. I remember being intensely aware only of the peeling sound of tires on concrete and the strains of the narrow metal bridge as the bus carried us across the River Jordan. September 6, 1996, was a day I had waited for and imagined for most of my 25 years. It was the day I entered Palestine. . . . The following May, I returned to Palestine with my parents, who had not been to the West Bank since 1967, or to West Jerusalem since 1948. "I didn't think this city really existed anymore. I never imagined it was actually possible to come back here," my father said as we stood in the Jerusalem railway station that he knew as a boy.

But I think it is a place he visits every day. And what is so strange about that? Palestine exists because Palestinians have chosen to remember it. (ABUNIMAH 1998, 4)

Moughrabi admitted that the images he lived with could not prepare him for the reality he found, and the shock related to this reality, although he wrote and lectured on the question of Palestine and thought himself connected to his homeland through numerous channels of information.

I quickly discovered how far removed from reality I had lived for so many years. I also discovered the extent to which my cognitive structure had been impaired by American media coverage of events in the region. (MOUGHRABI 1997, 6)

Some returnees looked in vain for the homeland that they had left behind decades ago, and were embarrassed to admit that they did not recognize childhood places anymore. Barghouti expressed the feeling of shame and confusion that he felt on the way to his native village:

> I could no longer recall the names of the villages along the twenty-seven kilometer stretch. But now here I was, with my friends, heading towards Dayr Ghassaneh and the home I had not seen for nearly thirty years. Ashamed to admit that I did not recognize anything along the way, whenever my friend Husam commented about a house or a landmark, I quickly replied "Yes, I know." But in truth, I no longer knew.

> My thoughts were confused. How can we sing songs for our country when we hardly know it? What is left for one estranged from his rightful place save metaphysical love?　　　　　　(BARGHOUTI 1998, 59)

Recalling the big fig tree that shaded the family home and bore the tastiest fruits in the village, the author discovered that the tree had been cut down. While understanding the reasons that his relatives in the village had had to cut the tree and plant other things in the courtyard, he could not really forgive them for altering the place of his childhood and memories (62). Returning to his experience of exile, he described the feelings of Palestinians who had been uprooted and did not have a homeland in their reach:

> When you are kept from taking possession of a place, what really is taken away from your life is that part that is connected to that place. Yearning is the breaking of the will. A displaced person does not set down roots— he is afraid to do so, cannot do so.　　　　　　(64)

After meeting his relatives and searching for his village and its images in his mind, he concluded that he had not found the place he had come to find, but a village that had changed and was no longer home for him. Yet his narrative ends with his hope that his son will live in the village one day. Thus, the circle would close and the family would have roots in Palestine again (67).

One of the earlier returnees had to find a new answer to the question of where he was from. He also encountered a welcoming attitude toward returnees:

> In the past, I'd always said that I was Palestinian or that I was from Jerusalem, but what was I to say to the Jerusalemites themselves? I settled on an answer with a paradoxical ring: "I'm from Jerusalem, but this is my first visit." To my amazement, this answer never raised an eyebrow, and I was taken in like a long-lost son returning home after a long period

of wandering. A friend explained this degree of acceptance by the local peoples' keen awareness that the Palestinians in the diaspora are not there by choice.   (M. A. KHALIDI 1995A, 79)

This is indeed an early account, because in 1994 local Palestinians were still thrilled "at the mere contact with the outside, even while they expressed deep disappointment with PLO policies and leadership style" (79).

Ghassan Zaqtan, after realizing that he could return, found himself attempting to memorize exile and homeland, while knowing that neither place would ever be the same.

> That is why I was busy remembering in the weeks that preceded my return, remembering the journey, in a painful and unorganized attempt to protect everything and confirm, conserve it in my memory, before it turned into "other places" whose change and transformation is difficult to control. . . . Suddenly I realized that the place had ended, had died, and that it was on me from this moment on to keep restoring each corner from my memory of it and to protect it in those distant corners of my memory from being scattered, to hold on to my future in this place with both hands, because I could not rely on the land to recollect the scenery or protect it.   (ZAQTAN 1997, 143)

Some reflections draw a bleak picture, full of disappointment and frustration.

> The human does not return, he only goes forward. If you left your homeland, you will never return to it. If you swim in a river once, you will never swim in it again. . . . What I came back to see and touch had disappeared before I arrived. I know that there is something negative about every return, something sick and unwanted, something that time wants to eat and erase. . . . I return to the past, not the homeland only. The past is gone and shattered, shattered by time and the Jews of the occupation. My return and each return is a disturbance, a defeat and a failure.
> (MUHAMMAD 1997, 126)

Intellectuals like Moughrabi coped with the disappointment by calling for change. In his reflections titled "A Year of Discovery," Moughrabi shared his observations of major problems in Palestine and called on the Palestinians to address these issues to develop a better society. He suggested better care and more knowledge about public space and the natural beauty of Palestine; the development of infrastructure, civil society, and a viable economic basis for a Palestinian state; a more open Palestinian society, aware of its distortions and fragmentation; and not least a democratic culture of participation (Moughrabi 1997, 6–14).

A change in identity is one of the central features of the return experience:

> In the best case I was "Zakariya Muhammad, the Palestinian" and in the worst cases I was "the Palestinian Zakariya Muhammad." But there was something worse than that, because at some moments I didn't know if I was Palestinian or Jordanian. . . . Now I am only Zakariya Muhammad. In exile I got lost in my identities, identity was before and above me and I was following it. Now I am only Zakariya Muhammad, that is the only great gain. No one points out that I am Palestinian, here everybody is Palestinian. . . .
>
> But I was mistaken. I lost this heavenly unity to a simple fact. I only learned of my difference in steps. Now I am the returnee Zakariya Muhammad, the characteristic returnee is primary and Zakariya Muhammad secondary. I am a returnee and the returnee is the authority and the authority is Yasir Arafat, so I am Yasir Arafat too. Or say he and I are both responsible for everything.　　　　　(MUHAMMAD 1997, 132)

And yet, he resolved that he would not leave again, even though Palestine did not feel like home to him. He recognized that his son, who had never seen Palestine before, did feel at home and had returned faster than he himself (140).

One of the most outspoken accounts of return concludes that going back into exile was not an option. Instead, the solution lies in building a better Palestine and thus in developing a new or expanded Palestinian identity.

> For myself, I am hostage to those years of exile, and I strain under the burden of living in an unmitigated Palestinian homogeneity. I may indulge silly whims, but I feel no desire to return to exile, nor do I feel a yearning for a land I have lived in and come to know.
>
> The homeland cannot be remolded into a lost paradise. The homeland is right here in front of us; it is divided and distorted, awaiting salvation. Our identity is in the process of formation; the scope of that identity will expand with every meter of land we can salvage from occupation, with every road we build, every book we print, every window we open in our lives (to escape the stagnant air suffocating us), and every decision we adopt in social and political organizations and in the field of human rights.　　　　　(KHADR 1997, 93)

Palestinian returnees, intellectuals, writers, and scholars have, in their particular ways, dealt with the experience of return. Their writings about first encounters with Palestine touch upon many of the questions discussed in this study. These encounters are different from those of the young second-generation returnees that I interviewed in 1998 and 1999, but they can be used as a starting point for finding patterns of return.

Two Groups of Young Returnees

I conducted sixty personal interviews and talked to many more young diaspora Palestinians and returnees. The organization of the data pointed to the existence of two distinct groups and four subgroups, thus it was possible to make comparisons between and within the groups. In the process of reviewing and analyzing the interviews, I found patterns and features that allowed conclusions about the nature of the return experiences and the process of challenging and rewriting aspects of their Palestinian identities. The individual stories told throughout this study provide the more personal aspects of the narratives.

The respondents of this study are divided into Aideen and Amrikan, with the members of each group sharing a number of similar life patterns and return features. Within the group, they are divided into voluntary and involuntary returnees, as the analysis shows that the question as to who made the decision to return is of vital importance to the subsequent return process. The groups are labeled with terms that the local Palestinians used for the returnees, because the returnees themselves were challenged by these terms and developed their own perceptions in response.

YOUNG RETURNEES FROM ARAB COUNTRIES: THE AIDEEN

The members of this group typically were born and grew up in Arab countries. Some lived all their lives in one country, such as Jordan, Lebanon, or Syria, while others moved several times, often because of political events in which the Palestinians were involved. Few of many examples are the war in Lebanon, the Palestinian withdrawal from Beirut in 1982, and the Gulf War of 1991.

Their fathers most often worked for the PLO or in the surrounding Palestinian communities in Arab countries. They trace their origins back to the 1948 area, to villages and towns depopulated and destroyed by Jewish and Israeli forces during and after the war. A minority was from 1967 areas. Of the 1948 refugees, many became refugees for a second time upon leaving the Occupied Territories. Related to 1967 and/or in search of better education, they went to study in Egypt, Lebanon, and Syria, where they got in contact with the PLO. The majority of those parents did not have the opportunity to visit Palestine before their return in the wake of the Oslo process. Several of the young returnees had non-Palestinian mothers; nevertheless, their Palestinian identity took precedence over any other national identity.

For many of these Aideen, the parents made the decision to return, often after consultation with their children, but sometimes assuming that the return wish of the younger generation would be as strong as their own. Usually the father would return first after applying for a national number and being accepted to work for the PA or police.[10] Others acquired visas to return through connections within the PLO without working for the PA. A third group consisted of people who returned because of hardship and suffering for the Palestinian cause, such as the families of martyrs and PLO members imprisoned in other countries. In cases in which the father came back first, the mother and children would follow after making preparations for housing and school.

A number of the young returnees came back after making their own decisions and organizing the logistics themselves. They were some years older and were either young professionals in their country of residence or had just finished their studies.

The young Aideen had to cope with the negative perceptions of local Palestinians. The pejorative use of the term Aideen and the general attitude toward returnees and the PA affected this group of young returnees who were often the children of those who were criticized and targeted.

YOUNG RETURNEES FROM WESTERN COUNTRIES: THE AMRIKAN

This group consists of young returnees who grew up in the United States, Canada, and, in some cases, European countries. *Amrikan* is the term often used for them by local Palestinians. They also identified themselves as Americans, distinct from local Palestinians, who they often called Arabs. Part of this group was still in high school or had recently graduated. Those of the Amrikan who were involuntary returnees usually had not been asked if they wanted to come to Palestine long term. Often they thought it would be just another summer vacation with relatives there. The parents of this subgroup were originally all West Bank residents, most of them from the Ramallah/Al-Bireh area. Many of these Amrikan told me that their parents had gone through the same experience of growing up in the West to then be sent back to Palestine for high school, language study, and culture. Many of them left Palestine again for college, had families abroad, and, in closing the circle, sent their own children back. This form of return was not as clearly related to the Oslo process, but the numbers of these returnees had increased because the situation in Palestine was considered more stable.

The other subgroup, voluntary returnees, had a number of features in common. They decided to come to Palestine based on their interest in finding out about the Palestinian aspects of their identity. Often they surprised their families with their decision. They usually started with an intellectual discussion of current questions, with studies in the field of the Middle East or political science; others worked for NGOs serving Palestinians and the Middle East.

Most of them worked for various NGOs in the West Bank. They came to help Palestine and, simultaneously, to find out about the country and their relation to it. The future plans of this group were flexible, and none of them came intending to stay for good.

Two stories of return may illustrate the experiences of the two groups. Najma belonged to the Aideen, and Ibtisam was a member of the Amrikan group.

Najma's Story

All our lives we lived as strangers in places and then I come to my country and I am a stranger again.

Najma was introduced to me as one of the Aideen. She was twenty-one and had returned to Palestine in 1994. She lived in Nablus and studied at Birzeit University.

Her migration history reflected the career of her father as a member of the Palestinian Liberation Army. Born in 1977 in Syria, she lived in Syria and Lebanon until 1982, then spent three years in Yemen, then went to Egypt from 1985 to 1989, and then spent 1989 to 1994 in Iraq. She got used to traveling, changing schools, and leaving places and people behind. Adjusting to new environments and cultural settings, as well as to new people, was a familiar feature of her life. Her mother was a housewife, and Najma had three younger brothers.

Her father was from Nablus and had left at the age of eighteen to study in Egypt, where he got in contact with Fatah and later became a PLO member. Her mother is of Palestinian origin, from Hebron, but she grew up in Syria as the daughter of 1948 refugees. Najma described how the decision to return was made in her family, and that it was in part because of the situation in Baghdad after the Gulf War in 1991:

> When the solution came about, my father didn't expect it, but he was only dreaming that we could return to Palestine. When it turned out that we could return, he was one of the first to apply to return with the military, and then we of course decided that we would return. It was a joint decision for all of us to go and even more so because we were in Baghdad, which was under siege, the pressure was really scary and we never knew what would happen next.

Although her father was by profession involved in politics, Najma said that her family was not very interested in politics. She was aware of her Palestinian identity but described herself as nonpolitical. When I asked her if she still felt Palestinian after all the moving around, she answered positively, saying:

> Outside, that was important for me. I even tried not to change my language; only in Egypt I felt that there was a change in my language. But in general our being Palestinian was the only thing we took with us; you can't leave your country alone.

Her image of Palestine was built on the stories and memories of her father, as her mother did not know the country herself. For Najma, it seemed like a mythical place that somehow, somewhere existed, but she did not imagine it to be a real place with real people.

The actual arrival, the journey over the Allenby Bridge at a time when only Gaza and Jericho were under Palestinian administration, turned out to be impressive, but also shocking:

> When we first came to Jericho and I saw the city, honestly, I started crying. They took me from Jericho and then I saw Anata, and it was so unorganized. I couldn't stop crying and my mum cried for some days most of the time. I cried all the time, and when my dad came I told him I don't want to stay in this country. I know my country is my heart and soul, but this is so different. I lived my whole life in countries like Lebanon and Syria, Egypt, and Iraq; all of them have big cities. When we came to Jericho, it was not like that; I didn't expect that at all.

She admitted that she did not feel at home in Palestine and also that somehow she did not feel the connection she had expected to feel.

One prominent topic throughout our conversation was the issue of the returnees and their troubled relationship with local Palestinians. She was deeply disappointed about the image of Aideen in the eyes of the locals.

> They say about us who came back that we are the returnees, they started calling us the returnees. All our lives we lived as strangers in places. And then I come to my country and I am a stranger again. I come here and they give me this name, the returnee.

After a number of disappointing experiences, she limited social contact with locals. She felt more comfortable with other returnees who shared her experience and her sentiments about the situation. She felt that blaming the returnees for all the problems was unfair, and was very frustrated about the situation:

> I feel that they blame us for a lot; there are a lot of negative feelings, not the way we had expected it. Even in our generation, when I see someone who came back from outside like us, I feel that we have something in common. Like my friend Rima, we were in Baghdad together and our families are connected since the time in Lebanon. I come back to my homeland, my country, and we dreamt of that outside and left everything behind . . . and then we come here to hear that we are just garbage?

These problems do not imply that she did not get along in daily life. She managed her studies, commuted daily between Nablus and Birzeit, and felt more concerned about her mother who seemed to have little social contact outside the family. After finishing her studies she planned on working in her field:

> I personally want very much to work with the representatives of the PLO somewhere. My nature is that I like traveling; I don't like to stay in the same place for four years, not even in my own country. I like the changes, the departures and arrivals. Possibly I will connect to this place, I don't know if I can settle here. . . . Who knows if it is my fate to leave the country again. . . . I want to be close to my family, because I am their only daughter, so I don't want to be too far.

She attempted to integrate her past migration experiences with her present. She did not interpret exile as suffering for herself, but rather as a challenge and an opportunity to learn about others and herself. Suffering was present in the life of her father and the family:

> My father has always been a fighter. He dedicated his whole life to the struggle, thirty, forty years he lived away from his family, his parents. My

grandmother cried so much when my father left. He was the youngest in the family and after so many years he finally came back to Palestine; she cried again and couldn't stop. If I hear stories like this, he didn't know his brothers, he had to leave his parents, all for Palestine, all for you, and then we come back and they talk like that about him?

She could feel at home in other places and related strongly to the way other people interacted with her and her family. Even as she recalled the first Gulf War in Baghdad, the bombings and the fear were, in her memory, something that connected people to each other, drew them closer, and made them realize that all one has in life are relationships with other people.

At the same time, she tried hard to see the positive sides of being in Palestine and belonging there. At this point, her language became more political and general as she abandoned the personal tone that she had used earlier in the interview and attempted to demonstrate her Palestinian identity:

> We have to shoulder our responsibilities; we have to work together to make this a state. Despite all the complications it is good that we got something; it is good that we have an ID, a passport now. We didn't even dream of that before. I thank God and Abu 'Ammar that we returned here and I at least got a passport. Whatever people say against it, it is better than nothing. Before that anyone could look at our documents and say, You cannot enter the country.

She used "we" as opposed to "I," to emphasize the group identity, meaning her family, the returnees, and all Palestinians. She did picture herself as part of a larger structure, which was also expressed in her wish to travel and work for the PLO or a Palestinian state. She connected to a lesser degree to Palestine as the land and the people, but instead connected to what she called the Palestinian entity.

> When we were in Yemen and Abu 'Ammar would come to us he used to say, "We will meet in Jerusalem!" We used to laugh about him, when he said we are going to meet there. We used to laugh, what was he talking about? What Palestine? And now we did return and something with the name Palestine emerged; whatever faults it may have, it exists. We have a Palestinian ID card; we have a Palestinian passport. There is a Palestinian entity for us, no matter if it is autonomy or a state.

Najma had spent more than four years in Palestine, and her distance and disappointment were apparent in every sentence. She took the interview as an opportunity to vent her anger and frustration. And yet, she did not seem helpless. Her strong connection to her family, the care for their well-being, and a positive self-image, together with an optimistic outlook on the future, made her convincing in her criticism of the place that she wanted to be her homeland. Thus, her conclusion about exile, return, and homeland:

> And until now I don't have the feeling that this is my country, my home, or what I expected it to be. But I am ready to live here in sweet and bitter days.

Ibtisam's Story

> I would like you to keep in mind that although we were born as Americans, we will die as Palestinians.[11]

I met Ibtisam during a class discussion about Palestine and America, and identity and home at the Friends School. She was raised in Florida, together with six siblings; her father owned a grocery store. Her parents were both from Al-Bireh. Her father left Palestine in search of better job opportunities, following other male family members to the United States. He met and married her mother in Palestine and then took her to the United States. She did not know why exactly or in what year her father emigrated. It was something that her parents did not talk about. Certainly, she did not know there was a political motivation for his migration.

Ibtisam described life in the United States as the only life she knew, and thought of it as the best life possible. She had a sense of being different from others, but took that as normal because she knew nothing else. There was little social integration into American society and little contact outside the family. Her life revolved around home and school, with occasional visits to cousins and other members of the extended family. Her immediate family would visit Palestine every summer, as would many of her relatives, but everyone was coming to see family, not so much to see Palestine.

At home she spoke more English than Arabic. English was her first language, and her command was impressive. By the time we talked she could also manage conversations in Arabic, and during the interview she used many Arabic words.

She thought that her parents made the decision to return jointly, because they were worried about the safety and well-being of their children. They had not told the children about their plans, but took them for the usual summer holiday to Palestine and then announced one day that they had decided to stay, and only her father would go back to keep the business running. He promised to bring them whatever they wanted and needed from the United States to make the transition easier for them. That was in the summer of 1994, so she had been in Palestine for a long time compared to many of her classmates.

Looking back, she admitted that she had at first hated the thought of living in Palestine, but said she would now find it hard to leave for college. She was about to finish high school and planned to attend college in the United States because she realized the greater job opportunities that a U.S. education afforded. But she also considered studying at the American University in Beirut or even Birzeit, if it turned out that she missed Palestine too much.

Her family was not interested in politics—they just followed the news —but living in Palestine had made her more political. She did not think that shopping in West Jerusalem conflicted with her new commitment to Palestine. She said that she would not get "involved" in politics but that she had written poems about political issues. That was her way of being part of the struggle.

> Part of being in Palestine is that if we lose our land we are not going to have a home, we are going to spread out and eventually we are going to become nothing. So in order to be Palestinian, you need Palestine to have a place to go to.

Ibtisam wrote poetry in English, and some of her poems were intense statements about her views on the Israeli-Palestinian conflict as it unfolded before her eyes. One of her poems, called "Yesterday We Purchased a New TV," and inspired by TV clips of the First Intifada, describes Israeli soldiers beating a Palestinian boy and ends with a call to take responsibility for change:

> But, who is to blame?
> The soldiers who have no shame?
> No, we are to blame . . .
> If we let it all stay the same.

In her statement about Palestine as a home for the Palestinians, she also pointed to the Palestine she wanted, and expressed concern about the pace of change.

> I don't like the way it is changing. Not that its becoming modern is bad, but I just wish that they couldn't change the culture. If you compare

Palestine now to how it was all the way back then, people . . . had more traditions; they still have the traditions, but they are changing a little bit more and a little bit more. And I am scared that by the time I come back it [will have] changed so much that I won't be able to recognize it.

Related to her concern about tradition and change, she pointed somewhat defensively to her conviction that being religious had nothing to do with where one lives:

There are a lot of people . . . that were born in America and they pray, they do the five prayers. And there are a lot of people that were born here and they don't even do the five prayers.

Ibtisam's notion of home was closely linked to her family and people in Palestine. To her mind, restrictions imposed on her by her parents, and their granting her some freedom were as much related to trust in her as they were to trust in other people.

I think my mum just didn't trust Americans. And I am not saying that she was unjustified. I think that if I was a parent in America, I wouldn't trust Americans either. We came over here and because my mum knows everybody is connected, it is like one big tree that branches out. . . . It is not like she is prejudiced against one race, but because she knows them. If she knew the Americans the way she knows the Arabs in this country, she would trust and give me equal opportunities to go to their house.

Ibtisam wanted to live, and, more importantly, raise her children, in Palestine and not in America. Another aspect of keeping tradition and strengthening her identity was her plan for choosing a husband.

I don't want to marry an Arab American because I feel that if I do, some of my culture and my traditions will be lost, because I don't know everything, and if I marry another Arab American, I am sure he is not going to know everything either. If I want to get married I am going to come over here to marry an Arab.

In Ibtisam's story we find Palestine on two different levels. It is a place where she belongs together with her family, a place where there is more safety and trust than in the United States. At the same time, her "public expressions," such as the poems she published in the school yearbook and the speech she gave at her graduation ceremony, were more political, recognizing the battlefield character of the country and taking sides in the conflict. She summarized these feelings when she addressed her classmates and teachers, as well as parents and relatives at the graduation ceremony:

Speaking more strictly on behalf of the English-speaking class, I say the following—practically all of us were forced to come to Palestine. Initially we hated it—we wanted to return [to America]. As the years passed, the desire to return home lessened and then disappeared. We no longer wanted to go home because we had succumbed to truth: We were already home—our home is Palestine. Despite this, some of us are going to America to continue our education. I would like you to keep in mind that although we were born as "Americans," we will die as Palestinians.

Not all her classmates would have agreed with her statement about being at home in Palestine. It was all the more interesting that she decided to say this on their behalf.

The young returnees to Palestine are part of a larger social, historical, political, and cultural framework. Their experience cannot be understood without considering the dreams and hopes of Palestinians in the diaspora to return to Palestine. They are part of the political struggle for the right of return, even if they are not aware of that. The perceptions and ideas they are confronted with upon their return are based on Palestine's social and political setting, the dispute about Palestinian identity, and questions about economic and political power sharing and distribution.

CHAPTER 5

The Return Process
in Comparison

All of us speak of awdah, "return," but do we
mean that literally, or do we mean "we must
restore ourselves to ourselves"? The latter is the
real point, I think, although I know many
Palestinians who want their houses and their
way of life back, exactly. But is there any place
that fits us, together with our accumulated
memories and experiences? (SAID 1986A, 33)

Many factors need to be considered for the description and understanding of the experience of returnees to Palestine, which is shaped by a combination of ideology, memories of previous generations, notions of exile, experience of diaspora, and yearning for homeland. The experiences of the two groups of young returnees in this study are part of this larger framework of return. How then did their return come about? What were the distinguishable steps of this process? The returnees in the two groups and four subgroups have a number of features in common. Their experiences of the five-stage process of return will be described and compared to each other.

Return is a journey or a process in which an individual or group passes through stages in order to get from one point to another. Since a process is continuous, characterized by constant movement and fluidity, it is difficult to tell when it starts and when it ends.

The young Palestinians who were born and raised abroad cannot base their expectations of Palestine on their own memories of the homeland. For the group that had the opportunity to visit before returning to Palestine, the country is less idealized, but still not a familiar place to return to. Return to Palestine is more symbolic than real. The return story started long before the return; in fact, it began with the emigration of their forefathers at the beginning of the twentieth century. Could there be a "happy ending" to the return process? The migration and cross-cultural upbringing experienced by the young interviewees of this study have resulted in a life that will time and again pose the question of whether to stay or move on.

It is also their age that poses this question; many have to make life decisions with the knowledge of their many options. There is as much a sense of opportunity as a sense of burden. There is no end, let alone a happy ending, to their being "between" cultures, homelands, and loyalties. We will see that individual choices may differ considerably in this respect, but only time will reveal the direction that their lives will take. Such a proposition, however, does not automatically imply that they lead unhappy lives. People long for things, places, and people, but manage to cope with undesired circumstances, and amazingly still make sense of their life stories. For these young Palestinians, much of their life story has yet to be written.

Return and Liminality

In developing this scheme of the return process, I took inspiration from Victor Turner's concepts of liminality and the rite of passage, and two studies in which this idea was applied to returnees. In the first study I found a three-stage scheme of return, namely, return, liminality, and resolution (Wernefeldt 1997, 36).[1] It was based on van Gennep's concept of three steps in passing a ritual: the pre-liminal, liminal, and post-liminal (Gennep 1909). Turner worked with this idea and emphasized the importance of the liminal stage. This stage suspends the social rules under which usual circumstances regulate daily life. This lack of rules is critical for understanding the importance of the prevailing order. Those undergoing the described ritual are put in a marginal position, completely at the mercy of those who organize and supervise the ritual. This stage of social invisibility is the precondition for acquiring a new social identity. Later, Turner transferred the idea of liminality from the ritual context to processes of social and political change. Liminality is then defined as a stage in which hindering circumstances are overcome but new stabilized ones have not yet been reached. It can thus describe different processes of change, which bear the dangers of marginalization as well as the chance for innovation. From the perspective of those who undergo the change, the process requires reflection, which has the potential to encourage creativity and active change (Wernefeldt 1997; Wolbert 1995, 33).

The original idea of "rite of passage" was applied to rituals, such as the initiation of adolescents into adulthood in traditional societies. In order to use the idea for migration, including return, one must widen the definition of societal ritual. There is no formal ritual involved in the return to one's country of origin, but it is a process that changes the individual and his position/identity in a society and has the potential to change that society as well.

Developing a Scheme of the Return Process

One major difference between the respondents was the voluntary or involuntary character of their return. Those who did not have a say in the return decision could be described as not in control of their fate and position in society. Those who voluntarily returned to Palestine have more control over the liminal stage and its resulting in a new social status. However, the examples show that the options are even more diverse.

We will divide the return process into five stages. The five stages are the return decision, arrival, meeting Palestine, living in Palestine, and staying in Palestine.

They do not exactly match the pre-liminal, liminal, and post-liminal steps, for three reasons. First, considering the complex circumstances of cross-cultural migration, it is difficult to isolate the particular return process from other processes taking place in different parts of Palestinian society. Second, the stage that could be defined as liminal involves a number of sub-stages that will be described in more detail. The third and most important reason is that migration as a life experience creates a situation for the migrant that can be described as endless liminality. Wherever he or she lives, there is no chance of complete belonging; there will always be a distance caused by having had different experiences and an awareness of "otherness." The individual can view this position as a comfortable space in different societies, but can also perceive it as a lifelong burden.

The Return Process

There are no boundaries between past, present, and future. What was the future a minute ago is the present now and will be the past in another minute. Correspondingly, peoples' imaginations do not clearly distinguish among memory, experience of the moment, and plans for the future. How we see the past is informed by how we live now, and both these aspects influence how we imagine the future.

The reconstruction of the return processes as it appears in the stories of my respondents reflects the temporality of narratives. Palestine in 1998 and 1999 was a different experience politically, socially, and personally for each respondent. One has to bear in mind that the interviewees were in different stages of the return process, and so each reflected on his or her own situation differently. Some were not clear as to whether or not they would stay, while others seemed firmly committed.

Especially during the process of change, which is characterized by resistance, upheaval, and possible rewriting of identity, telling one's story can be either a painful or an eye-opening process. Respondents told me that they considered it helpful and soothing to talk openly about their experiences to someone who was an outsider but was familiar with the nature of the problem. Being in the midst of the process, the interviewees reflected the confusion they felt, the daily struggle for meaning and understanding, and the possible endlessness of their struggle. At the same time, they often expressed a surprising certainty in their wishes and life plans and displayed considerable patience in confronting situations that others forced them to face.

We have already seen how different the images of Palestine, created before their return and remembered while in Palestine, were within the two groups. For the Amrikan, the experience of Palestine as a cultural homeland and a place to spend summer vacations would facilitate their return and settlement; for the Aideen, for whom Palestine was an entirely imagined homeland, created through memory, stories, and art, return and settlement would be experienced differently.

STEP 1: THE RETURN DECISION

Who made the decision to return, and what were the reasons for and circumstances of the decision? For the Aideen, the decision to return was clearly a result of the peace process. After the signing of the Oslo agreement in September 1993, it became clear that for the building of a Palestinian National Authority, PLO cadres would be needed in Palestine. As part of the agreements, spouses and dependent children were allowed to return as well. In all cases in this group, the decision was made in consultation with the children. Instead of calling them voluntary and involuntary returnees, we should instead call the Aideen dependent or independent returnees, the former being those too young to remain abroad alone.

The dependent returnees were not always happy about returning. Some fathers felt obliged to apply for a national number because of their position in the PLO, and for their self-image it seemed unthinkable not to return when the opportunity arose. For their children, return proved to be difficult, as return had been a dream for them, not a real possibility.

Muna recalled that from her father's perspective, there was no question about return both because he would have lost his work in Egypt and because he spent all his life in exile dreaming of return. Muna's mother hesitated at first because she had been brought up in Lebanon and was afraid that she would not get along with her in-laws in Gaza or integrate into the society in general. She was socially more integrated in Egypt and was described by her daughter as less nationalistic than Muna's father and Muna herself. This situation demonstrates the different quality of attachment to Palestine as a homeland as more imagined for her mother than for her father who grew up in Palestine and left at seventeen. Though he had left in 1948, most of his family had remained in Gaza, even after 1967. Muna sided with her father but returned with her mother some while after her father had returned.

In Najma's earlier narrative we saw that her approval of the return decision, which was made jointly by the family, was facilitated by strong family ties and the danger of remaining in Baghdad at the time. Najma did not explicitly point to political or ideological reasons for return.

Sulayman was given a choice between studying in France and following his father to Palestine. He returned because he wanted to see the homeland that he had only imagined. In Marwan's case, it was the mother who raised the question, because Marwan's father had died.

> It was my mother: She sustains the family, so she can decide, and we have to follow. She asked for our opinion: my brother was eighteen years old at the time, one of my sisters was twenty and two sisters were younger than seventeen. So she said, What do you think? Do you want to return? We all agreed, but they had some doubts because of their friends and also about school here. In the beginning I desperately didn't want to return, but I wouldn't say no.

Basma was most outspoken about her resistance and tried to explain her complicated and confusing feelings:

> It was a dream of life, but it's coming true. And when it's coming true, then it is not the time it should be coming true. It was just a fantasy, it will never come true, and it just came true. When I came here I didn't cry. My mother cried and my brother cried; they were all crying tears of happiness. I wasn't, because I felt that what I left behind was really worth crying for.

In talking about her mother's reaction, she strongly emphasized the importance of loyalty and family relations:

My mum has been married to my dad for more than twenty-five years. So if she said no, that would mean she doesn't want my father anymore. Because when he decided, he believed in his decision: I worked, I struggled, I did everything to come to Palestine, and when I have the chance, this opportunity in life, why don't I use it? Otherwise I will be a big liar. I won't be a patriot. My mum believed in him and she still does. She believed in the way they lived, the love between them. She came here because of two reasons: She didn't want to lose her family and she believed in her husband a lot.

Those in the group who returned based on their independent decisions mentioned more political reasons for it. Majid told me simply: "Because it is my country and I had to come back." He was the only respondent who returned without applying for residency status and was illegally staying in Palestine.

Dalia listed several reasons for her decision, both personal and political. She was trying to leave behind a failed marriage in Egypt and wanted to continue her studies. Her parents had already returned, and she wanted to be closer to them. She was certain that she wanted to experience her dream of being in Palestine and finding the home that she never had because of all the moving and traveling.

Kamila recalled that she had just finished university in London and was looking for a new orientation in life. Together with her upbringing as a Palestinian, she felt that not trying to return would have amounted to hypocrisy. Her father was already in Palestine and working for the PA when she contemplated her return.

We always used the term "going back" to Palestine; we are definitely going back to Palestine. I think deep down I knew that we would never ever go back, but we would talk about it and say one day we will go back. I asked my mum, If Palestine actually was liberated, will we go back, will we leave everything here and go? And, you know, she didn't have an answer. So when I did get the chance, I couldn't not come, even though I was really worried and scared about it.

The interviews show that the decision to return to Palestine was based on political as well as social and personal concerns. Once the opportunity arose because of the peace process, it posed a challenge to lifelong convictions and the dream of Palestinian nationalism. The father or the head of the family usually initiated the actual decision, and the young Aideen followed their parents to Palestine.

The collected data do not support the conclusion that young Aideen are more often male than female. The young women I interviewed had enough independence and family support to return on their own initiative, to study, for example. Some were bound to a family network of relatives in Palestine, but even they were not under the family's control. Studying in Palestine, at a prestigious university such as Birzeit, was a popular reason to return to Palestine, to claim it temporarily or permanently as home.

For the group of the Amrikan, there is a clear demarcation between voluntary and involuntary returnees. Those who were involuntary returnees were often minors. It was mainly their parents' decision, and it was not directly related to the peace process as such.

The principal of the Friends Boys School pointed out that it could be called a tradition in Palestinian migration patterns that Palestinian Americans send their children back to Palestine to attend high school.[2] It was a pattern over several generations in which parents repeated with their children what their parents had done with them earlier. He defined these return patterns as "oscillating migration." Though always a familiar presence in the Ramallah area, Palestinian American high school students had increased in numbers and visibility. The number of Amrikan returnees at the Friends School had decreased since the first months of the First Intifada when families grew weary of the unstable situation. After frequent school closings, many of them decided to leave for America again. However, the peace process had revived the return pattern of this segment of Palestinian society.

The reason most often given for the return decision was that parents wanted their children to learn about Palestinian culture and to improve their Arabic. Concerns about their children growing up in a hostile and dangerous Western environment where drug use and premarital sex are more common, and feeling a lack of control over the safety of their adolescents forced parents seriously to consider return. In many cases, only the mother and the children returned, while the father stayed abroad to provide for the family. He would only occasionally visit. In previous decades, children between thirteen and seventeen would sometimes be sent to Palestine alone to stay with grandparents or other relatives.

Western immorality and the danger to children was not only a concern with regard to girls, although it was often the eldest daughter's reaching "that age" that catalyzed the fears and ultimately the decision to return. At that same age, some of the boys, depending on where they had grown up, had already been involved in minor crimes, gang fights, and trouble with the police. There are differences in the traditions of Christian and Muslim families, but the anxiety of adopting Western lifestyles for their children is shared by Muslim and Christian Palestinians alike.

Despite the advantage of knowing the place from summer vacations, the young returnees usually did not have a say in the decision. Some were not even informed that this summer vacation would instead be a return. Jane recalled her father's main concerns:

> My father was scared how we would grow up in America, he didn't want us to be involved with drugs and boys, he is really against dating and that stuff. He doesn't think that a guy and a girl can just be friends. So he didn't want to take the chance of me getting involved with someone or clicking drugs.

'Aziz pointed to tradition as an important factor in the decision:

> My parents wanted me to see our country and learn more about my culture and my religion and finish my high school here. To show what our background is, how our grandfather and grandmother were born and raised here and where they come from. It is not really a big deal to them, but to us it is a big change.

In some cases the return decision was more closely related to the situation of the grandparents. Most of the parents of the respondents were at an age at which their parents were getting older and ailing. Sometimes they tried to bring them to the United States to be closer and take care of them, but older people often refused to be uprooted, and preferred their children to come back to stay. Amira returned after her paternal grandmother died and her grandfather could not manage living alone and asked Amira's father to come back.

> My grandfather was lonely; he wanted some family to live with him. He kept calling us. He was here and we were living in Cleveland and he kept calling. So my dad said that we had to come here and stay with him.

Because the family's financial situation was not very stable, the father decided to go back temporarily. After six months the parents agreed that Amira, her siblings, and mother would stay with the grandfather, and the father would return to the United States. The children were enrolled in different schools, and the family moved in with the grandfather. By the time he passed away, leaving was not even a point of discussion anymore.

Ayat told me that she was given a choice about returning, and her decision was made based on her increasing awareness of how different she was from mainstream American society. In two cases, the return of the family was related to business in Palestine. Both families decided to open or reopen a business in Ramallah and were happy about the opportunity to resettle in Palestine.

Clearly, the young Amrikan came from similar backgrounds and shared a number of characteristics. Their families had all been economically successful in America, whether as rich shop owners or grocery stores employees. Sometimes mothers and fathers had themselves been born in America, brought back to Palestine for high school and for "learning culture," and then had emigrated like their parents. None of the Amrikans' parents had been involved in any way in Palestinian politics or had left Palestine for political reasons. This does not mean that Palestinian Americans are not politically involved, just that the families in question were not.

Return presented the voluntary returnees with different issues. These respondents were considerably older, had finished college, and had developed their ideas of return based on their own questions about their identity as Palestinians or Palestinian Americans. This group was more diverse in their biographies and much clearer about their expectations. Almost all of them had prepared for their return by trying to find a job or internship with an NGO in Palestine. It was a special form of return to come to Palestine and stay for an unlimited period of time, thereby claiming their belonging to the place and testing the exact nature of that connection.

The questions about one's identity were inspired by events in college and by the pro-Israeli atmosphere that prevailed on university campuses, combined with the lack of information about Palestine in American media and society. Many of the respondents related their growing awareness of being Palestinian to the First Intifada and the first Gulf War, which politicized the Arab American community and the Palestinian communities in other Western countries.

Allen, who grew up in Australia with a loose cultural connection to the Palestinian community there, related his returning to Palestine to his growing political awareness, and recalled the anger and frustration he felt about the one-sided media coverage of the Gulf War. It was then that he started to see a connection between the pro-Israeli stand of the West and the distorted picture of the Palestinian predicament. This political interest coincided in time with questions about his professional future after finishing a teacher's degree and working as a teacher for some time. At twenty-five, he decided to visit his father's relatives in Jordan as a "cultural warm-up" before going to Palestine.

Tariq had told a similar story, just like Hiyam, who also went to Jordan before she made her way to Palestine. Rayda reflected upon the process of internal debate:

> I had a lot of reasons. I really didn't like the situation I was in and I needed to get away from it. And a good place to get away was here, because it is a place that I can come to alone, even though I have very few relatives here. But I thought I could go and it would feel okay, I wasn't just escaping from something, but that I was going to learn something. And after finishing college I didn't know what I wanted to do with my life and figured that a year would give me some time to think and to see what I wanted to do. And if I don't know what life is like here, I feel like I am ignoring a huge part of myself. It used to drive me crazy that I couldn't speak Arabic with people. . . . Also I felt that if I was ever going to have kids, the biggest crime in my life would be that I couldn't speak to them in Arabic. So coming here had a lot to do with just filling out the empty places in my life with a little bit more understanding.

For all of them, the decision to return was the result of searching for a clearer picture of Palestine and their own place in this picture, the only way of finding out about the Palestinian component of their identity. Their stories are the most difficult to categorize, with amazing turns and twists and fascinating reflections on their situation and self-perception. Their return to Palestine was not a return to the place of origin of the parents, as none of the families originally came from the Ramallah area.

For them, political or nationalistic motivation was important in the return decision. But it was often combined with cultural and economic considerations, and only the combination of these factors accounted for the actual return. All return decisions were, directly or indirectly, related to the changes in Palestine resulting from the Oslo process. One can clearly differentiate between voluntary returnees who made the decision to return and those who were dependent on their families and thus had little say in the decision. In cases of voluntary return, the decision-making process was linked to the individual's reflection about the life situation as well as questions and tensions shaping his or her identity. An important factor was the concept of Palestine as an imagined or cultural homeland.

STEP 2: ARRIVAL IN PALESTINE

If the return process is described as part of a ritual, then as far as the idea of liminality goes, arrival marks the beginning of the liminal period during which the individual or group departs from his or her former environment and circumstances and enters a phase characterized by uncertainty, difference, and unexpected changes. One can expect arrival to be staged as a memorable special event. Traveling from one place to the other involves the crossing of borders, both physically and mentally. Khalidi has called crossing borders at airports and checkpoints "the quintessential Palestinian experience," something that always and forcefully reminds them of their identity as Palestinians (R. Khalidi 1997, 1).

It is no mere coincidence that two Palestinian writers, Khalidi and Turki, chose the picture of a Palestinian crossing a border to introduce their readers to the common experience of Palestinians. It is this experience that reminds Palestinians of their identity as a people.

> But if you are a Palestinian, you worry more. You know that you have no recourse to justice. You have no state, no embassy, no institution of any kind to protect you in a moment of crisis. . . . You have worn your sense of otherness all these years as a consciousness more intimately enfolding than your own skin. (TURKI 1988, 6)

Although many Palestinians have, over the years, acquired passports or travel documents from other countries and legally travel as citizens of those states, the Arabic names, and in some cases their places of birth, written in the documents single them out as suspicious and different. For arrival in Palestine, each Palestinian returnee has to cross a border controlled by Israel. Even American passports have not saved Palestinians from hassle, security searches, and long hours waiting at airports and borders. Countless are the stories of crossing the Allenby Bridge from Jordan, waiting in line in the scorching summer heat, with children, harassed by Israeli soldiers, and put through intimidating and embarrassing luggage and body searches.

As an important step in the return process, the arrival itself takes on an additional symbolic meaning, loaded with expectations, excitement, and anxiety. This symbolic meaning was heaviest for those returnees who had never seen the country before, which was true for most Aideen in this study. The stories also speak of the double meaning of this journey, not only that of arriving in Palestine but also the counter-story of leaving behind one's old life. The returnees went on a journey; for some it was long and complicated, as from Yemen to Saudi Arabia, to Jordan, and then to Palestine. Others had to go to Egypt from Jordan to cross the border into Gaza. Those with foreign passports could travel by plane and arrive at Tel Aviv Airport, actually seeing Israel before Palestine, though many of them consider this territory to be "stolen Palestine."

In comparing the interviews, I found that the women talked in strikingly more emotional ways about their memories of arriving in Palestine. If the men responded at all, it seemed rather unemotional, as if they did not want to talk about those feelings.

There was a pattern among the Aideens' experiences of return, namely, that it was the first direct confrontation with Israelis. The Israeli soldiers stood as a barrier between Palestine and the returnee. Not only did the young returnees know that the soldiers had the power to decide who could reach Palestine, but they had a frightening image of Israeli soldiers from their childhood. For Hanadi the prevalent feeling was fear:

> I remember the first time I came to Palestine I felt so many things. I was very nervous; I was very happy and afraid at the same time. The first time I saw an Israeli soldier, I was very afraid, very scared. . . . He didn't talk to me at all and didn't do anything to me, but from what I had heard and seen in the news I became very nervous.

Because the Israelis were seen as enemies, there was a profound feeling of hatred that the male respondents found less embarrassing than their fear. The experience at the border altered Sulayman's image of the Israelis:

> First of all when we crossed the border I saw the Israeli flag, so I had this hatred in myself, because I have always seen what they used to do to my people; they used to break their arms and kill them. . . . I just wanted to pick up a stone and throw it at the soldier. . . . When I first crossed the bridge I had my first dialogue with an Israeli, with this Israeli soldier, and my stereotype began to decrease for me. . . . He was kind with me and apologized for the delay and problems. I had this idea that they are very tough people—they aren't human beings like us; they are like machines.

Marwan recalled a similar situation:

> When I entered the bridge I was of course happy; then I saw the Jews, I felt hurt from the inside. I hadn't expected to see Jews. I imagined that after Oslo, after the peace, Jericho would be ours: You would go there and only find Palestinians, nothing by the name Jews. So I looked at this Israeli. Of course, if there is Israel at the border it means the area behind is Israel too. Why is there no Palestine, no Palestinian flag? This question might seem silly when you know the realities, but it comes to your mind. There were two military checkpoints on the way, and we had to leave the car. They searched everything in the car, the bags and all, and their behavior was mean, so I became even more tense.

Many of the respondents mentioned their first encounter with an Israeli before speaking about the impression of Palestine itself. Not only did the women cry at the bridge or upon arrival on Palestinian soil but they talked more openly about their emotions than did the men. The way Kamila laid out her narrative about arriving in Palestine illustrates the different aspects of the passage.

> It was really shocking and touching; I was crying a lot. When we crossed the Allenby Bridge, I had seen photos of people coming over that bridge, I couldn't believe it. And the Israeli flag and the Israeli soldiers, that shocked me, I didn't expect it to be that obvious and intense. And it was just that horrible journey to get across to this side, but when we crossed I thought this is it, I am in Palestine. I was crying nonstop, and I kissed the ground in Jericho. It was so touching, I couldn't speak for a day. I went to Jerusalem that same night, to the Mount of Olives, and we stood there and I was looking and I was crying so much, I just couldn't stop crying, it was so beautiful. It was more beautiful than I imagined, Jerusalem was just wonderful. . . . I didn't know much about Palestine at all; I just assumed that everyone here was Palestinian. You go on the street and everyone is Palestinian, I have never seen so many Palestinians in one place. I just felt like going up to everyone and saying, you know, I am Palestinian, I am here, we are all one people here.

Kamila's narrative has many of the features one would expect in a homecoming story. To kiss the ground of the homeland upon return is a common image from many parts of the world when exiles reach the soil of their native country. The tears, the inability to speak for a day, and the overwhelming beauty of the homeland tie in with the emotional connection to Palestine and the unearthly beauty of the homeland in the exile's imagination.

In a parable of loss, Amina told the counter-story of return, the story of losing her previous life:

> I felt that my soul was crying. I left a life behind, and I didn't cry openly because I didn't want my family to worry. . . . We came through the bridge, which took very long, there were a lot of flies and they also bothered us a lot. When we arrived at the Jewish side, we were kept waiting there for about four hours. The intelligence questioned my mother. I remember something that happened there. I had a small bag; I had put into it all the things my girlfriends had given me, little silver pieces from long ago when they went to India before my father was detained. He was

a military attaché in India and Pakistan and was trained there for some time, so my mum came back from there with a lot of silver things. And when we grew up she gave these things to us. And my dad sent us from jail a piece of wood with his name on it. I had all that in this box. So I had that box in my hand, and the Jewish soldier who checked us insisted that this goes with the big bags for inspection. I tried convincing him that there was nothing in it and that I could open it for him and he could check, but he refused. Then we were standing and waiting for four hours until the Jews were done questioning my mother. When we finished, my mum and brother started taking the bags and I helped them, but I was looking for my little bag. It was lost; I couldn't find it. It had all my souvenirs, my memories in it, things that were very dear to me. I didn't care about the material value. Maybe they were simple things, but they were very important for me. At that point I exploded, I started crying and screaming at the Jewish soldiers and I yelled at them. I told them that they were not to tell me where to go and that this country is not theirs.

The loss of things dear to her, things symbolizing her memory of the past and her father, would later be linked to her discontent and disappointment about living in Palestine.

For the Amrikan there is no similar arrival story to tell. Many of them knew Palestine from previous summer vacations. Most of them were too young at the time to remember the first visit. What they recalled was the excitement about meeting relatives during the vacations, the ways they managed the language problems as younger children, and the feeling of being with others like them. Also, parents would allow their children more freedom to play outside the house and socialize with other children, because in the neighborhoods of Ramallah and Al-Bireh people knew each other and were often related. This summary holds true for more than half of the Amrikan I interviewed but is limited to the younger ones, the group that was brought back for high school. If they mentioned something like a first impression at all, it was how Palestine looked different from the United States. They spoke about dirty streets and the lack of streetlights and order.

The narratives of the voluntary returnees in this group are similar to those of the Aideen. For some of them the "return journey" was the first visit to Palestine; others still remembered their first trip. During interviews in the United States, I found that young Palestinian Americans, the second or third generation in the United States, often visited Palestine for the first time in adolescence. In some cases, the family decided to take all family members back for a visit; in others, Palestinian American organizations and youth groups organized trips to Palestine. A third option was summer courses or summer camps at one of the Palestinian universities, such as Birzeit. For them, the first encounter with Palestine was not a return trip but an educational journey. Consequently, they describe their impressions in different terms. On such trips there is less pressure to recognize the imagined homeland in the reality.

As Allen arrived in Palestine crossing the Allenby Bridge from Jordan, he not only experienced the "special treatment" reserved for Palestinians but he also observed how people around him were treated during the procedure.

> I will never forget my going through the bridge. There was one old man who was going back; he was from Palestine, he was coming to visit for the first time and he was with his grandson. I remember one of the young Israeli soldiers asked him something and she spoke Arabic to him. And then she went away and he said, he whispered to his grandson, "They speak Arabic!" It was very shocking to see that and to think that the reason this man is over there and not where he should be is because of what this woman's parents or another generation above did. That was a very moving experience. And then I went through two hours' worth of searching and everything. It was a good introduction to here because you see the racism straight up.

The shaping of arrival as a stage in the return process in its intensity and importance varies greatly among the respondents of the two groups. The Aideen share some patterns, such as the first confrontation with Israeli soldiers, the anxiety and excitement about reaching the homeland they have never seen before, and the simultaneous exposure to leaving behind the previous life and seeking a new one. The loss is certain, but the promise is not. The first impression was linked to many emotions, but sounded rationalized upon telling the story. The narratives contained elements that were expected, and it is possible that the respondents wanted to meet my expectations. Gender played a role in the expression of emotion, as did the distance between the actual event and the moment of remembering. For all respondents, arrival was now part of the past, and they were much more involved with managing the present.

In the narratives there is no clear line between the arrival stage and the next step in the process defined as "meeting Palestine." The meeting or encounter starts with getting the first glimpse of Palestine or meeting the first local Palestinian or somewhere between the two.

STEP 3: MEETING PALESTINE

Depending on the time of their arrival, the young returnees found very different political situations in Palestine. Those who came with the first wave of Aideen in early 1994 had to go to Jericho or Gaza first, as these were the only two pieces of land under control of the Palestinian Authority at that time. In many cases, fathers had arrived earlier to evaluate the situation before bringing the families. Many Amrikan (or their parents) were attracted by the seemingly more stable situation; for other parents, the return was mostly related to their children's being young and their wish to protect them from "American life."

Many practical aspects had to be considered; the country had to be rediscovered and the search for stability begun. Also, one would meet local Palestinians as well as one's relatives. When I asked in interviews about these first impressions, three important features emerged. The first was the amazement about a country in which everyone is Palestinian and so being Palestinian is not special or unusual. The two other features are divided into meeting Palestine as a place and meeting Palestinian people. For both, the young returnees had to compare their expectations with the actual findings and cope with the enormous gaps between imagination and reality.

Meeting the Place   Young Palestinians found the land to be as beautiful as their parents had said. But it turned out that the land's beauty and the sweetness of its fruits were not the most important aspects of their return, when compared to the daily difficulties they faced with the local Palestinians. They could not isolate their feelings about Palestine from their connection to the Palestinian people.

Some respondents mentioned that seeing the Palestinian flag, Palestinian license plates, and Palestinian postage stamps gave them a new feeling of pride, although these were all only symbolic in a state that did not yet exist. Special value was attributed to visiting Jerusalem. I asked them how much traveling they had done and how familiar they were with Palestine as a place. The ability to travel in Palestine and Israel depended on several factors besides their personal interest in traveling. Those who were dependent on their families could not travel without their parents, school, or university. Very few members of the two groups had their own car and could move around freely.

For the young Aideen, a Palestinian identity card or passport was a major obstacle to traveling around the country. They needed special Israeli permits to enter Israeli territory, and these permits were difficult to obtain. This prevented many of them from going to Jerusalem; many who did entered illegally. For others, it delayed their first visit to Jerusalem until long after their arrival, although they had a strong wish to see the city that holds so much religious and national symbolic importance. It was equally hard for them to travel between the West Bank and Gaza, meaning that those who had families in Gaza but studied in the West Bank often did not see their parents and siblings after leaving for their studies.

Qasim had his own car and had been appointed to various workplaces in the West Bank and Gaza by the PA, so he had explored much of the two territories. Whenever he came to a new city (Tulkarem, Ramallah, Bethlehem, Jericho), he would drive around the town and the surrounding villages for the first couple of weeks. Basma got to know Palestine through a special experience: She organized a play for children at Birzeit, and the group traveled around the West Bank and to Gaza to perform. But she said:

> There are a lot of places, names of villages in Palestine, I hear them in the university and I don't know where they are. And I am ashamed to ask, because you know when I ask such a question I feel that I am not Palestinian, so I just go over it. . . . I don't consider the West Bank as Palestine, or the Gaza Strip. Palestine for me is Jaffa, the place my grandfather left . . . and it is much more beautiful than Tunis and Lebanon and Syria and all the places I have seen, and Cyprus. The view there over the sea and the sun, it is hard to describe. It is really nice. If it wasn't nice, I don't think Israel would have thought of taking any of those areas. Because it is beautiful they would take it.

Most of the Aideen who were students at Birzeit University had been on trips to Jaffa, Haifa, Nazareth, and Tiberias (inside Israel). They went to visit the West Bank cities of Nablus, Bethlehem, Jenin, Hebron, and Jericho with family or other students. They were much less familiar with the villages of Palestine, even those around Ramallah. Amina discovered the beauty of Palestine on these trips:

> I was very disturbed. I saw that the nature of our land is wonderful; I feel that the olive trees and the almond trees are different from those in any other country. In Amman I would not look like that at an olive tree and think how beautiful or at an almond tree blossoming. I find it beautiful, and I know that the Jews are very interested in these things. I feel that they took the most beautiful places in this country.

For those of the Aideen who were originally from 1948, their return to Palestine only seemed complete when they visited the villages or towns from which their parents or grandparents had come. It is often mentioned that part of Palestinian identity is expressed in the ability of every Palestinian to tell where he or she originally came from, even though it might be two or three generations since anyone in the family lived there. Many people mentioned the name of the place when introducing themselves to me. We have already seen how Nimr returned to Palestine with his father to fulfill his father's dreams — to die and be buried in Palestine, and to connect his son to the homeland. Though his father did not get a chance to see the land that once belonged to his family, Nimr ultimately did.

Many times, returnees did not find that these places matched their images of them. They realized that their parents had painted a picture of Palestine that was lost to them. Majid, whose family was originally from a village near Ramleh remembered the stories he was told as a child about the village in which his family found refuge after 1948. He did not find the trees, the jasmine flowers, or any of the things he had expected. Instead, he saw sun, dirt, and dust.

The Amrikan adolescents had American passports that allowed them to travel more freely, even without valid tourist visas. Traveling in Palestine for them included educational sightseeing with the school, as well as shopping in West Jerusalem or going to the beach in Tel Aviv. Many of them knew the villages around Ramallah and Birzeit because they or their friends and relatives lived there. One of their clear observations was that places in Israel were better taken care of.

Rami got tired of the trips that his father took the family on every weekend. He pointed out that Palestine was such a small country that he had already seen all the interesting places several times. The only exception he made was Jerusalem; in his view it was a place that one could never tire of because of its history and its meaning for the region and the world.

Those who came voluntarily had better opportunities to travel the country. However, they were very involved in their work and had less time for such trips, unless they traveled for their job. Every time we talked, Kamila told me about her plans to see all the fascinating places in Palestine; when I left, she still had not had a chance to realize her plans. Sandy got to know Palestine better when her mother came to visit Palestine for the first time. Her mother was Palestinian but had never seen the country before. Together they explored the place with an enthusiasm that brought them closer together and helped them understand each other better.

Hiyam perceived a trip to the north of Israel and the Golan Heights as a difficult experience and a challenge to her Palestinian identity; it left her pessimistic about the future of the Palestinians.

> Our encounters during those three days unsettled each and every one of us, each for similar and individual reasons. We spoke about it briefly upon our return, but since then have not externalized the effects which it had on us. For me, it was another delve into identity, an identity which I have been struggling to comprehend.[3]

Familiarity with a place, especially one that has been perceived as homeland in a symbolic and cultural sense, can help develop a feeling of actually being at home. The traveling either related or disconnected the images and expectations about Palestine developed before return to the physical realities of the land. The experience of checkpoints, settlements, and restricted movement demonstrated to the young returnees the problems and limitations of life in Palestine. It often had a clarifying effect on their political awareness.

Jerusalem holds a special meaning for Palestinians in general and for the returnees in particular, whether in political, historical, or religious terms. Some remarks about visiting Jerusalem will add to the picture of how meeting Palestine as a place was an important step in the return process.

Many respondents of the Aideen group were not immediately able to visit Jerusalem. Because of travel restrictions, it often took a long time for them to get to the city with whose image they were familiar through pictures, posters, and carpets remembered from childhood. For those of the respondents who were Muslims, praying at the Haram al-Sharif—both at the Al-Aqsa Mosque and the Dome of the Rock—held special meaning.[4] For Christians it was the Church of the Holy Sepulcher, as well as the Via Dolorosa and the Mount of Olives, that made Jerusalem the most important religious site. In addition, Jerusalem was perceived as a national symbol because of Palestinian aspirations to see Jerusalem become the capital of a Palestinian state. Hanadi expressed the religious importance of Jerusalem and her feelings about going there for the first time:

> Because that is where the night journey and ascension of Prophet Muhammad took place in Al-Aqsa, that is why it has a very high importance religiously. Going there had a big psychological impact on me. When I entered I felt very comfortable and I didn't want to leave again. It was very different from all other mosques.

In Amina's memory of her first visit, her sense of Jerusalem's religious significance affects her impression of Palestinian society:

> I went and prayed and cried a lot also. . . . In a long time I hadn't cried like that, I felt that I was very far from Allah, that my life was full of mistakes I made. . . . I love Jerusalem so much; I wish I could live there. . . . In the Old City the buildings are so beautiful; it amazed me. I have the feeling that the people there are closer to each other maybe because of the construction of the houses, they are so close together. I loved Jerusalem very much.

Mukhlis, one of the Amrikan, and a respondent who was otherwise not very emotional, surprised me with his remarks about Jerusalem:

> It is holy, it is one of the most beautiful things God created; it is not basically the structure of it, it is the place. Usually people get it wrong, it is not the way it looks, a temple or whatever it is. It is when you go in and you go down the steps there is that rock where Prophet Muhammad went up from there to heaven; that is what is beautiful about it.

Rami emphasized the historical meaning of Jerusalem and vividly imagined the events that have taken place there:

> In the Old City, because Jesus walked through there, and the Prophet Mohammed, and the Crusades, just the whole city itself. The Crusades took place over here, you look at the walls and you know people fought, they sacrificed their lives for this place; they didn't do it for nothing. This is the center of the main religions in the world.

For Sandy, Paul, and some of the other volunteers with foreign passports who lived and worked in Ramallah, Jerusalem acquired a special importance because they could go there, especially to West Jerusalem, to feel like they were in the West again and "relax" from being in the Middle East. Going out at night, watching movies, and enjoying other activities had a place in their schedule, though they were never particularly comfortable about these trips. Sandy told me:

> I love Jerusalem; it is very beautiful. I only can't stand the normalization with the Israelis that is taking place. And I can go there and hang out, but the way that I so quickly fall into feeling normal about being there, that is something I don't like in myself. I feel that I am in Palestine here; I am not in Palestine there. Although Jerusalem should be Palestine, it is now just Yerushalaim.

To meet and discover Palestine as a place proved to be important, but it was not the experience itself that the returnees perceived as the central part of their return. The interviews spoke of the difficulties and disappointments not with the place, but with the people. For this reason the second and more important aspect of meeting Palestine was meeting the people of Palestine. Muna put it this way:

> Palestine as a land, as nature, did not change. But the homeland only becomes a homeland because of the people in it. And I imagined the people to be different.

Meeting the People   Upon arrival in Palestine, the young returnees were confronted with not only the political situation in Palestine, but with the realities of Palestinian society. They were raised with images of the Intifada, as many of them grew into awareness during the time that the Intifada started. Their parents told them that people in Palestine were more educated, politically aware, and friendlier than other people in the Middle East. Through TV and newspapers in the Arab world and the United States, they saw the brave stone-throwing Palestinian youth, fighting and sacrificing themselves for the freedom of Palestine. The image of the Palestinian people is intimately linked to the image of the homeland Palestine, the political, historical, and cultural homeland. Before they were confronted with local Palestinians' attitudes toward them, the Aideen and Amrikan learned about the tensions and problems in Palestinian society.

Majid could not wait for a national number and so came to Palestine illegally. He simply considered it the right to time to return, and he was happy about making the journey. He told me how he and his friend were so happy about returning that they laughed all the way from the Allenby Bridge to Ramallah, and once there it took him three days to stop being so happy and to realize that people in Palestine were not happy.

One Palestinian intellectual, upon visiting Palestine after decades abroad, described Palestinian society as a "distorted society," with social Darwinism and a lack of courtesy prevailing (Moughrabi 1997, 10).[5] The interviews revealed shock and disappointment about the situation in Palestine and the attitude of the local Palestinians. Basma expressed most clearly what many of the Aideen felt:

> I was living a nice life, but believe me, when I used to see Palestine on TV, I used to cry when I was a kid. Oh, I felt they were all my cousins and my friends, it is the Palestinian soul, they were more than relatives for me, when I saw them on TV. When I came here I found things differ-

ent; the boys that used to throw stones in the Intifada are now the boys that are standing in the streets saying rude words to girls.

Kamila, who was so moved and fascinated by Jerusalem and the West Bank described reaching Gaza as a major shock. When she started working for the PA in Gaza, other feelings surfaced:

> And then I went to Gaza and I was really shocked by Gaza. It is really underdeveloped and the mentality is so straight. I just couldn't believe it; I thought Palestinians are so open-minded, because the people that I met in Lebanon and London and everywhere were different, and I thought they were all very highly educated and intellectual and knew what they were doing. I was so shocked; people in Gaza are more similar to Egyptians than they are to Palestinians. And their mentality, it was very hard to live in Gaza, very difficult, and I went through a major depression in the beginning.

Amina had a nervous breakdown after a small incident in her uncle's house, but in her view the breakdown reflected her general feeling of discomfort about being in Palestine in general, and Gaza in particular. She then decided to study at Birzeit, which improved her situation somewhat, but she was confronted with new problems and the same attitude of locals toward returnees. In addition she had to face the negative image of Gazans in the eyes of many West Bankers.

MEETING RELATIVES For the younger Amrikan, the image of Palestinians was the image of friendly relatives whom they knew from their summer vacations. Some of them recalled language problems from that time, but memories were generally positive, dominated by family gatherings, playing with cousins, and a freedom of movement that many of them did not have in the United States.

With their return to Palestine, their impression of relatives changed. Their relatives turned out to be more demanding and less tolerant about the differences in their American cousins. I often heard people complain about those strange American youngsters who did not know how to behave, did not speak Arabic, and showed little respect for the elders. An Associated Press report from July 1999 describes it as a conflict over not speaking Arabic, dressing improperly, defending one's own views, and not eating Arabic food.[6] These observations reduce the conflict to one between traditional Palestinians and more "modern," or Western, American returnees. In reality, matters were more complicated than that.

It is true that many of the Amrikan had problems communicating in Arabic, which prevented them from understanding their relatives. However, they knew many of these relatives from before and had maintained contact through extended family networks.

For the volunteers who did not arrive in Palestine with parents and were not introduced to relatives, it was their own choice as to whether to keep in touch with them or not, and they were cautious about doing so. They were aware that there were expectations that they might not meet and also feared the social control that involvement in a family network could entail. Tariq did not have any relatives in Palestine that he was aware of. Sandy and Nigel wanted to wait before meeting them, to first discover their Palestinian identity. Rayda regularly visited members of her extended family and enjoyed their hospitality but refrained from living with them despite several offers. Hiyam, who had been in close touch with her relatives, encountered problems only when she started talking about a Muslim Palestinian she had met. Her Christian family disappointed her with their prejudice.

The situation was different for the Aideen. For their parents and families it had been more difficult to stay in touch with the extended family. The political nature of their work, their dispersal around the world, and the difficulty of communicating with Palestine and Israel had contributed to the problem. Occasional letters and basic knowledge of the whereabouts of family members had to suffice. Accordingly, the expectations upon meeting those relatives after long years of separation were high. In many cases parents and children, brothers and sisters, uncles and cousins had not seen each other in decades.

Palestinians tend to think close connections within the Palestinian family are what have kept the Palestinian identity alive since 1948. Family links have in reality often been reduced to occasional letters, brief phone conversations, and messages from travelers. This is not to diminish the importance of these links. Families have been present in spirit at weddings, circumcisions, and funerals, and pictures of new babies have traveled all over the world to keep a sense of connection. But realistic pictures of how people really are and how they change over time cannot be transported this way. Surely, the first meeting after such a long separation was overwhelming to those brothers, parents, sisters, and grandparents who were apart for decades. But in due time, living close together revealed personal differences and tensions.

For the young Aideen, meeting those relatives most often meant meeting people that they did not know at all. Their parents might have had emotional reunions if they had family left in Palestine, but the children only knew those relatives from pictures and stories. They were expected to get along with their cousins in the same age group. In some cases the Aideen and their families had to stay with their families in Palestine for lack of other housing and as an expression of accepting the hospitality extended to them. These living arrangements eventually turned out to be problematic.

The Palestinians described here had lived in Arab countries and had had a family life that was centered on the core family, often with no members of the extended family around. They were not used to the expectations and the social control of their new living arrangements. As a consequence, they tried to move to their own places as soon as possible. The interviewees were hesitant to admit that there were any problems when I asked about relations with relatives.

Lana told me that her family had always been in contact with relatives, but added that they did not stay at their house when they arrived, and maintained rather formal relations. They disagreed on many issues, so she preferred not to socialize with them too much. Muna reported that her parents lived close to her father's family in Gaza and that she did not have any problems with these aunts, mainly because she did not live with them. Hanadi voiced disappointment about the weakness of her relationship with her father's relatives:

> I thought that my relationship with the family of my father would be stronger. But because of the long time that we didn't know each other, the relationship stayed weak, even after we came here. It is not a relation where you can say you have known the people all your life.

Zaynab openly rebelled against meeting her relatives in Nablus and told me about her father:

> He hates it when I say, I don't want to go to Nablus with you. I don't get along with my cousins; they are too close-minded, they have been here all their lives and they are idiots.

The young men had fewer problems with these family matters. Marwan told me that his experience with relatives in Palestine had been more positive than with those in Jordan. There he had met his father's family, but because his father had already passed away, he had the feeling that they did not care too much about him and his immediate family. In Palestine things were better; only travel problems posed obstacles to closer contact:

My aunts are here and also aunts of my father. The relations are very
good; we are really friends with them. They are in Abu Ghosh, in 1948,
and they even have Israeli citizenship. The contact is good, they visit
us and we go to their houses. There is my aunt in Jerusalem and I have
one uncle in Hebron. The geographical distance keeps us, it is far away,
but they always come for 'Eid, in Ramadan, and when there are other
festivities of the family.

In both groups, meeting relatives challenged the idea of strong Palestinian
family connections and put it to the test of everyday life. The Amrikan
could at least rely on the fact that they already knew many family members
in the Ramallah area. The Aideen were confronted with relatives whom
they had not known before. Depending on their places of origin in Palestine, relatives lived in Gaza, Nablus, Hebron, or even Israel, but rarely in
the Ramallah area. This fact helped avoid open conflict but did not necessarily facilitate closer connections.

In both groups, the young women voiced more concern about connections with relatives. One explanation for this might be that women were
expected to pay social visits, behave according to tradition, and carry on
conversation more than young men. Socializing within the family network
is an acceptable activity for young women, while young men can choose
from a wider range of leisure activities and do not need to be protected.
The pressure on young women could result in stronger resistance, while
young men could be more relaxed about these issues. For the returning
families, the behavior of their daughters and the impression they made on
relatives often functioned as proof of their proper upbringing, thus much
more was expected of young women than of young men.

NAMING THE "OTHERS" An intriguing aspect of meeting and being
met by people in Palestine was naming the different groups to which one
belonged and those to which one thought the'others belonged. It was the
first step in specific group formation.

The terms that local Palestinians used to name the returnees were introduced when I defined the groups for this study. "Aideen," those who are returning or have returned, is commonly used for those returnees who came
to Palestine after spending a long time or all their lives in Arab countries. It
applies to those who work for or are related to the Palestinian Authority or
police. The connotation has changed from a very positive one, the hope of
Palestinian diaspora members and their families being reunited and living
in a liberated Palestine, to a synonym for corruption, privilege, and the

takeover of political power. In the opinion of local Palestinians, there is no way to differentiate between those Aideen who are corrupt and abuse privileges and power and, for example, their children or other returnees who do not work for the PA. There is a correlation between the political or professional position that someone has and the society's resentment against that person. Everyone knows that policemen do not earn enough money to be called privileged.

For Palestinians who returned from the United States or other Western countries and were not directly linked to the PA, local Palestinians use a different term. They are called the Americans: Amrikan. Not surprisingly, group assignment was more important than the details of someone's life story. Zaynab, who grew up in Kuwait and Cyprus, and Yasin and Hamdi, born and raised in Sweden, were called Amrikan as well, simply because they were usually found speaking English with their fellow students who were Palestinian Americans.

Among the Aideen I found a number of terms for local Palestinians. The most common ones are *ahl al-balad* (the people of the land), *al-nas huna* (the people here), and *al-muwatinin* (the compatriots or citizens). The first term emphasizes the connection and right of the local Palestinians to the land; similarly, "the people here" means "the people from here," as opposed to the returnees who are from somewhere else. Al-muwatinin is an interesting term because it assigns those Palestinians to a status that they do not yet have, that of citizens of a Palestinian state. None of these terms is pejorative. The Aideen resent the negative meaning of the name used for them but do not attempt to find or use a similar term for the others to defend themselves. The feeling they express is that of disappointment with unfair treatment rather than outright anger.

More resistance and anger toward local Palestinians is expressed in the most common term that the Amrikan use for local Palestinians: They call them Arabs—those Arabs—clearly distancing themselves from them. Considering the fact that it is exactly this term that is commonly used for Palestinian and other Arab Americans in the United States, the irony is striking. "In America we are Arab. . . . Here we are American. . . . It is very confusing" (Janet).

The boys in particular subscribed to the linguistic divide by using expressions like "us Americans" and "them Arabs." Sometimes they also use the Arabic word *'arab*. Voluntary returnees were rather careful in using any term. When I asked about their relations with local Palestinians, they would usually call them "the people here" or "the Palestinians." Their definition of themselves as well as that of other Palestinians was more careful, expressing the troubling process of assessing and rewriting their own identities in the return process.

This part of the return process has been described as part of the liminal stage. Here the old environment and familiar setting was left and lost just as a new unknown or relatively unfamiliar one was reached. The process of meeting the place and the people is characterized by confrontation between the previously developed diaspora identities and images of Palestine, and the reality of the land and its people. The meeting stage forced the returnees to become aware of their own identities by realizing how they were different from the local people, and by recognizing the discrepancy between their own expectations and reality. From the perspective of local Palestinians, it is also a question of recognizing differences and naming the newcomers. It is impossible to put a time limit on this stage. What needs to be emphasized is the individual nature of each confrontation.

From "meeting Palestine," they take the next step to "living in Palestine," a process that is marked by constant negotiation, a quest for relative stability in a rather unstable setting, and the search for a group with which to identify. These groups temporarily offer needed protection and stability and initiate the rewriting of identity.

STEP 4: LIVING IN PALESTINE

This step of the return process has to be viewed as part of the liminal stage. For the returnees in this study, life in Palestine was centered in Ramallah. The study focused on that city, a place where the two groups of returnees lived side by side. They interacted with each other to an extent, but interacted more with local Palestinians.

Living in Ramallah Historically, Ramallah and its sister town Al-Bireh have not been towns at all. Both were villages prior to 1948, Ramallah having a mainly Christian population, and Al-Bireh having a predominantly Muslim one. It was the influx of refugees from what would become the state of Israel in 1948 that increased the population of these two villages and turned them into towns. Strategically situated in the middle of the West Bank and close to Jerusalem, Ramallah has developed into a center of Palestinian life, economically, socially, and politically. A relatively large number of Christians have left this place of origin and migrated to the United States, Latin America, or elsewhere. A similar type of economically induced migration occurred in Al-Bireh. Chain migration and "oscillating migration" between different countries and Palestine have provided Ramallah and Al-Bireh with various influences from outside as well as with money from migrants in many countries.

The city evidenced these facts in the large number of houses that had been built over the years, many of them only inhabited in summer when families came for vacations. More recently, Ramallah has been turned into the de facto capital of Palestine, with many of the PA institutions, ministries, and offices there. Various NGO offices have preceded or followed them. Aideen, returnees from Arab countries, have settled in and around Ramallah to work for the PA administration.

Was Ramallah changing and becoming more open because of the influx of returnees, or was it attracting returnees because it was more open than other places in the Palestinian territories? Before the Intifada, Ramallah was famous for having a nightlife with bars, restaurants, music, and movie theaters. During the Intifada, nightlife ended because Israel imposed curfews, and Palestinians stayed home, feeling as though they were at war. Since the Oslo process began, which also marked the end of the First Intifada, Ramallah has opened up again. It was certainly the most cosmopolitan place in Palestine and saw the fastest pace of change. As a result, Ramallah's infrastructure and society seemed to be developing too quickly.

Housing was a big issue for returnees. The question of where and how returnees and their families would live might explain their feeling at home in Palestine. Comparing the two groups, the difference is striking. Many of the Amrikan returnees had their roots in the area in and around Ramallah, and consequently they most often lived in houses that were owned by their parents or their extended family. They often stayed with relatives until their own house was renovated and furnished, but at the time of the research none of the Amrikan youngsters lived in a rented apartment. The situation was different for the voluntary returnees; they lived in rented apartments, usually sharing them with foreigners working for NGOs in Ramallah or studying in Birzeit.

Partly because of the influx of returnees, Ramallah saw a boom in construction. Initially the town could not accommodate large numbers of new inhabitants. The new buildings were usually high-rise apartment buildings, housing unfamiliar to people in the region.

Generally, the idea of renting a place to live, as opposed to owning a place, is not traditional for Palestinians. The appearance of such forms of housing has considerably changed the social structures and the relations between neighbors and relatives in the area around Ramallah, creating anonymity. The PA has never considered programs to provide housing for the Aideen. Many of them had to stay with friends or relatives while looking for a place to rent. All the Aideen I interviewed lived in rented apartments.

This living situation caused them to feel only partly settled, just as they had felt while in exile. It also distinguished "real locals" from newcomers to the area or to Palestine. Very few of the Aideen were able to buy houses upon their arrival. The price of land in and around Ramallah had risen enormously, and much available land had been used for other construction projects. Many locals who owned land, especially in Al-Bireh, had turned from peasants into rich city people by selling their farmland for construction.

Housing is important for developing a sense of being at home, as the safety and reliability of private space is one major component in creating a feeling of stability. The situation of most Amrikan was better in this respect, and even if they did not stay after high school, they knew that there was a family home that they could always return to. For the Aideen the housing situation was more difficult and offered less opportunity to feel settled. Living in a rented apartment also further distinguished them from local Palestinians. Najma told me about the situation in the building in which her family lived, saying that neighbors were not supportive and that they did not establish lasting ties with them. Kamila, who lived alone, felt considerable pressure and control from neighbors who frequently gossiped about her comings and goings and about her guests. It was the contact with neighbors, colleagues, and fellow students that proved decisive in the development of group identities.

Group Formation The formation of group identity is determined by external and internal factors. Group identity occurs with different groups at different times, and individuals can operate with identities that depend on time, setting, and circumstances. A number of identities possessed and utilized by a person can be overlapping, coexisting, and at times even contradictory. The focus here is on group identity, in particular the question of how the returnees of the two groups perceived their respective identities.

In this step of the return process, the young returnees attempted to solve the problems created by losing their pre-return identity and suffering the tension they felt in Palestinian society. To protect themselves and find a shared identity, they formed a group, mainly as a reaction to the critical or even hostile attitude of local society. This group identity was also based on shared previous experiences and the need to be with others who understood the specific process of change that they were undergoing. After all, they were labeled and perceived as the "others," as Aideen, Amrikan, or *Ajanib* (foreigners or strangers). They displayed different behavioral patterns, interpretations of tradition, concepts of personality, and political attitudes. They were distinguishable by their way of dressing, their speech, and their body language.

The two groups of returnees in and around Ramallah did not merge into one larger group of returnees, nor did they ever mention that they had recognized the other group, either as a problem or as a source of allies. None of the Aideen ever voiced criticism of the Amrikan, although they must have recognized them as different, just as the locals did. The Amrikan rarely talked about the Aideen; their criticism was directed at the PA in general and did not mention the Aideen in particular. One can conclude that the members of both groups were too occupied with the group conflict between themselves and local Palestinians to consider more complicated constellations.

In many of the interviews, the respondents spent considerable time and effort explaining their situation vis-à-vis the local Palestinians. The nature of the clash between them can be described on two levels. The first conflict was political and, although the respondents of this study were too young to have themselves participated in political activity, the clash reflected the conflict between "inside" and "outside" in Palestinian politics.

The second conflict was cultural and surfaced because of the different cultural and social norms of the returnees and the locals. Both conflicts played a role in both groups, but to different degrees. The political one was predominant among the Aideen, although they also had cultural problems. The Amrikan lacked political knowledge, but, more importantly, they had different concepts of behavior.

The Political Conflict   The nature of the political conflict described here is closely linked to the clash of power interests and an awareness of the political past; it is a conflict between the local Palestinian elite—the inside, and the returnees—the outside.

The nature of this conflict also explains why the Aideen are criticized more harshly than are the Amrikan. In the eyes of Palestinian locals, the Amrikan and their families were not considered part of the "outside," and those who came voluntarily were seen as foreigners more than as a threat to local political and power interests. On the other hand, all the young

Aideen mentioned the problems that they had coping with the negative perceptions of the Aideen as a group. The discussions reflected their deep disappointment and resistance.

Basma, whose father did not work for the PA but was instead a re-searcher and journalist, felt very challenged in her convictions when she was first accused of not having suffered and not being a real Palestinian.

> I used to hear a lot of things in class. Oh, yes, you lived in Cyprus, you could go swimming and you had a happy life, whereas we were living the most terrible days in our life. We were having war and our friends were dying and our brothers were in prisons. We were living a really bad life, whereas you were living the most lovely life, so you are not Palestinian; we are the Palestinians, the people who are living here in our country. We are the real Palestinians; you are not real Palestinians. You are nothing. At first I started to cry and then I wanted to say, No, that is not right; I wanted to find a reason, a convincing reason, but it was like this. I think I was living a nice life.

Muna described a similar experience:

> And it happens a lot to us that people attack us; you are returnees, you had a good life, you had fun. Just when they hear Beirut, Syria, Egypt, you lived but we didn't and we were fighting the Intifada. Sure, you can explain and explain, but they have a picture in their minds that we didn't suffer. I think, okay, I didn't suffer, but my father did suffer and my mother did too, but me as Muna, I didn't suffer. I know they suffered a lot, they had the Intifada, they always had curfews and the schools were closed. Sure, I lived a better life than someone in Jabaliya in Gaza, I am sure I had more joy in my life. But that is not my fault; I didn't choose to be there and not here. And the same way he sacrificed, we sacrificed as well, for example, in Lebanon, many people there, our relatives, suffered, my brothers did. I was just too small.

For Hanadi it was the most disappointing part of her return experience that local people put her in a category that she felt to be unfair. In our conversation she explained to me how the treatment of local people had made her feel unwelcome:

> I thought that my relation with the local people would be better, but it is not very good, because there are people who say that I am a returnee. You are Palestinian and I am Palestinian, Why do you tell me I am a re-turnee? The only difference is that I couldn't come and live here and you

lived here. But you don't love your country more than I do. I love my country as well, like you and maybe even more. We were hated outside by the people we lived with, and we couldn't believe that we would come here and there would still be a difference.

Maybe it is because the people have problems with the PA and they think that all returnees are alike and that they are all with the PA. That is not true, and I tell them always that it is wrong. People tell me a lot, You are a returnee, and I tell them, No, I am a Palestinian.

Najma found the explanation for locals' behavior in their anger about privileges and corruption. Like her, many of the young Aideen recognized this problem but felt that they were not personally responsible for it and neither were their parents. For that reason they expressed resentment against being categorized as Aideen. Najma added that she thought the Palestinians expected the PA to be able to perform miracles and solve all problems immediately. Because this expectation was unrealistic, they needed someone to blame for their disappointment, and it was only logical to choose the outsiders, namely, the returnees.

Marwan explained to me that he had not expected being a returnee to be a problem. He did acknowledge that some returnees had abused privileges and were corrupt, which in turn reflected on all the other returnees. He thought that Palestinians everywhere had suffered and sacrificed in different ways, and thus both had a right to live in Palestine, side by side.

When I talk about how much we fought or sacrificed, I don't expect anything in return. My father, when he offered his soul, he didn't expect a car or a house. He didn't expect a reward. The reward would be to live in Palestine. The people who sacrificed didn't do it for rewards.

Many of the Aideen pointed out that it was exactly this feeling of being treated unfairly and lumped together as outsiders that most often led them to turn to other returnees for close friendships. But some returnees made a conscious attempt not to let that happen, instead choosing friends from among both returnees and locals. The longer a returnee lived in Palestine, the more likely he had close relationships with locals and thus a growing feeling of integration.

The young returnees felt that they were treated unfairly by being blamed for not suffering enough, especially since they had been born outside Palestine and, in fact, had never had a choice about living there. Historically, the "inside" blames the "outside" because they believe that the refugees betrayed their homeland by fleeing, while those who stayed were the true heroes. The returnees understood the motivation of the locals, but at the same time they strongly resisted being treated accordingly. For their age, the returnees were astonishingly understanding and patient. Many of them recalled having heated discussions about this topic and making drastic decisions not to socialize with friends anymore when they voiced this type of negative stereotype of returnees.

Returnees' treatment by the local population had caused an intense feeling of alienation, in some cases leading them to want to leave Palestine, or to fear that they would never feel at home, or in a few cases, to take active measures to change people's perceptions about returnees. None of them demanded political solutions, but all of them believed that personal contacts and good examples would change the picture in the long run.

For the Amrikan the political issue was less important. They had to cope with their own immense lack of knowledge about Palestinian politics, having grown up in a less politicized environment, with parents who had little political involvement and, in fact, had left Palestine for nonpolitical reasons. Interestingly enough, this segment of Palestinian society, the work and study migrants, were never blamed for betraying Palestine by leaving it. In the ongoing conflict between "inside" and "outside," that fact might be related to the fact that their return did not result in a change of power distribution. They often brought money to Palestine to sustain their families, and some of them have opened small businesses, catering to the needs of the growing Palestinian American segment of society (Associated Press, July 30, 1999).[7]

In their attempts to integrate into Palestinian society, the Aideen were confronted with a conflict of political interests and power balances. Their strategies of coping with this conflict had to recognize that it was not their conflict, but rather that of their parents' generation. Many of them solved it by keeping a low profile politically and by defending themselves verbally in confrontations. They showed much understanding and patience with the locals' image of returnees but rejected the assignment of negative images to them personally.

The Cultural Conflict   It can be said that Palestinian society is politicized and politically structured, but it is also characterized by cultural and social diversity, not least because of migration. Thus, a clash between the cultural and social ideas and norms of locals and returnees was likely to occur.

One would have expected that Palestinian society inside Palestine would not "develop" and change as fast as diaspora communities, because these communities were exposed to different cultural influences, especially in Western countries. Returnees would be morally lax, less integrated into family, more individualized, and not as respectful of elders as local Palestinians. Of course, the conditions were much more complicated than that, and it is good to realize how the common dichotomies of traditional and modern, conservative and progressive, Westernized and non-Westernized fail to explain developments in non-Western societies. It is almost impossible to draw a line here when one talks about migration. Is a Palestinian who was born in Lebanon and spent half of his life in Canada an Eastern or a Western individual? One should be aware of the pitfalls that these terms and categories create. To clarify the situation, the cultural conflict will be described in the terms of the returnees themselves.[8]

As well as the political conflict, the Aideen experienced an almost equally important clash of cultures. Two things were mentioned in most of the interviews: morality and social control.

Many of the girls told me that locals expected them to be more open about dating and socializing with young men than local Palestinian girls. They expressed frustration and anger about bold offers. Basma told me:

> It is because they think I am a returnee I must be the kind of open-minded girl, I don't care about anything, there is no limits for my casual life. I used to tell them no, and then after a period of time I understood the reason why they asked me to go out on a date. It is because I am a returnee. When I say I can't go out at night, they say how come, you are a returnee. And they say it unconsciously I think.

The young women (for example, Basma, Najma, and Hanadi) were often judged by the way they dressed. Except for Amina, none of them wore *hijab*, thus they were assumed to be less religious and more open to dating. In Palestinian society, recent years have seen a sharper division in dress and behavior between religious people and those who are considered modern or secular.[9] This is not the place to discuss these matters in detail, but for the Aideen, no correlation could be found between hijab and the level of religiosity.

Many of the girls who dressed according to the latest fashions and did not contemplate wearing hijab were religious. They did not see a contradiction in their public appearance and the upholding of their religion. Patterns of morality and behavior might have been different when Palestinians lived in exile communities in Arab countries. This fact is less related to the "openness" of the host society and more to the "outsider" role of Palestinians in relation to the host society. Outsiders in a society often enjoy greater freedom because they are not considered a part of the body of that society.

The assumption that they would be more liberal than the local Palestinian society in the West Bank and Gaza overlooks the changes in this society itself. The West Bank and Gaza were not completely isolated from the rest of the world. Several influential factors can be identified: migration and interaction with migrants, TV and other media, the proximity of Israeli society, the Israeli occupation, and not least the considerable number of foreigners working for NGOs. One major complaint in the interviews was the danger and intensity of the harassment of women in the streets of Ramallah. The women in the Aideen group did not actively protest this treatment but rather avoided those parts of town, such as the main street in Ramallah. Another option was not to go out alone.

The situation holds true for the Amrikan. Although the clash was more a cultural one than it was for the Aideen, in their actual experience both groups of returnees had a lot in common. However, two aspects differentiated the Amrikan experience considerably from that of the Aideen and from the experience of local Palestinian women confronted with the problem of harassment: One was the fact that most of the Amrikan had had a very traditional upbringing, whether they were Christian or Muslim; all were raised with values like preserving one's virginity, behaving modestly, and respecting one's elders. One reason these teenagers were brought to Palestine was because their parents wanted to protect these values, a task they considered easier in a more traditional society.

The adult women in this group who returned voluntarily also showed an awareness of the moral rules and expectations but more freely and consciously broke them, although they avoided public censure by keeping a low profile. At the same time, even the young Amrikan women considered dating in the form of meeting young men in public places and talking. They told me that premarital sex was out of the question, even for the young men, but meeting a person before marriage was both desired and possible.[10] Their beliefs were a mixture of Western ideas of individuality, the right to actively look for happiness in life, and the holding on to traditional values.

A number of the respondents in this group said that matchmaking by their parents would be acceptable, as long as they could reject suitors. This holds true for the young women as well as a number of men. The best protection the Amrikan teenagers found against harassment on the streets was their peer group.

The second component of conflict as reflected in many of the interviews is "the talking." The social control exercised in the context of Ramallah, the surrounding villages, and the university is a phenomenon most of the returnees did not expect and do not know how to deal with. It was accompanied by a feeling of constantly being under surveillance. This was more open and direct for the girls and women, as they were considered to be the bearers of honor and reputation. It is a mechanism that threatens their feeling of safety in society. I heard several stories of how someone would spend the afternoon in Ramallah, and later people from the village, relatives, and so on, would carry the story to the parents and cause problems by inventing details and questioning the parents about their children's reputation. Jane, who lived in Birzeit with her family, said:

> We would do things that are not bad, and the next day my parents would hear about it and they would say, for example, I was sitting at Checkers with a bunch of guys smoking. I am not that dumb to do something like that, because I know how people think. I just want people to mind their own business and not care so much about other people's lives.

Not surprisingly, when I asked them what they would change in Palestine, many of the respondents said that people should gossip less. With most of the Amrikan coming from bigger cities in the United States or elsewhere, they had no concept of social surveillance. In Palestine, this behavior is a tool of social control.

In the Palestinian context, it can be said that this social control substitutes for the existence of a state. Because of the lack of legal and administrative bodies to rule the country, social control is used to keep people in line. In a relatively small society, gossip and reputation are powerful tools. The power that just a few gossipers can wield over many other people is obvious. And so is the imbalance of power between older and younger people, with the older generations controlling and setting the standards, and the younger ones being threatened. Especially during and after the Intifada, when political power rapidly shifted from the older to the younger generation, this insistence on moral control kept some power in the hands of the elders.

According to the respondents, women mainly, but not exclusively, exercised the power of gossip. It is a myth that men do not gossip: In the Palestinian context, high unemployment rates meant that large numbers of younger and older men spent their days in the streets and cafés doing exactly that, gossiping. One can assume that control is stricter in Gaza, the refugee camps, and the villages, where people know each other even better.

The formation of the groups of returnees, and the political and cultural conflicts constitute the stage of the return process called "living in Palestine." Looking at it from one perspective, it was mainly outside images that assigned the returnees to their respective groups, and only as a reaction to these assignments did they start socializing within their groups for protection, support, and understanding of their specific problems.

The coping strategies were as different and diverse as the people interviewed. At one end of the spectrum, there was acceptance and understanding of the actions of local Palestinians and their sentiments and even of the obviously unfair treatment. At the other end, there was verbal resistance and negotiation in critical situations, refusal to socialize with local Palestinians, and ultimately the choice not to stay in Palestine. The most extreme way of "coping" with Palestine was expressed in acts of resistance to being in Palestine.

Acts of Resistance   The examples of acts of resistance described here are those of the dependent Amrikan. The reactions described here are only possible and make sense within this group. The other returnees had other ways to change their situation. In addition, they participated in the decision to return and supported it. Some of the Amrikan were forced into returning or did not even know that they would be staying for good. One form of protest was simply to run away. I heard several runaway stories during my research, two of them from respondents in this study.

Aziz grew up in Chicago and came back to Palestine in 1996 at age fifteen. A year later and with the help of a friend, he made it all the way back to the United States, first to Miami and then to Chicago. There he got in touch with his favorite uncle who eventually convinced him to talk to his father and go back to Palestine. His escape was a freeing experience that allowed him to express his objection and gave him the feeling of having control over his life.

Another way of showing one's resistance concerned speaking Arabic. The young Amrikan found learning Arabic in the West difficult. None of them was fluent, and all of them had problems reading and writing. Some could understand most colloquial Arabic; others were able to express themselves as well. There was no correlation between the length of their stay in Palestine and their command of the language. Several respondents seemed to resist openly the attempts to improve their Arabic.

Amira had been in Palestine for almost three years. She was fifteen when her family moved from Cleveland to Al-Bireh. She did understand the basics of the Palestinian dialect but could not carry on a conversation with someone who did not speak English. I knew her family, and I noticed that her younger siblings had picked up much more Arabic from school and from the streets. She told me that she had always felt forced to learn Arabic and that people had pressured her too much. She had become a very quiet girl because she simply would not speak if it was not absolutely necessary. She needed a friend or her mother to speak for her when dealing with Arabic speakers.

Jimmy had been in Palestine for eight months but was certain that he would leave again soon, mainly because of his poor integration into the society. He spoke some Arabic but did not read or write it at all, and he openly told me that he could not see the point of improving, because he was going to leave anyway.

Mukhlis said he understood about 60 percent of what people said to him but had problems with reading and writing; it took him very long. He added that his younger brothers and sisters spoke and read better Arabic and that he had not learned it because when he arrived four years earlier he did not want to stay and did not want to learn.

Ultimately, all the English speakers' Arabic improved: They learned on the streets, they had instruction in school, and as part of the "integration process" they realized the importance of understanding the language of their parents.

Finding Spaces Space, or the occupation of space, has been identified as an important aspect of expressing one's identification with a social group. In this context, only the use of public spaces can be analyzed in more detail, as I did not have access to the private homes of my respondents.

The young returnees had found several spaces that supported their expression of group identity. The spaces, both in educational and leisure facilities, were not exclusively theirs, but they provided meeting places for the respective groups. In educational facilities, these spaces were to be found in Birzeit University and the Friends Boys School (FBS) in Al-Bireh. Leisure spaces included restaurants, Internet cafés, and gyms. As access to all these places required a certain amount of money, not all returnees could use them. Poverty excluded both local Palestinians and returnees from these spaces.

BIRZEIT Both Birzeit University and FBS required that parents have the financial means to send their children there. Birzeit is considered the best university in Palestine, where tuition and fees are low compared to American universities, but they are nevertheless high for the average Palestinian. Access to university programs is also determined by entrance exams.

At Birzeit, one can find both returnees and students from all parts of the Palestinian territories. Birzeit has a reputation for being a reflection of the political situation in Palestine. The student council annual elections are said to measure the political mood of the Palestinian people.[11]

Discussion of the returnee issue at Birzeit was complicated. At the Public Relations Office, an employee set up appointments and brought returnees to the office to meet me. But he refused to organize a meeting of a group of returnees to discuss their particular problems and experiences, arguing that Birzeit was not interested in creating a group structure that differentiated among students. I was also unable to get official statistics or additional information about how many returnees were students there. Another researcher heard the same argument to explain why Birzeit did not offer special study groups or courses for returnees from non-Arab countries to improve their command of Arabic and to allow them to fully participate in courses (Wernefeldt 1997, 31).[12]

For returnees, the university is often the most important opportunity to socialize and to have a peer group, especially for those who live in the dormitories. Some students socialized only with other returnees, building on the group feeling and shared experience that created a special bond between them. Others studied and socialized with a mixed group, but these respondents often reported negative experiences and situations in which they felt excluded and offended by local students. Najma told me such a story:

> Once it happened to me here at the university; I was sitting and talking with friends and then we came to the PA as a topic, so I of course defended the PA. One of them told me, Darling, every country has its garbage. So I tell her: And we are the garbage? And she replies: You can understand that as you like. She was a very good friend of mine! I told her, You have been living with us on a daily basis and you have seen how we interact and you know what we have inside, how can you talk about us like that? See, she was my friend and I became so sad that I started crying.

Amina had a mixture of problems. She lived in one of the dorms but did not get along with the girls there for political as well as personal reasons. Her friends next door were all returnee girls. She felt that she could share memories and the feeling of being rejected by the local society with them. She also changed her style of dress from wearing the *jilbab* (headscarf and coat) to wearing just a headscarf (*hijab*) and modest clothes, because she felt that people in Ramallah and Birzeit were looking at her strangely.

Dalia, who studied at Birzeit, lived in a student house. She was upset about her negative experience with people at the university and was also frustrated about the amount of social control exercised by the people around her. She had become very cautious about whom she talked to and what she said to them and claimed that people were always misinterpreting things.

For returnees and local students, Birzeit functioned as a meeting place and at the same time as a place for confrontation, whether open or hidden. It allowed for the crystallization of group identities but at the same time facilitated a slow process of mutual adjustment. Returnees could learn to deal with the Palestinian "mentality" and learned the rules of social control and the power of gossip. Simultaneously, local students saw returnees daily and got a chance to differentiate and create their own image instead of just accepting society's perceptions. In addition, "local" and "returnee" students were not the only groups on campus. There were tensions between political factions, and between groups of students from different parts of Palestine, such as the West Bank and Gaza, Ramallah, Nablus, and so forth. Social differences played a role, as did the prestige of families, the connections to the PA, and the educational and professional backgrounds of the students. By getting involved in these other groups, returnees went through an adjustment process that could integrate them into the different folds of Palestinian society. And in this regard, Birzeit could be viewed as a reflection of the larger Palestinian society.

FRIENDS BOYS SCHOOL   At FBS, a high school in Al-Bireh, the divisions between returnees and locals were clearer because the school had one program for English speakers and a different one for Arabic speakers. FBS is a private school, run by Quakers, with both Palestinian and non-Palestinian staff.[13] According to Jim Fine, the principal of the school, most of the students in the English-speaking program were children of parents who migrated to the West, mostly the United States, and brought them back to learn the language and culture.[14] He spoke of the tension between the two groups of speakers, even for those who were competent in both languages. The issue was their different pasts, their cultural differences, the English speakers' lack of political knowledge, and the differing fashions and music.

Having different opportunities in the future seemed to me another potential source of conflict. The majority of the English speakers had firm plans to attend college in the United States and, even if they were to return to Palestine, which was only one possibility, they would have better job opportunities and would most likely also get more money to start.

Like Birzeit, FBS was a microcosm, and here returnees also found peers with similar experiences. Approximately 30 percent of the students at FBS were returnees. For the school, Amrikan were a familiar phenomenon, and although there were more of them than in years past, the students themselves had not changed much. Their numbers had increased, and the demand for places at FBS was still growing, despite the fact that a number of other private schools with English instruction had been established in the area.[15] The new phenomenon was that there were now children of returnees from Arab countries (about 10 percent of the students), but they generally had fewer problems fitting in and were hardly recognizable in the school environment.[16] The major division at FBS remained that between Arabic and English speakers.

Language played an important role at FBS outside class as well. During ethics classes with Carleta Baker, and in conversations with her, I learned that, as they became more integrated, students would speak more Arabic and often started to use it as a "secret language" to say things that she should not understand. They also often cursed in Arabic. The English they spoke was of course mostly American, but I learned to detect differences corresponding to the place of upbringing and social class. Those who had not grown up in the United States, like Nabila (Austria), Yasin and Hamdi (Sweden), and Zaynab (Kuwait and Cyprus), had already acquired an American peer group accent. Writing skills showed differences in style, command, and spelling.

The division between the English and Arabic speakers was apparent in school. During breaks, groups would form and, as in the streets of Ramallah, the Amrikan were clearly distinguishable. The topic surfaced in classroom discussions, and the Amrikan explained the difference between "us" and "them" as a matter of "them not accepting us," not knowing about their American background and acknowledging the different upbringing. In the interviews themselves, the issue was usually downplayed, as if the youngsters did not want to talk about it outside school.

For Ibtisam, who had been in Palestine for six years when I talked to her, the problem was the returnees themselves. She emphasized that the locals, or Arabic speakers, would only feel that the returnees or Amrikan were different if they themselves acted in this way. For her, it was the problem of the returnees' putting too much emphasis on being different and being made outsiders that actually created the division and group boundaries. She would respond to Arabic speakers in Arabic and confront them with their negative attitude, thereby also speaking on behalf of her class.

For the Amrikan, FBS was a space that functioned as a place both to meet and to confront. While English instruction separated the youngsters from the local Arabic-speaking students at the school, the shared daily school life and interaction provided space for developing a group identity as returnees, or Americans. It also offered opportunities to develop shared features of identity—in attending the same school, going on school trips together, and communicating during breaks.

One particularly integrating aspect was political activity. The administration of the school was naturally concerned about the safety of the students but had pro-Palestinian political attitudes. Some students were related to political factions and rallied on the school campus. FBS students were involved in demonstrations against the Israelis and in the Intifada, until the school was closed along with the other schools and universities. During my fieldwork, there were several demonstrations at the checkpoint between Jerusalem and Ramallah, and FBS students participated in them.

SPACES FOR LEISURE ACTIVITY   The choice of where to spend the time after school and university was more in the hands of the young returnees themselves than was the choice of attending a particular school or university. Of course, there were certain restrictions, more so for the girls than for the boys, and all of them had to adhere to restrictions related to transportation, as many of them lived outside Ramallah, while the leisure spaces were all in town. The surrounding villages and distant suburbs of Ramallah, as well as more distant places, such as Nablus or Jerusalem, could only be reached by taxi or service buses. The money required for accessing leisure spaces was another restriction.

None of the spaces described here were exclusively reserved for returnees; rather, they functioned as meeting places for them and, thus, enforced group identity. Similar to Birzeit University and FBS, they also facilitated meeting and socializing with local Palestinians and had the potential of being "integration spaces" where similarities and shared interests could be discovered as a starting point for mutual adjustment.

The reason why Ramallah had attraction for returnees was the existence of a diverse social life and a considerable number of places for recreation, which they used as voluntary meeting, grouping, and integrating spaces. Most of these places had been opened after the Intifada and, in the wake of the peace process, were possibly also intended to cater to the different needs of the returnees. As Ramallah grew in size and many new buildings, mostly apartments and houses, were constructed, a large number of bars, cafés, and restaurants appeared. They completed the scene of new shops and mall buildings, especially at the center of Ramallah, surrounding the main street. Not only returnees frequented them, but local Palestinians as well.

The first example is Checkers, a franchise of an American fast-food chain, owned by a Palestinian American woman who had returned a few years earlier. Business was going very well and the restaurant was always crowded and full of noise and music. Approximately half of the customers were local Palestinians who often took their children to eat out.

The Amrikan youngsters were a familiar feature of the restaurant, and there were always more guys than girls. They started coming in the afternoon when school let out, many of them still in their school uniforms. They sat there and chatted, talked about homework and school, or met with others who went to other schools but belonged to the same peer network. It was also a very public and thus safe dating place. Boys and girls would sit together in pairs or larger groups. Checkers had a sitting area especially designed for families. The more traditional restaurants and cafés in Palestine always had a section, usually upstairs, that only families and groups of women or girls used. It was hidden from public view and separated from the downstairs entrance area where only men sat. It was an opportunity for women to go and eat out without obviously being in public. The family section in Checkers was a compromise; it was not hidden from public view, but there was a separate area where only families and girls went. It functioned as a way for women to express that they did not want attention from men. I never saw young men crossing this line of symbolic separation. The later the time of the day, the fewer girls would be there. They had to be home earlier than the guys, and it was considered inappropriate to be out after dark.

Located in the same building as the restaurant was Palsoft, one of two Internet cafés in this building, and one of seven existing at the time in the center of Ramallah. Palsoft was one large room with ten computers and many people crowding it. Many of the young Amrikan would come in groups, talking to each other in English, chatting, and surfing the Web together. It was a part of their leisure time spent with the group, and sometimes they also did homework there. They would go to chat rooms, rarely alone, more often with a crowd of them around one screen, commenting on the responses. For some of them it was also a way of keeping in touch with friends in the United States whom they had not seen in a long time.

The second Internet café in the building worked with a slightly different concept. It was in a remote corner of the building and provided more private spaces to browse, read, and write. It soon became the favorite place for some of the Amrikan girls, removed from too much public attention and still a place to go besides home. Reputation and gossip, and being seen or not in public, were an important concern for them, so this place catered to their particular needs.

For the Aideen, a number of cafés acquired importance as meeting places. One in particular, Kan Bata Zaman, in the main street in Ramallah, was popular at the time. Centrally situated in Ramallah and in an easy-to-find location for meetings, its comfortable and private atmosphere was inviting. It was a place that played Western music, was owned by a Christian, and served alcohol. Even this place had a separate upstairs area with the familiar sign "For families only," but here it seemed to be a game played with tradition. Downstairs there were only two tables, never enough for young men coming in, so groups of young men as well as mixed groups, secret couples, and groups of girls crowded the much larger room upstairs.

There were many more expensive and extravagant restaurants and bars, and I often heard local people say that only the Aideen could afford to go there. For Palestinians the bars had a decadent and "immoral" flair, especially for those who could not or did not want to frequent them. Though in general Palestinians did express pride in the cultural variety that Ramallah displayed, this type of nightlife was not considered a source of such pride for most. It was an artistic, intellectual scene with secular overtones. It was as if nightlife, alcohol, and "decadent" pleasures were a way of escaping the depressing realities of Palestine, at least for the night. For the older returnees it was a way of socializing, showing off their taste and lifestyle, and escaping the disappointment about all that Palestine was expected to be, but turned out to not be.

A type of leisure space that both Aideen and Amrikan used were gyms. As far as I know, Ramallah had at least three. The one I knew best was not in the center of Ramallah, but on the way to Jerusalem, about ten minutes away by car. It had been opened by a Palestinian returnee who had spent most of his life in South America but came back after the Oslo agreement. He was fluent in Arabic and Spanish and was a bodybuilder himself. The gym was spacious, with saunas and showers, fitness machines, and a weight-training section. Sensitive to the local situation and customs, the gym was open only to women in the mornings, and no man, not even the owner, would be around during that time. From early afternoon on, the members were mixed, but the trainers were very conscious about possible harassment, and "protected" the women working out there. Two groups of people caught the eye, men who were familiar with fitness and bodybuilding from where they came from, namely Aideen and Amrikan, and many more Christian than Muslim women. The second important characteristic of members was, again, that they could afford membership. A monthly membership was worth a quarter of the wage of a policeman or teacher. Nevertheless, it was a successful and popular workout place, not least for the foreigners in Ramallah who perceived it as a familiar "Western" place to relax and maintain a healthy lifestyle.

All these places had in common that they provided space for group contact. People could differentiate themselves from local Palestinians by reinforcing their identities as people who were more liberal, more educated, and more conscious of health and fitness. For returnees they meant familiar terrain, something that connected them to their past and a different type of life, often the more pleasant aspects of exile or diaspora life. Returnees attempted to recreate familiar lifestyles and transport them to Palestine in order to feel at home. It made living in Palestine bearable, smoothed the process of adjustment, and enabled the returnees to switch between the comfort of group identity and a local environment that they perceived as strange and unfamiliar.

Visibility as a Group Two aspects of visibility in Palestinian society caught the eye (and ear) when observing the returnees in Ramallah, namely dress and language. The question of how people dressed in public played a role in many of the interviews. Usually the respondents brought it up. They pointed out to me that their way of dressing made them recognizable to others as non-local Palestinians. Surprisingly, it was the young males of the Amrikan who most often talked about it. They wore wide, saggy trousers, oversized shirts, sneakers, and baseball caps. They reflected the American hip-hop culture images in an idealized and unchanging form. Locals looked at this way of dressing with suspicion, branded it as strange and different, and often made fun of it. There was also envy and curiosity, and some of these outfits became so popular that local Palestinians started to copy them. Some of the Amrikan youngsters started dressing this way only in Palestine, like Rami, who told me that he belonged to the group and wanted others to recognize this fact. He came from a better middle-class background and, in the United States, had little connection to this social culture. He adopted the peer group style together with the music they listened to, though he was used to classical music.

For the girls, it was different because dress was related to morality and religion, to ideas of honor and respectability. The boys in the peer group told the girls how to dress and behave in order to avoid conflict or friction with local boys in the streets.

In comparison, Aideen girls often told me that they were blamed for dressing too seductively. Often this was related to the earlier-mentioned idea that girls who grew up in supposedly more liberal Arab countries such as Lebanon, Syria, or Tunisia had loose morals and a lack of modesty. They defended their taste in fashion and insisted that modesty (and also religiosity) was not a matter of dress, but one of inner values and behavior.

The volunteers in this group told me that they consciously adjusted their way of dressing to the local situation, simply to avoid harassment. They spoke about the feelings of the local people with much concern and acknowledged the need to fit in rather than provoke. Age played a role here too. For those between sixteen and twenty-two, dress played a more important role in peer group attitudes, acceptance, and communication. Young professionals above that age had developed a more independent personal style of dress and showed more confidence in their own personality together with an increasing awareness of their visibility and role in society.

The topic of hijab rarely came up in the interviews. Only two of the girls wore a headscarf, one of the Aideen and one of the Amrikan. Ibtisam surprised me with her statement that she wanted to start wearing a headscarf after her wedding, as she thought it hypocritical to take it off for this occasion and later be embarrassed about it. She did not want to wear hijab in her wedding, so the implementation of her plan was just postponed.

In general, the returnees had not picked up on the discussion about female dress and religion taking place in Palestinian society. Two main groups of women were emerging in this debate: First, there were those who demonstrated religiosity by taking the hijab or other forms of covering hair and body according to modern Islamic interpretation. The other group comprised those who rejected this idea and wore what is commonly called Western dress, either to show secular inclinations or to express their opinion that religiosity and dress have little to do with each other.

In the life context of the young returnees, and regarding the return process, dress codes were a marker of peer group identity, and at the same time demonstrated one's difference from the "others," that is, local Palestinians. For the young women it was more a matter of preserving their modesty and reputation and avoiding harassment and comments in public, than a question of religious expression. Presumably, the "integration process" of the returnees also entailed a process of adjustment to local tastes in fashion and expectations for dress; thus, after some time returnees became less recognizable through their outfits.

Living in Palestine, the fourth stage of the return process, is characterized by returnees' forming groups. This formation is only partly voluntary in character, as the definition and naming of the groups is initiated by the surrounding society. It was as a reaction to this definition that the young returnees looked for consolation and understanding within the group and chose to socialize within this safer circle. The conflict between locals and returnees took place on a political and a cultural level, reflecting the problems between "inside" and "outside" of the parents' generation, and the different pace of change and development in Palestine and the diaspora countries. For the Aideen it was more of a political, and for the Amrikan more of a cultural, conflict. They showed considerable understanding for the sentiments of the local Palestinians, both politically and culturally, but rejected the negative definition as Aideen and Amrikan. Different spaces were occupied and used to simultaneously facilitate group identity and a mutual adjustment process.

Following the inner logic of the return scheme, the last stage of the process should be called "integration in Palestine." That would assume that the process was successfully completed, the liminal stage finished, and a new social identity acquired. In reality, processes did not always go full circle, and consequently return to Palestine does not always end happily in integration. Thus, the following section looks at the different possible outcomes of the return process.

STEP 5: STAYING IN PALESTINE?

The fifth stage of the return process has a question mark for the reasons introduced in the beginning. The systematic way in which the experiences and expressions of this group of people has been categorized and analyzed here cannot hide the constructed nature of the scheme. The stage of liminality might never end for many migrants, and yet they might find ways and strategies of coping with their situation. Integration or reintegration as part of the return experience is difficult to measure. Who would decide that a person is integrated, has a social identity, or completely rewrote the one he had before this process? At this point, we will look only at the plans of the respondents for the near future, while questions of home and homeland as well as long-term plans will be addressed in a later chapter.

Things change quickly at this particular age, especially for those who have finished high school or are just about to. This research was intentionally not based on the expectation that return to Palestine would be a permanent settlement for the respondents. It is in the fifth stage of the return process that the young returnees make the choice of staying in Palestine and making it home, or leaving. Like the return decision itself, for a number of them, to stay in Palestine was not entirely a matter of their own choice, while others could make their own decisions.

Majid told me during the "official part" of the interview that he would of course stay in Palestine. After all it was his homeland, no matter how difficult the situation was. Only after turning off the tape recorder did he admit that he was contemplating leaving again. Mainly what kept him in Palestine were his illegal status and consequent problems with leaving the country. His best friend, who had accompanied him throughout the journey from Tunis to Palestine, had left again a number of days before, incapable of coping with the disappointment.

Kamila, who quit working for the Palestinian Authority, was an independent journalist and had plans to develop her own business:

> I don't know, it scares me to say I will stay here forever. . . . I miss London, I miss my friends there, and it is hard to think this is going to be completely out of my life forever. Maybe I live here and I go to Britain for visits. But, yes, I am staying here for a while; I got plans, I am working on my own business now.

> It is a studio for editing, filming, video production, documentaries, films, sound, adverts, news reports, things like that. Everything you can think of will be needed in this country. I thought I could give Palestine something in the Ministry of Planning, and I don't think that is true anymore.

For those Aideen who were still in university, continuing their studies abroad was an option that they seriously considered. Some of them would have problems with passports (Arab or Palestinian), a fact that limited their possibilities for leaving the country. Najma wanted to study in another country but was concerned about staying close to her family, thus the farthest she could go would be a neighboring Arab country. Muna, Lana, Amina, and Sulayman had firm plans to finish their degrees at Birzeit University and then seek higher degrees in other countries.

Basma was most outspoken about her plans:

> The most important thing is to finish Birzeit and to move either to Syria or Cairo to continue studying theater, and then I'd love to go to theater and do acting and things like this. That is my dream of life, and I won't give that dream up. Why won't I give it up? Because I don't find anything

in this country that deserves losing my dream of life: nothing, not a man, not the situation, not a country. Everyone is leaving Palestine and going out to live in America, and why would I stay? Because of my dad? Leave him, let him live here, and I'll go. I can't continue here; you can't find a theater here to study with. There is no theater in Palestine; theater is in Israel and I am not ready to work with Jews.

Hanadi connected her decision to stay in Palestine to finding work after university, but more importantly to having her own family:

I study journalism and, as a minor, English. I hope to find work quickly, but it is very difficult to find work. I want to work and help my father. I want to take care of myself. I am afraid that I finish university and then I won't find work because with journalism there is not much of a chance. I have hope that the country will be better in the future, that the economy develops and there are more jobs and also that it develops socially. People, hopefully, will accept new ideas better. *Inshallah* (God willing) I will get married and I don't want to leave the country. I want to marry and stay here. I tried living outside and I tried moving around all the time, and I didn't have a feeling of security and stability. For me it is better to settle here; wherever one goes he is not going to feel as good as in his country, and also the people won't treat him like the people in his country.

Zaynab was the only respondent in the group of the Aideen who preferred to go to the United States and study art. Partly, she took inspiration from the future plans of her classmates, as she attended FBS and would have the necessary high school degrees to study at an American college. Her problems were financial; her parents could not afford college in the United States, and she carried a Jordanian passport. She was determined to study art although her parents did not approve of this wish. It was obvious that living in Palestine was not an option for her in the near future.

For Dalia the decision was bound to her daughter because her own migration experience and the time in Palestine had helped her realize that the constant movement and instability made her restless. She doubted that she would ever feel at home anywhere. She had professional aspirations, dreams of studying in the United States or some other place, but said that she would either find a job and stability in Ramallah, for the sake of her daughter or, if that did not work, she would leave and settle in another place for good. No looking back and no searching for a homeland for herself: She wanted stability only for her child.

For the Aideen, the plans for the near future were related to their professional (and to a lesser extent) personal aspirations. Only a few would completely rule out leaving Palestine again. On the other hand, most of them had developed an attachment to Palestine as a place and identified themselves with it as a homeland. On a different level, the choice not to leave again could be a result of settlement and adjustment in Palestine, the wish to belong in a place and never experience the instability of exile again.

For the Amrikan the situation presented itself differently. Those who were about to finish high school had firm plans to leave Palestine and study at different colleges in the United States. Some of the girls considered staying in Palestine and studying at Birzeit or one of the other Palestinian universities. Their considerations were related to fears of their parents allowing them to live in the United States without their families. From the discussions at FBS I learned that a number of the girls were faced with their parents' demands that they get married immediately. Some could hope to continue their education in Palestine; others would follow their husbands to the United States and might have a chance to go to college there. Marriages were often arranged between parents and relatives or acquaintances from the United States, thus the girls would also leave Palestine, but not on their own.

Of those who came back based on their own decision, many did not have a plan to settle in Palestine to begin with. Their stay was intended to be temporary, and most of them ended up staying for longer than they had expected. Sandy, for example, who came with a minimal "amount" of "Palestinianness," but with much curiosity as well as a plan to do human rights work in Palestine and for Palestinians, admitted that she did not have an answer to my question:

> Yes. I feel privileged to be living here most of the time. I say to myself that I am the happiest I have ever been. I feel very privileged to be here; I feel this is something really special. Not always: Sometimes it is really difficult as well. . . . I don't want to go home, not home, I don't want to go back to England. Back to England is not home, although I just said it was. It never was, and if I went back now, I would constantly feel like I haven't got to the bottom of anything. But at the same time I could take all the confidence that being here has given me and take that back to England and this idea that I can do anything, which I never had there. . . . For the feeling this place gives me, I would love to stay. Now, integrating myself wholeheartedly into society here I don't think it is something I could do. . . . I really don't know if I want to stay here, if I want to marry a Palestinian and stay.

Munir had made up his mind and was determined to stay. He planned to finish his degree at Hebrew University in Jerusalem, while he also worked at his father's store and helped build the family home. He said:

> That is what I decided; my parents are going to go to America once in a while to take care of stuff and they are going to sell the house. They are asking me to go with them, and I said I won't. I don't know why, but I don't feel like going. I can't remember what I miss over there; I lived there my whole life and experienced everything, and now it is suddenly not where I want to be. At first it is going to be hard to change the way things are going right now, but I will get used to it.

Allen and Hiyam, who both worked at Birzeit University, originally did not plan to stay for so long, but they did not seem to have a plan to leave Palestine in the near future:

> At this point I don't have any plans on leaving here, but you know that might change. If I leave, then I will probably come back at some point. I am enjoying the work that I am doing, you know. I think it is useful work, and I am still learning a lot of new things about here. I don't have any desire to leave at this point. (Allen)

> I don't know. I see myself being here for a little bit longer; I don't know how long though. A year, two years, it could be longer; it could be forever. It is really uncertain. I love my job now and I am very happy, and for me that is the most important thing that keeps me here. It is one of the most important things. If I didn't have a good job that I felt comfortable with, then I wouldn't be able to stay here. It really depends on what happens in my life. (Hiyam)

For most of the involuntary returnees of this group, leaving Palestine was a matter of their plans for a professional or, at least, educational future. Female returnees were more likely to stay in Palestine, mostly because they would probably get married and go along with their husbands' plans and decisions for the future.

For the voluntary returnees, the short-term future was connected to their wish to accomplish something in terms of helping Palestine and the Palestinians. They had experienced the difficult process of not only learning about their Palestinianness but also about their differences from local Palestinians. The presence of a foreign community in and around Ramallah allowed them to live in Palestine, yet at a certain distance to local Palestinians. They were appreciated for their work and engagement and also did not face the problem of having a negative image that many of the young Aideen had to face. They all spoke about discovering the Palestinian aspects of their personalities, and considered living in Palestine an inner journey to come to terms with their cross-cultural identities. Only the long-term future would show which path they would take.

The return process has been described chronologically, as a series of five steps from the decision to return to Palestine, to plans for the near future. As the study argues that return to Palestine for the young respondents entails a process of rewriting aspects of their identities, this chronological approach is only one way of looking at the process of return. In the following, the rewriting of identities will be approached by dividing "identity" into different aspects in order to then investigate how the respondents remembered these aspects from their childhood and youth in different diaspora countries and which changes might have occurred in the process of return.

CHAPTER 6

Rewriting of Identities in the Context of Diaspora and Return

> *I stood up in class one day and let my teacher*
> *know that I was a Palestinian, and that we did*
> *exist as a nation, as a people. My love over the*
> *ocean wasn't enough to stop the rubber bullets*
> *from killing or the bulldozers from demolishing*
> *homes, but I've kept my eye and heart on*
> *Palestine, since I saw the first stone thrown.*
> *I haven't turned away. I haven't blinked.*
> (HAMMAD 1996B, 60)

Return as a process involves different stages and confronts the young returnees with a challenge to their previous identity as members of Palestinian diaspora communities. In order to substantiate the thesis of a rewriting of identity during and as a result of the return process, this chapter describes different aspects of identity as they developed in the diaspora situation and how they changed upon return to Palestine. Thus, what is of concern here is not the return process itself but the status of identities before and after return.

If identities are defined as multiple and fluid, dividing them into subcategories might seem rather arbitrary. For the purpose of a more detailed analysis, three aspects of identity are singled out. These three categories are political identity, cultural identity, and religious identity. They are not exhaustive or exclusive, but are chosen from the mosaic of identities of the young returnees. In some ways the identities fall into more than one category.

Political Aspects of Identity

The political aspects of identity are often emphasized as most relevant for Palestinians, while this study has pointed to the complexity of identity issues among the young returnees. The discussion focuses on two aspects, namely, the political commitment of the respondents and their knowledge of Palestinian politics. Both topics were discussed in each interview and both were difficult to measure. Questions revolved around whether and how the respondents and their parents were interested in politics and how that translated into participation in Palestinian politics.

The answers show that Palestinians who grew up in Arab countries definitely knew more about Palestinian politics than those from Western countries. The simplest reason is that they were raised in a Palestinian community and, in many cases, near PLO institutions.

A study conducted in the late 1970s to determine how Palestinian children in Kuwait experienced political socialization showed that Palestinian children at the time were almost completely supportive of Yasir Arafat. They learned this identification through their parents and the peer group. It found that children's political activities, such as membership in Fatah's youth organization, or the type of school they attended did not play a significant role in shaping this support. The trust in Arafat as a father-like figure and benevolent leader was directly translated into trust in the PLO. The children were asked to choose between their parents and their country, and 86 percent of them chose Palestine! Neither gender nor socioeconomic status played a significant role in these findings (T. Farah 1977, 1987).[1]

Pointing in a very different direction, a more ethnographic study conducted almost a decade later argues that the Palestinian community in Kuwait centered around family more than politics. Based on research in Kuwait, it extends this main conclusion to Palestinian communities in both the homeland and the diaspora. These findings point to the importance of cultural and social identities (Ghabra 1987, 1988).[2]

Studies in Lebanon have shown that Palestinian political identity was stronger among camp residents than among those residing outside the camps. In the camps, the presence of political groups combined with the pressure from the host society, and the political and economic exclusion created a politicized environment (Peteet 1987 and 1993; Sayigh 1977a, 1977b, 1993, and 1995). Even after 1982, when the PLO institutions and military units were driven out of Lebanon, the camps remained strongholds of national identity.

Most of the members of the Aideen group expressed interest in politics and said they followed the news and were informed about political events in Palestine. With the exception of Nimr, none of them was actively involved in a political party or organization. The respondents did not see themselves involved in Palestinian diaspora politics before their return, although the parents of the young returnees had worked directly for the PLO or close to Palestinian institutions in the diaspora. Some occasionally participated in youth activities such as youth camps; Nimr, Marwan, and Dalia recalled such activities. Najma described her family as not very political, despite the fact that her father was a military commander in the West Bank and had a similar position before the family returned. Political talk about Palestine was common in most families. The young Aideen did not typically use a Palestine-specific political language that would include such terms as *thawra* (revolution), *dam* (blood), and *watan* (national homeland).

Dalia, Najma, and Hanadi expressed that they were initially interested in political participation but got discouraged by the petty politics of the student blocs at Birzeit University, and also by their treatment as Aideen. Najma emphasized the lack of knowledge about domestic Palestinian politics and related it to her and the other returnees' absence from Palestine during the Intifada.

Majid, who returned because of his commitment to Palestine, was so disappointed with what he found that he retreated completely from political activity. Nimr was an exception because he returned with direct support from Arafat and the Palestinian leadership. His activities were concentrated on creating a political movement of refugees, both inside and outside Palestine, to ensure the representation of their interests in Palestinian politics. It was intended to bridge the gap between inside and outside by emphasizing their common fate as refugees and the shared interest in return and/or compensation.

After their return, Kamila, Nimr, and Qasim worked for the PA and were thus somewhat politically involved. Later, Kamila chose to quit this work and concentrate on independent journalistic activity in Palestine. The other respondents of the Aideen group were still in school and university.

Regarding knowledge about Palestinian politics, it became clear that despite being brought up in Palestinian communities, many respondents of this group had rather scattered knowledge of Palestinian history. One reason might be that Palestinian history has never been properly taught as a subject in school in the surrounding Arab countries, and the respondents either attended local schools or were taught curricula heavily influenced by the host countries' governments. As Najma put it:

> When I came to Iraq I had been to an Egyptian school where I learned things about Egypt — geography, history, all about Egypt. Then in Iraq it was the history of the Baath party, and Saddam Hussein. . . . In some way

it was the same when I came to Palestine. I came here and did not have any idea about the politics here.

On the other hand, there was a strong attachment to Palestine. This attachment to the homeland, especially in its symbolic terms, can without doubt be considered political, even if it is not directly translated into active participation.

Respondents from the Amrikan group showed different attitudes toward political involvement. The scattered character of their knowledge about Palestine was more obvious, as they lacked both the Palestinian political communities in the diaspora and the Palestine-specific schooling. On the other hand, because many of them were able to visit Palestine throughout their childhood, they reflected a certain amount of situational knowledge of Palestine.

A study of Palestinian Americans claims that, compared to other immigrant communities in the United States, Palestinians showed an unusually high degree of consciousness and involvement in the politics of their homeland, a fact that in turn blocked their full political acculturation in the United States and kept them as a distinct group (Christison 1989, 19). My own interviews in the Palestinian American community confirmed this claim. I also found that Palestinian Americans were generally interested in politics and seemed especially well informed about events in the Middle East.[3]

The political activity of Palestinians in the American context has been part of the activities of Arab American organizations. These organizations were created around the issue of Palestine and later developed stronger features of community representation in the United States. Studies show that only 10 percent of the Arab American community was actively involved in these organizations. In the years since the first Gulf War, these organizations have gradually retreated from political statements on the Middle East and have instead focused on community interests (Shain 1996). They have always been entirely secular in their orientation.

A relatively new phenomenon is the growth of Muslim American organizations, which, because of the traditional Islamic support for Palestinians or because they are specifically Palestinian Muslim organizations, offer new grounds for identification. This does not indicate a growth in religiosity but reflects Palestinians' choice to be part of a larger minority group in the American context to enhance their chances of representation.[4] This only applies to the Muslim part of the Palestinian American community. According to estimates, roughly half of the Palestinian American community is Muslim (Christison 1989; Shain 1996).

Those of the Amrikan who returned voluntarily to Palestine had made their decision to return after learning more about Palestine. They all made an effort to learn about Palestinian history and politics and were often involved in pro-Palestinian activities or work in their diaspora countries. Upon returning to Palestine, they turned their knowledge and commitment into work for Palestinian NGOs. These organizations and institutions represented civil society in Palestine and thus operated on a different level from political parties. Nevertheless, their activities were highly political, whether for civil or human rights, or on behalf of women, refugees, or other interest groups. Paul, Hiyam, and Sandy were involved in human rights work, while Tariq offered his journalistic and language skills in order to benefit Palestine. Allen employed his knowledge about computers and Web design for his activism.

The younger and involuntary returnees were still in high school and came from families with no political involvement. But even they listened to the news regularly and gained more knowledge about Palestinian politics. In some cases, this translated into active commitment, as was the case for Ibtisam, who started writing poems about her feelings about being Palestinian. Many of the boys participated in demonstrations and clashed with the Israelis. The experience of group coherence, shared suffering, and political outrage was certainly a defining factor for their Palestinian political identity. Munzir, who was injured by an Israeli rubber bullet in clashes in 1997, said that he never felt more Palestinian than following his injury (Associated Press, July 30, 1999, and my interview with him). In addition, this incident inspired Ibtisam to write a poem about him, which had an impact on many of his classmates. At the graduation ceremony at the Friends School in May 1999, they applauded him for the fact that he had graduated despite the long time he had spent in the hospital after his injury.

The language of the Amrikan respondents had no room for political slogans, partly because they expressed themselves better in English than in Arabic. The Palestinian national movement never developed a political English terminology because the center of their activities was always in Arab host countries.

Regarding their political identities, both groups showed an increased political awareness and knowledge of Palestinian politics following their return to Palestine. This is not surprising, considering the obvious importance of politics for the Palestinian situation. In their self-perceptions as Palestinians, everything tended to be political, and all groups in society were, in one way or the other, involved in politics. Considering this fact, the Aideens' relative disinterest in politics is surprising, especially since their parents were often active PLO cadres. The main reason for the Aideens' lack of political participation was their disappointment with the realities of Palestinian domestic politics and their being assigned the label "Aideen" by the local community. To an extent, the Amrikan, like their parents, showed a lack of involvement, but they experienced a special political socialization through living in Palestine. Moreover, the age of the respondents has to be considered. It seems to be a general truth worldwide that adolescents spend their time on activities other than politics and often feel disconnected from political participation.

Cultural Aspects of Identity

The term "cultural" is a dangerous and debated one, but I use culture as a concept to approach the aspects of identity I want to discuss here. Language can be said to be an important aspect of cultural identity, especially in the context of migration. Language can reflect the level of integration into a host country as well as the differentiation between native culture and host culture. In the process of migration, migrants usually develop language skills, with many becoming bilingual. In the second and third generation, it may be increasingly difficult for the parents to pass on the native language, as life in a host country requires that one master that country's language and seldom affords one the opportunity to learn one's parents' language. Sometimes parents urge their children to learn the language of the host society to facilitate integration; others insist on their speaking the native language at home and leave it to school and the street to teach their children the second language. Verbal expression in one or the other language can be seen as a choice made to emphasize one or the other aspect of identity. At the same time, the choice of language can be related to the hostile attitude of the host society toward the immigrant minority. In those cases it might be considered safer to conceal the native language in public and only speak it within the community.

Observing changes in these language choices can tell something about the negotiation between identities. Many of the respondents used code switching (that is, they used both languages in one sentence) in particular situations, but more generally, according to the interviews, their use of language changed following the return. In the case of the Aideen it seemed somewhat easier, as they had all lived in Arab countries most of their lives; their native language and the host language were both based on standard Arabic. However, because Arabs in different regions of the Arab world speak varying dialects, even this group saw some adjustment in their language.

With the exception of Nimr, Qasim, and Kamila, all members of this group spoke the Palestinian dialect during the interviews. Nimr and Kamila had a strong Lebanese accent. Both of them had grown up in Lebanon and both had Lebanese mothers. Qasim's mother was Egyptian, and he grew up surrounded by Egyptian relatives. The three of them seemed not to have made an effort to change the way they spoke. Sulayman, who grew up in Morocco and was fluent in French and Moroccan Arabic, had some difficulties expressing himself in the Palestinian dialect.

All the others told me that they had learned different Arabic dialects throughout their childhoods, depending on where they had lived and how often they had moved. To speak the Palestinian dialect was part of their upbringing. Muna explained to me why she spoke Egyptian dialect on the streets:

> I wanted them to understand me. The Egyptians don't understand Palestinian or any other dialect, so I spoke Egyptian; but in the beginning it was difficult. When I was small they couldn't understand me in school, but step-by-step I learned it. At home our father didn't allow us to speak Egyptian. He wanted us to speak Palestinian, and we got used to switching between house and street.

They also all recalled adjusting to the local situation and choosing to speak the host dialect in order to feel accepted and to avoid conflict. In the context of Lebanon, being recognized as a Palestinian through language could, during the civil war, mean danger and even death. Consequently, parents urged their children to be cautious and not to use Palestinian expressions on the streets. As Muhammad, a returnee of the older generation, recalled in his memoirs:

> They were all Palestinians and they all spoke the Palestinian dialect and I felt joy and peace as I never did before. . . . No one can understand these words except an exile Palestinian. The one who tried how the dialect can be a danger, the one who tried to escape his dialect and cover it with the dialects of the others. . . . Palestinians were killed because of the difference between *bandora* [Palestinian for "tomato"] and *banadora* [Lebanese for "tomato"], yes, they were killed for the difference between *fath* and *sukun* [vocalization signs in Arabic script]. . . . I walk in the streets of Ramallah and my dialect is the dialect of the people, my

identity is their identity and for that I do not have to point to it day and
night.   (MUHAMMAD 1997, 131)

It is part of the Palestinian exile experience to speak different Arabic dialects, and I have often noticed that exile Palestinians play with these skills.
Many jokes are based on expressions in Lebanese, Syrian, or Egyptian
dialects. (Egyptian is well known through television and is understood
throughout the Arab world.)

Many members of the Aideen group said that they had adjusted their
speech and used the Palestinian dialect when they returned. Lana recalled that she could understand her father speaking Palestinian dialect
but would reply in Algerian, mainly because her mother is Algerian. Since
she returned, she had learned to speak Palestinian Arabic. Basma said:

> But the problem in this country is the accent; I've got that Syrian accent,
> and there is some words I say, and they say, You talk with another accent,
> so you are a returnee.

To be recognized as a returnee by one's different accent means added difficulty integrating into Palestinian society. Thus, the young Aideen were
faced with similar pressure to adopt the local speech, a pressure with which
they were already familiar from time spent in exile. For those Palestinian
returnees who were born in Palestine, returning to Palestine and speaking
their dialect meant coming home, but for second- and third-generation
returnees, there was no such feeling, even if they could appreciate the return to Palestine and the existence of a specific dialect on an intellectual
level. Ultimately, all those who chose to stay did adjust to the Palestinian
dialect to facilitate their integration.

For Palestinian Americans, it was more difficult to teach their children
to speak fluent Arabic because English was more important, not for integration, but for functioning in American society. Consequently, many Palestinian Americans have urged their children to focus on learning English.
Arabic is considered important only for domestic conversation. Only in
the last decade or so has there been a change in attitude, a greater acceptance of ethnic and cultural differences in American society that has
supported learning one's native language. This change is not attributable
to Palestinian or Arab efforts. The main obstacle to proficiency in Arabic is literacy in Arabic. It is more difficult to learn the Palestinian dialect
through hearing and speaking than if oral and aural skills are simultaneously supplemented by formal study in reading and writing standard
Arabic. As these children are not taught Arabic in school, they are mostly

illiterate and thus dependent on the oral efforts of their parents and the community. Thus, they cannot access Arabic literature, and understand little of the standard Arabic on television and radio. As a result, they are bilingual only to an extent because they have different levels of proficiency in the two languages.

A case study of Arab American bilinguals showed that the respondents were all "coordinate bilinguals"; that is, they had learned the two languages in different contexts: Arabic at home, and English at school. They were divided into sophisticated and naive bilinguals.[5] All the respondents in the study scored higher on English tests than on Arabic ones, while interference from English into Arabic was higher than from Arabic into English. Nevertheless, the respondents were emotionally involved in both languages and recognized Arabic as the socially dominant language of the community, while English was the language of the country in which they lived (Rouchdy 1974).

My interviews confirm many of these findings. In addition, my respondents recalled having learned some Arabic whenever they visited Palestine and/or were in contact with older relatives. When their parents spoke Arabic with them they would often respond in English, and it seems as if many parents at some point gave up on the issue. Some made an extra effort to send their children to mosques and community centers to learn Arabic in Sunday school. Others even had tutors at home.[6] When children lived in Western countries and had only one Palestinian parent, learning Arabic was even more difficult.

Clearly, the expression "mother tongue" reflects the reality of learning languages. It depends more on the mother than the father if a child learns the native language in a foreign environment. This is not to say that the limited Arabic of many Palestinian Americans is the fault of the mothers, but in most societies mothers spend more time with their children than do fathers. In Western society, children spend much of their time outside the home while growing up, and thus parents have less influence. School is more important than family to socialization. It would require a more conscious effort on the part of both the families and the larger community to create an environment in which Palestinian children could become proficient in Arabic. Motivation is key, as Rayda explains:

> And my parents tried here and there, but somehow we always found other things that seemed more important to us. People here, when they find out you don't speak Arabic, the first thing they do is they blame your parents, like it is their problem, they should have taught you, they are the ones who are wrong. But they tried; we just weren't accepting.

None of the Amrikan I interviewed were literate in Arabic before their return to Palestine. It can be assumed that lacking proficiency in the native language (native to their parents) also makes it more difficult for this group of exile Palestinians to learn about other aspects of their culture, as many of these aspects are reflected in language.

Upon their return to Palestine, language thus proved to be a bigger problem for the Amrikan than for the Aideen. They could not be enrolled in Palestinian schools or universities and had to go to schools with English instruction. Their communication with local Palestinians, including their relatives, was in many cases limited, if not impossible. Those who attended private schools with English instruction found a group of fellow students in the same situation. They spoke English among themselves, providing one another comfort and support.

The instruction in school, as well as the emergence of this peer group, prevented them from being forced to learn better Arabic through daily practice. Some of my respondents actively resisted learning Arabic to protest their return to Palestine. Others pointed out that they had made progress over the years since returning, but most were still not comfortable having a conversation about more complicated issues. Despite Arabic classes, their reading and writing ability was not comparable to that of their Arabic-speaking schoolmates. Some could not read newspapers at all; others would take a long time to decipher a sentence. I also found that the girls invested more effort in improving their Arabic, emphasizing the importance of communication with relatives or other Palestinians and, generally, the cultural importance of speaking one's native tongue. The following exchange was part of my conversation in English with Amy and Shuruq:

How much Arabic do you speak now?
S: I speak, but it is not that well. I understand a lot, but I can't speak it that well.
What about reading and writing?
S: I can read and I can write. . . . I have a tutor who comes to my house and teaches me how to read and write, so I have improved a lot. He can show me something and it won't take me that long to read it.
A: Same with me, I can read and I can write, but I am still in the lower level.
Do you find it important to speak Arabic?
A: You are Palestinian; you have to know your language and where you are from. See, she is Palestinian, how can she not speak her language? It is important to know your language.

S: And the Qur'an is written in *'Arabi,* so we have to know it to read and understand the Qur'an.

How do you speak to your relatives?

S: I talk to them in *'Arabi;* my *'Arabi* is not good but I can talk to them.

So what do they say about you?

S: I think they look at us as a little lower than them because we are not the same and we will never get the language. We can, but it takes time. They have been here their whole lives and it can take time as it would if they went to America; they won't expect it from them right away.

A: Maybe it is because we've lived in America and we just didn't go through what they went though especially during the Intifada. And so they see us differently because we were in a different world. We spoke differently, we dressed differently, we lived different lives.

The boys seemed more comfortable with their marginal position as a group. The fact that the Amrikan spoke English with each other, often quite loudly in the streets, was a frequent cause of friction with local Palestinians who complained about the Americans' ignorance of local language and culture. Language skills were also applied in a situational fashion. When the youngsters wanted to talk to a particular person or wanted to conceal a conversation from an English-speaking teacher in school, they knew how to express themselves; but confronted with an older relative or a person on the street, they made their Arabic sound weak.

Most of the returnees recognized and appreciated their parents' desire to return with them to Palestine to teach them the language and culture. And despite all their difficulties with the language issues, many told me that they intended to do the same with their children in the future, as they wanted them to speak Arabic and know their cultural heritage.

Of the voluntary returnees of this group, only Paul spoke Arabic fluently, as he had grown up in Lebanon. Rayda, Sandy, Allen, Nigel, and Hiyam all had difficulties with Arabic but made an effort to learn it throughout their stay. Socializing more with foreigners in Ramallah and working within the NGO community made this more difficult.

In both groups, respondents recognized that speaking Palestinian Arabic was part of their cultural identity and generally made an effort to achieve a better command of it. Learning or improving language skills was hindered by a certain rejection by the local community; the use of an in-group language among members of the returnee groups; and, for the Amrikan, the fact that Arabic was perceived as a difficult language to learn.[7] Improving Arabic language skills is a time-consuming process and ultimately was most successful if it was not interrupted by leaving Palestine again. The command of Arabic was directly related to the returnees' access to their cultural heritage, particularly literature and music.

Poetry, fiction, and music were important to me because a review of the repertoire of Palestinian poetry, short stories, novels, and nationalist songs shows that they can help young exile Palestinians learn about their national culture. In many cases, they directly reflect on political issues; in others they simply reflect that the preservation of the Palestinian heritage is an important part of preserving national and cultural identity.

Most important is the case of poetry, a genre with a long tradition in Arab literary culture. Reciting poetry, as well as inventing rhymes on the spot, are considered impressive proof of language mastery. The importance of the Arabic language is directly linked to the Qur'an, and thus considered sacred. Poems support the expression of emotions, and a shared set of well-known poems can enhance the feeling of group cohesion within and for a people. In the absence of a national homeland and an institutionally preserved national culture, poems have been significant in keeping Palestinians connected to each other, and as a symbolic means of traveling between diaspora and homeland. Palestinian poets are held in high regard, as they are perceived as able to express what everyone else feels. Poetry and fiction, as well as other art forms, play a role in creating an image of the homeland Palestine. The responses about poetry and fiction reflect a wide variety within the groups and a large gap between them. Only the Aideen, by virtue of their language skills, would have been able to study Palestinian poetry and fiction by reading the original Arabic. Majid told me that he knew poetry by Mahmud Darwish and Samih Al-Qasim and fiction by Emile Habibi and many other Palestinian writers and poets. He had read most of their books between the ages of twelve and eighteen.

Kamila remembered that she had grown up listening to Ghassan Kanafani's children's stories, calling them her childhood fairytales. Many other respondents in this group recalled having had books of poetry, fiction, and nonfiction about Palestine at home because their parents read them. Some could recall names of poets and considered these poems part of their upbringing as Palestinians. Muna told me:

> We knew Mahmud Darwish and Samih Al-Qasim. Samih Al-Qasim came to Egypt to read his poems in an event. My dad wanted us to know our language and to know what Palestine is. It was also because we were brought up in a very Palestinian environment; Dad is a fighter and was

in the resistance. For us it was normal to listen to Fairuz and to Marcel Khalifeh, the national songs, and we had books by Mahmud Darwish, Samih Al-Qasim, and Taufiq Zayyad.

And Marwan said:

> I think the majority of the people outside did read Palestinian poetry and fiction. Like I would find my father reading Ghassan Kanafani and would ask, who is that, and he would tell me; so I grew up being interested and then myself started reading Kanafani. It is the same with the poetry of Mahmud Darwish, Fadwa Tuqan, Ibrahim Tuqan, the ones who had the strongest connection with Palestine. Well, after I came back, I also started reading the poetry of Nizar Qabbani, Muzaffir Al-Nawab, and Ahmad Mattar, the people whose books you would find with Palestinians reading them. Because they somehow described the circumstances they lived in and the stand of the other Arabs toward them. They also say in their poetry how the Arabs betrayed the Palestinians.

Others, especially the younger ones, had difficulty remembering names of poets or writers or titles of books. Differences in knowledge were most influenced by the political commitment of the family (not the fathers' work!), the age of the interviewees, and the educational level of the parents. The migration situation, such as the temporary character of any settlement, has to be considered as well, since it can prevent one from acquiring books. In addition, reading is an individual activity, and the transmission of cultural knowledge would more likely happen through recitation in social gatherings, such as in political discussions and at weddings, and on other occasions.[8] When I asked about poetry and fiction, a number of respondents told me that they planned to familiarize themselves with such materials and regretted that they had not done so earlier.[9]

For the Amrikan, the situation was different because they could hardly read Arabic. And although a number of poetry collections have been published in English (e.g., Elmessiri and Boullata 1982; Elmessiri and Elmessiri 1996; Jayyusi 1992), along with short stories and novels by Kanafani and others, the respondents in this group knew little or nothing about Palestinian literature. Even specifically Palestinian American poetry by Turki, Hammad, and others, or biographical accounts, such as books by Turki, Ashrawi, and Said were not familiar to most of them. The younger respondents typically came from a different social background, and their parents were not interested in politics. Schooling for them was not about knowledge for knowledge's sake; it only mattered to better one's chances in life.

This view of education did not encourage them to familiarize themselves with Palestinian literature. When I asked them about it, I learned that they often did not even realize that Palestinian literature existed.

Those of the Amrikan who had finished high school had often read some Palestinian literature and were interested in reading more. My research in the United States confirmed that this interest is often related to studies about the Middle East; that is, it is not until college that Palestinian Americans become familiar with Palestinian literature. Their interest often derives from learning Arabic as an academic subject but, even then, many students prefer nonfiction to fiction.

Something Palestinians in all parts of the diaspora have in common is the music and poetry of weddings. For example, before the Gulf War the community in Kuwait had combined traditional elements of the Palestinian village wedding with newer elements, resulting in a "semitraditional" wedding. Folk songs performed during a wedding point to changes in the social structure and views of tradition (Alqudsi-Taghreed 1990).

In the Palestinian American context, traditional weddings are often cited as proof that the community preserves its cultural identity through these celebrations; in fact, places like Jacksonville and Cleveland are the only places in the world where one can see a traditional Ramallah wedding of the 1960s.

At weddings, young Palestinians also learn about Arabic music and, in many cases, about oriental dancing. Whether or not men and women dance together depends on the families' orientations. Weddings are also family gatherings where ties between relatives are reinforced, and the social links within the community are refreshed and strengthened. Hanadi told me:

> Whenever we had an opportunity, like a celebration or something, we liked wearing the Palestinian dress, the traditional peasant dress. At weddings we would wear it and also at other cultural events, especially outside. You won't find that much here, but when you would go to a wedding outside you would try to wear the *thob* (Palestinian embroidered dress). Here it is different, because now we are in Palestine, but when we were outside we gave more attention and meaning to these things.

Only young women talked about the cultural value of these weddings; they seemed not to play an important role for the young men. Basma, especially, appreciated traditional weddings, characterized by Palestinian dress and the use of henna, in the camps and villages in Palestine, and rejected "modern weddings" as a loss of national culture.

Music is an important part of cultural expression on different levels. One has to distinguish clearly among "political songs," folk songs that can be political in their function to preserve Palestinian identity, and Arabic popular or classical music. The study revealed that "Western" music played a role in communication between different parts of Palestinian society as well.

"Political songs" were familiar to most of the Aideen. Famous Arab singers, for example, Fairuz and Marcel Khalifeh, have written and performed songs about Palestine and are held in high regard for that. Other kinds of political music include revolutionary songs, mostly from the 1960s and 1970s. Many Palestinians in Arab countries grew up with these songs, and the Palestinian national anthem "Biladi" has been part of almost every Palestinian childhood in these countries.

Arabic popular music was a familiar feature of cultural life for all respondents in my study, but in different ways. The growing popularity of world music as a genre creates a connection between migrants and locals, and simultaneously connects the migrant to his or her past and the "lost culture" (Chambers 1994, 77–83).

In the Middle East and North Africa, there is a large market for popular Arabic music. With the majority of popular singers coming from Lebanon and Egypt, the season's hits are heard all over the Middle East, blasting from car radios, played in taxis and buses, and enjoyed in restaurants, at home, and on radio and TV. Most of the songs and the singers enjoy a short-lived fame among teenagers and young adults. Other songs become classics for their lyrics, which are often poems by Arab poets, or for their music, such as those of Fairuz.

For returnees from Arab countries, music was ground they shared in common with the local Palestinians, a space to meet and share similar tastes and experiences. For those who grew up in other countries with other languages, such as the Amrikan, the lyrics were usually difficult to understand; thus, they were mostly excluded from this joined celebration. For them, Arabic music was the sound of their parents, the nostalgic longing for the memories of home conjured up by the music. They recognized it as part of their cultural heritage, connected to weddings and other family and community events.

Western music, rap, hip-hop, and English lyrics were common ground for all young Palestinians. Through media, radio, TV, and the Internet, Palestine is included in the global distribution of music. Often, illegal

copies of CDs and tapes are available the day a new song or album is re-
leased. Thus, tunes and lyrics are familiar to all: returnees, diaspora Palestinians, and locals. They are a common language for young people.

To a lesser extent, food can tell something about one's cultural identity.
As the "contest" between Israelis and Palestinians also takes place on cultural levels, the idea that Palestinians all around the world share the same
cuisine can, for Palestinians, be an aspect of identity building. Two stories
may illustrate this point. In an interview with Edward Said on Palestinian
identity, he told this story:

> A close friend of mine once came to my house and stayed overnight.
> In the morning we had breakfast, which included yogurt cheese with a
> special herb, *za'atar*. This combination probably exists all over the Arab
> world, and certainly in Palestine, Syria and Lebanon. But my friend said:
> "There you see. It's a sign of a Palestinian home that it has *za'atar* in it."
> Being a poet, he then expatiated at great and tedious length on Pales-
> tinian cuisine, which is generally much like Lebanese and Syrian cuisine,
> and by the end of the morning we were both convinced that we had a
> totally distinct national cuisine.   (RUSHDIE AND SAID 1991, 175)

Suheir Hammad in her biographical account recalled:

> I know that this story was in the olive oil we sprinkled on our hummus.
> In the tomato juice that squirted as we prepared taboulleh for parties.
> When it became cool to eat hummus, falafel, taboulleh, and pita with
> everything, it was too late. I had already wasted years trying to trade my
> labeneh sandwiches for peanut butter and jelly, which I didn't even like.
> (HAMMAD 1996B, 51)

For those who grew up in the Western world, ethnic food was more of an
issue than for Palestinians in the Arab world, mainly because the cuisine of
the Middle East only differs in detail in different countries. And even the
cuisine of North Africa uses similar ingredients and cooking techniques
and is thus familiar.

Cuisine travels as fast as music and has been globalized in recent decades. And although globalization can reduce the variety of recipes from
within a cultural setting by defining a global standard and adjusting it to
local tastes, it can also develop "ethnic pride" and thus enhance cultural
identity. Hiyam, whose parents ran a Middle Eastern deli in Canada, told
me that the place was not only the source of these specific foods but was
also a meeting place for community members, similar in its function to
the coffee houses of the Middle East.

Some of the respondents would even go as far as saying that eating ethnic food could "make you" a Palestinian. This idea of hummus and falafel turning one into a Palestinian can be interpreted as a symbolic extension of feeding from the "mother Palestine," as the same interviewee spoke in a conversation in class about the "blood connection" he felt to the soil of Palestine.[10]

Palestinian or Middle Eastern food was often related to feelings of home, as it reminded the young adults of their family. The mother cooked traditional food; the celebrations and family gatherings provided a sense of community and separated home from the outside world. Even for the Palestinian families in Arab countries, preparing Palestinian dishes was considered part of preserving their cultural identity.

Upon returning to Palestine, the previously special and different Palestinian cuisine became the norm and, in turn, those culinary traditions adopted from other places were emphasized. Ibtisam recalled that, in the beginning, her father would bring back American food whenever he went to the United States in order to make life in Palestine easier for his children. By the same token, an Associated Press article remarked that more and more businesses catered to the needs of Palestinian Americans, specifically in the Ramallah area (Associated Press, July 30, 1999).

The idea of home, or the feeling of being at home, centers on the image of the house as a physical space. Edward Said relates hospitality and the rituals of eating to Palestinians' need to emphasize the importance of this home space, even to excess, when he states:

> This compulsion to repeat is evident in the interiors of Palestinian houses of all classes. The same food and eating rituals organized around a table or central space occur with maddening regularity. The rituals of offering and hospitality are designed, I think, to be excessive, to put before a guest more than is needed, more than will be consumed, more than can be afforded. Wherever there are Palestinians, the same signs of hospitality and offering keep appearing, the same expectant intimacy.
>
> (SAID 1986A, 58)

The expression of hospitality may not be specifically Palestinian in all its aspects. But for Palestinians, the display of food and generous hospitality, as well as having the family gathered around the table or central space, carry a special meaning because of the constant threat of losing this home. Generous hospitality is a pattern in Middle Eastern culture in general, and to offer more than "necessary" is related to social class and wealth.[11] At the same time, the idea of generosity is based on giving all that a family has, not just what the family does not need.

Said has described the interior of Palestinian homes as having

> the same display of affection and of objects — replicas of the Mosque of Omar, plates inlaid with mother-of-pearl, tiny Palestinian flags — appropriated for protection as well as sociability. Naturally, they authenticate and certify the fact that you are in a Palestinian home. But it is more than that. It is part of a larger pattern of repetition in which even I, supposedly liberated and secular, participate. We keep re-creating the interior — tables are set, living rooms furnished, knick-knacks arranged, photographs set forth — but it inadvertently highlights and preserves the rift or break fundamental to our lives. You see this if you look carefully at what is before you. Something is always slightly off, something always doesn't work. Pictures in Palestinian houses are always hung too high, and in what seem to be random places. Something is always missing by virtue of the excess.   (SAID 1986A, 58)

It is precisely the absence of a safe, secure home and homeland that makes the creation of such spaces imperative. If there is something seemingly "off," it might just be because of different acquired tastes and a culture-specific sense of aesthetic.

The posters, Palestinian flags, and pictures in the homes of Palestinian friends triggered my interest in Palestinian identity. I asked the respondents if and how one could tell from their homes in the diaspora that they were Palestinian homes. Not all respondents answered this question, and I found that the girls and young women were more observant. Those who responded described their homes in very similar terms. For example, Hanadi told me:

> Not necessarily the flag but Palestinian heritage had to be there. You feel at ease when you sit, and this way you keep remembering. For example the art pieces would be Palestinian embroidery, the pillows, the tablecloths, that are things that stayed with us. . . . The walls were full of pictures of 'Akka, Haifa, and Jerusalem, souvenirs from Jerusalem, and a lot of books. There were books on Jerusalem, on Palestine, on other cities in Palestine, also Palestinian poetry, all these things; one likes collecting these things.

Sulayman, who grew up in Morocco, needed some help remembering the interior of their house, but then he said, "In fact, our house was full of

pictures of Palestine, posters and stuff, and of course the flag." Marwan
recalled what mattered to him in the houses they lived in:

> You would find certain things in all the houses we lived in. For example
> in Jordan we moved to four different places. Each house had the Pales-
> tinian flag, a picture of Abu 'Ammar, a picture of Abu Jihad, a picture
> of my father with the Palestinian flag, the flag that they gave us when he
> died. I don't think there was anyone who didn't see that we are Palestin-
> ians. And we also had the map of Palestine, souvenirs with the flag, and
> all that.

In many Palestinian houses one finds photographs of deceased family
members. Where people died for the Palestinian cause their photographs
have often been turned into shrines in a corner, or else they overlook the
central space of the house, thus making the home a place of remembrance,
a museum of individual and family fate. These memories define Palestinian identity as they remind the survivors of the loss and pain they have
experienced and of the hostility of the outside world.

In Palestinian homes in the United States and other Western countries,
the emphasis in decoration is less political. One rarely finds Palestinian
flags; instead there are "cultural objects," such as olive wood carvings,
mother-of-pearl items made in Jerusalem, and many pictures. Often, the
Dome of the Rock or the churches of Jerusalem are displayed, depending
on the religious inclination of the family. Nabila, who grew up in Austria,
remembered embroidered pillows and wall decorations as well as excerpts
from the Qu'ran in decorated frames. She also said that they had more of
these things now that they lived in Palestine, mainly because it was easier
to buy them. Munir gave a longer description about his home in the United
States and also called the things they had *tuhaf*, literally meaning a gift or
work of art.

> We used to have *argileh* (a waterpipe), we had *Ayat al-Qur'an* in the
> house, embroidered scarves and pieces, baskets and carpets, many
> things. Every time we came here we would bring more things, and people
> would come into our house and say this is really nice. We would tell
> them it is from our land, from back home. People would like our house
> because it was different, not like their normal houses.

And although he described the interior as beautiful and special, he also
considered it a deviation from the norm, thus declaring American cultural taste to be the norm. Others, such as Ranya, called their house in the

United States normal, and emphasized that they did not have any of the "traditional stuff." When I asked Hiyam about their house in Canada, we got into an entertaining discussion about tastes, which revolved around the use of plastic flowers in Palestinian decorations:

> Yes, we had all that: We had camels; and furniture, like puffs; a lot of embroidery; pillows. So it certainly had a Palestinian touch.
> *So you think that plastic flowers are also Palestinian?*
> Well, that is what I have learned coming here, that those are very much Palestinian culture! My mum did have plastic flowers as well, but a little bit more tasteful!

It is important to point out that women play a central role in decorating. Furnishing and decorating is one aspect of preserving tradition, as is language, food, and family memoirs. Thus, Palestinian mothers play a crucial role in re-creating aspects, in particular cultural aspects, of Palestinian identity in the younger generations.

The material and symbolic aspects of cultural identity take on a different meaning in the return process. On the one hand, the Palestinian features do not need to be emphasized as much as they did in the diaspora because they are the norm in Palestine. Other aspects, such as language, require returnees to adjust. Returnees' encounter with Palestinian society in Palestine challenged the returnees' perception of Palestinian culture. They found similarities in which they could relate better to local Palestinians, which helped their integration. When they found disparities, some adopted the newly found "Palestinianness," while others tended to emphasize that they were different from the local Palestinians. Suddenly, the Moroccan cuisine adopted in exile, the American taste in music, or the Lebanese style of dress was considered better because it was foreign and different.

Halima stressed the hybrid nature of her tastes in cultural things:

> Well, in Kuwait we were influenced by a lot of things. I loved the Gulf music the most. There are some things that we picked up in the Gulf, like incense; I love that a lot. In our house that is a tradition, even in Amman we would use incense and listen to Gulf music.
>
> But in Kuwait you could see that we are Palestinians; we were not so influenced that it would look as if we were Kuwaitis. The furniture in the house was normal, but the house was full of embroidery, because my mother loves it and she wants to see it everywhere.

There were some traditions that were just for Kuwaitis and that we learned about there, such as one day of the year when they make children go to houses in the morning with a bag or something with embroidery . . . and they ask for sweets and chocolate. That was very nice; we also did it in Amman, but with the Palestinian families who lived in Kuwait.

Cultural traditions are directly linked to what could be called social traditions, which in turn are often related to religion. In fact, in the perception of many of my respondents tradition and morality were based on religious norms and could thus not be separated. At the same time, when they discussed progress, they would point out how fundamentally different customs and traditions are from real religion. They would oppose "oppressive" customs but not religious principles.

Religious Aspects of Identity and the Role of Tradition

In the perception of many Palestinians, it is difficult to distinguish between religion and tradition, although they are different words: *din* (meaning something similar to "religion") and *'adat wa taqalid* (customs and traditions). Often, the difference between the two is stressed in discussions about women's rights and Islamic "fundamentalism." We will reflect upon their intersection in the discussions with my respondents.

I asked all respondents if they practiced their religion and what religion meant to their lives. The answers were as diverse as the people I interviewed, and in many ways they surprised me. The Palestinians in Arab countries could be expected to be similar to the people in those host countries. Lebanon and Tunisia would be considered liberal, while a country like Yemen is conservative. This divide overlooks the fact that the host societies are far more complex than their images imply. Southern Lebanon might be as religiously inclined, as say, Gaza. Egypt has more or less "Western," or "liberalized," spheres. The fact that Palestinians were outsiders in these societies allowed them some space to act differently from others in the host societies. As Ali Jarbawi explained, "Certain types of behavior would be accepted in Tunis, because the people were Palestinians and not Tunisians. They would point at us and say that they tolerate us as foreigners, not as a part of society. They would be more liberal than with their own members of society."[12]

Also, there are enormous differences between Palestinians of the upper class in Beirut or Tunis, and Palestinian refugees in the camps of Lebanon and Jordan. The camps are often described as preservers of tradition. On the other hand, the experience of flight and being uprooted had disrupted the structure of Palestinian society that had previously ensured this preservation of tradition. In conclusion, one may say that there are contradicting trends in both the Palestinian communities of the diaspora and Palestinian society in Palestine concerning religion and tradition.

Most of the issues brought up by the interviewees were in fact gender-related. The concept of modesty, especially for women, is linked to dress, public behavior, and dating. Dating and premarital sex are more or less taboo and are issues that people do not like to speak about. Many assume that religion (Islam as well as Christianity) demands that girls be virgins when they marry. Only two of the ten women in the group of Aideen explicitly said that they had a boyfriend. None of the men gave me any details about relationships, but at least one had a girlfriend in Tunis whom he was planning to marry. Obviously, dating is partly a matter of age, but in Palestinian society, even in "liberal" places like Ramallah, young people dated very discreetly, afraid of being seen by relatives and neighbors, which would ruin the reputation of at least the girl.

Ramallah, as local Palestinians claimed, had become "loose," as one could find couples sitting in cafés talking and even holding hands. They blame these changes mainly on the returnees, who brought their liberal ideas back to Palestine. By the same token, Aideen girls complained that they were more often asked for dates because they were considered liberal. Most of them refused such invitations with indignation.

Dress was often mentioned as a way of being different, as pointed out earlier. I asked the girls if they changed the way they dressed to adjust, and most of them answered in the affirmative; others said they were simply more conscious about the way they dressed. Kamila, who had had a boyfriend for some time and insisted on living on her own, summed up all her problems with tradition, behavior, dress, and gossip at once:

> There are so many things about me that I have to hide. With certain people I can't drink; certain people don't know other things about me, maybe that I have boyfriends or whatever. It is a perfectly healthy relationship in every other way, but it works so much better when they don't know these things about me, because they won't understand. . . . All the neighbors have their eye on my flat to see who has been there and who has not. If they see one man going up, it just gets blown out of proportion and they will start saying, "She always has men coming over."

It is not easy at all. When I first wanted to live alone everyone was telling me, Don't do it. It is a lot of hassle and they are right, but you just have to prove otherwise, and I am trying. I don't know if it is working. I feel that I have to prove them wrong, and that a woman can live alone and still be okay. I feel like I am doing something positive.

I did adjust, actually; I used to be really arrogant about it, saying I would not change the way I dress and behave. But you have to and you do. I don't go out wearing a sleeveless shirt; I am conscious about what I wear because it does save you a lot of hassle and I suppose it is disrespectful to people. Also, I don't have to drink heavily in public; I can live without it and people are more comfortable. So, yes, I think I really did change over time.

Because Kamila did not live with a family, her experience was more difficult than that of the other young women, as most of them were under the protection (or control) of the family. Najma described her family as reasonably religious and pointed out where she would draw the line:

And even I who was given freedom by my family, I don't feel that I am very liberal. For example, in our house there is no alcohol. We do not drink and we don't have any inappropriate clothes. No, we are conservative, but at the same time we go out to parties and dance. We live a normal life but without being more liberal than is good and reasonable. There are a lot of people here who call themselves Westernized and brought all these Western ideas. I don't like even the word Westernized because I think in the West there are a lot of conservative families. But look when the Arabs go there and come back, what do they bring with them? Only things like the clothes, and then they dress like it here and they think this is progress and civilization. And I think that is backwardness in thinking.

Concerning religiosity and religious practice, the responses confirmed the idea that because the Palestinian national movement is a secular liberation movement, members of the diaspora in Arab countries are less attached to religion. However, personal religiosity does not have much connection to political Islam, or even to a more or less open lifestyle.

The young men I interviewed had little connection to their religion. Nominally all Muslim, none of them prayed and only a minority fasted, and even that was for social more than religious reasons. They explained, in similar terms, that praying and fasting were not what mattered; how one interacted with people was what counted. In their families only the women, that is, their mothers and sisters, practiced the religion.

For the young women, the results presented themselves differently, with more variation within the group. Most of them fasted and prayed occasionally, with the exception of Kamila, who was brought up as a nonbeliever and claimed religious labels if necessary (her father was Muslim, but a Marxist, and her mother was Christian). But even Kamila would not tell everybody in Palestine about this fact.

For Najma, religion had its fixed place in her life:

> In our house there is no prayer. My family is not Muslim because you cover your head and wear a headscarf, or because you pray all the time. I think most of the Palestinians who lived outside are like us. But inside we have a lot of faith; we fear Allah a lot. My father has in his whole life not done anything that is forbidden and didn't allow us either. . . . My mother fears Allah very much. She doesn't wear hijab or anything; [when] we came to Palestine she said it is early for her; she is still too young for that. But from another side we have a lot of faith in God; you feel very much that we are believers. I personally speak to Allah when I am afraid; when I have an exam, when I want something or hope for something, or there is an occasion I pray. Whatever we talk about at home, any topic you will never hear us curse Allah; that would never happen. When I am angry or sad I just turn to Him and speak to Him.

Somewhat surprisingly, it was Amina, the only one in this group who wore a headscarf, who had serious doubts about her religion. She started wearing hijab when she was in school in Jordan, but "reduced" it to "more normal clothes," like trousers and blouses combined with a smaller headscarf, when she came to Birzeit. Her doubts went deep and were related to the issue of *haram* (forbidden) and *halal* (allowed) in tradition and morality:

> Yes, I do pray, but right now I am not in line with that. You know how the classes cut your days, and in winter I am not strong about waking up so early. What happened was that I finished school and with leaving I also left the religious atmosphere I was living in. I noticed that the school didn't build anything for us inside. . . . They should have built something inside of us: Why should I pray, why it is necessary no matter if my life is good or bad to be grateful to Allah; they didn't build on that. It was all only about appearance, that you don't laugh in front of men, that you don't listen to music, that kind of thing only. Now I listen to music, I

greet guys, I also wear sandals. . . . Sometimes when I feel bad and I have problems I wish I were closer to Allah and more religious. I feel that religion is important for one's life, no matter if showing from the outside or not. It is not necessary that I wear hijab or follow 100 percent of the rules, because I fear Allah I don't do the bad things. As they say, the religion is a matter of your intentions. I feel religion is like nothing else; it is hard to live without it.

In conclusion, we can say that religion and tradition are aspects of identity, which are considered rather personal. The young returnees were confronted with ideas about tradition and modesty that were sometimes stricter and sometimes more open than their own. They noticed an adjustment that focused on limiting tensions and playing down differences. The only one who made an effort to change the others, Kamila, also said that she had adjusted to the situation, not internally, but on the outside to please society and avoid conflict. At least the young women cannot be called secular in the sense of not having a religion. Rather, faith in God appeared as a factor of stability, an authority to turn to for guidance, principles, and help in times of crisis and doubt. The respondents in this group did not mention a change in this realm because of their return experience. Rather, the most influential factor for the religious inclination was the example of the parents, combined with school.

Tradition and religion played a more central role in the lives of the young Palestinians of the Amrikan group. The main reason for that is that many of the parents' and grandparents' generation did not leave Palestine for political reasons. And even if the initial reason had political dimensions, their path of migration and occupation in life did not lead to active political involvement in the sense of participation in the struggle for Palestinian liberation. That does not mean that they are not interested in politics or do not show any commitment to Palestine, but that the core of their Palestinian identity is cultural and religious. As a result, both culture and religion are more community or family issues and not just personal choices.

I had expected that Palestinians who returned from the United States and other Western countries would be "Westernized." After all, they had been immersed in Western lifestyles, and for many of the younger ones, it was the only life they knew. They, unlike their parents or grandparents, did not have the opportunity to make comparisons and try to take the best from both worlds. My expectations proved to be wrong, and I quickly realized that tradition and religion were central to these young people's lives.

When they tried to adopt Western ideas, they constantly had to negotiate between those ideas and the value systems they learned from their parents.

One major characteristic of the first group was that 25 percent of the Amrikan interviewed were Christians; therefore, talking about religion took on a different dimension. The rules drawn from religion (whether Islam or Christianity) to define proper behavior differed only in detail, as what was called religion was actually tradition based on the interpretation of religion.

For many youths, learning about Islam in the United States was linked to learning Arabic, as the parents sent them to school with both purposes in mind. But even if the children were not successful in learning the language, many of them did learn the basics of their religious rituals. Only one of the girls did not know how to pray when she came to Palestine, and learned it at the Friends School.

Whenever I asked about religious practices, the answers were somewhat apologetic. All respondents could tell me what they were supposed to be able to do by their age according to Islam, namely, praying and fasting. And those who did not regularly do these things felt compelled to explain, as if I were a moral authority judging them.

'Aziz told me that he went to Sunday school in the United States where he was taught about Islam, and thus he knew a lot about it. The school did not help much with Arabic, but he learned the fundamentals of Islam. But in the next sentence, when he told me that he did not practice, he blamed it on life in America:

> Yes, I am Muslim; I don't practice my religion, but I know it very well. A lot of the Americans that live here, they don't really practice religion because it is just not brought on us, the religion in America. Like kids from here, who were born and raised here, it is brought up on them a lot, because they live in this country and there is a lot of religion in this country, but in America it wasn't really that important for my family.

Thus, it was America and his family that were responsible for the fact that he did not pray and fast. He described his mother as very religious, but his father was not and, thus, the central element of the children's upbringing was being respectful, being good in school, and "not getting in trouble with the law."

When I asked Amira about how important religion was for her, she said, "It is very important, just like a lot of rules, like especially for girls, no dating. I never used to go to parties. . . . I fast in Ramadan, but I don't pray." Shuruq added that one has to turn to God before every important decision and that this was something she thought Muslims and Christians had in common. Among the high school girls, I found varying degrees of religious practice, mostly depending on how religious the parents were. While Shuruq fasted during Ramadan and only prayed during that time, Ranya explained that she prayed, but not regularly, and that she was aware that she was not practicing strict Islam because she did not cover her hair.

Ayat, the only girl in the Amrikan group with a headscarf, told me:

> Prayer keeps you intact and keeps you from temptation. It is a cleansing process, every time during the day, the five daily prayers that you have to do. I cleanse myself; I'd be feeling stressed out and then I'll go home and I pray the afternoon prayer. I will feel better after that with myself. After I have done that, I feel relaxed, I feel like I can continue now with my day.

Although they did not pray five times a day or fast, the Christian members of this group were very similar in their perception of the importance of God. They spoke of seeking God's guidance and following rules of morality. The only difference lay in a certain feeling of alienation from the Muslim majority, a sense of being different and somewhat threatened or at least not accepted.[13] The girls reported discussing these topics in school, "where they [the Muslims] acted as if they were the only ones who were right." At community occasions such as weddings they felt alienated because they had different ways of celebrating and were somewhat more tolerant of mixed parties.

Most of the boys in this group did not pray, although many of them fasted. When they spoke about religion, it was more about culture, rules, and the prohibition against dating, premarital sex, and alcohol. I learned that it was more than just talk when 'Aziz told me that he intended to marry soon:

> Yes, I plan to marry a Palestinian girl, the one who is my girlfriend; I am very much in love with her. Hopefully, you know how it is over here: The tradition is go and ask for a girl's hand with your parents and ask their parents if they are willing to give their daughter to that person. Hopefully, I will do that before I leave the country . . . not to get married right now, but to ask for her hand.

In this part of the group (those 16–19), four of the young men had a girlfriend, but dating did not go beyond talking to each other or holding hands at parties (according to the interviews). Of the girls, only a few cautiously told me about being interested in a young man or having talked to one. At school it counted as dating when a couple spent the breaks together in the courtyard, or two or more couples went after school to Checkers or some other place to have coffee or ice cream.

Concerning both religion and tradition, the situation presented itself differently for the voluntary returnees of this group. They were not bound to a family context and had proven their independence by coming to Palestine. They were confronted with a more traditional society than they had left, and faced stronger demands to conform to its rules. Strikingly, with the exception of Munir, none of them was devout, whether their families were Muslim or Christian. Explanations can be found in the different socialization of the Amrikan, and to a lesser extent, in the fact that the voluntary returnees were older.

Socially, Munir would fit in with the younger, involuntary returnees, and thus share their religious inclination and intense interest in the preservation of Palestinian traditions concerning morality, behavior, and family values. He fasted and attended Friday prayers, but apologetically admitted that he had girlfriends in the United States and also drank alcohol. He added that he should practice more and that his parents were an example for him. They never forced either religion or tradition on him and only demanded that he show good judgment in making his decisions. As he had returned voluntarily to live with his parents and assist them as they got older, values like respect and support for his parents, their traditions, and religious obligations were imprinted on his consciousness.

Rayda gave me the longest and most eloquent explanation for her problems with her parents' religion, Islam, and why she (unlike her sister) was not devout:

> My biggest problem with religion is that it is a way of life. And I am a really stubborn person who says no one is going to tell me how to live my life, when it comes to these very specific personal details. If I had agreed with everything that they were infringing upon me then it might be a different thing, but I don't agree with many things. And it is the very basic, foundational or fundamental beliefs that I have that are completely contradictory to what I am supposed to have been as a Muslim woman. When people ask me what my religion is, I say I was raised Muslim, my mother and father are Muslim, but I don't know and there is a lot of things that I don't agree with.
>
> There is things in religion, morals, like not hurting anyone, being good to people, loving people, sharing, not lying, not stealing: They are im-

portant to me. But I think that is just coincidence. But there are details, small and big, like having to cover my hair and not having sex before marriage, the idea that homosexuality is grounds for burning: These are all things I don't agree with at all.

Like covering your hair, okay, that is something I could deal with and that I could not deal with. I know Muslim women who pray and who are very religious and who choose not to do this. But when it comes to things that I think are very natural and I think are very right, they think these are completely wrong. Which is what makes me know that it is not my religion.

The others either had only one Palestinian parent or came from a more educated background. Christian Palestinians in the United States have better integrated into U.S. society than Muslim Palestinians, and as a result more Christian Palestinians belong to the upper class. They tend to raise their children in more Americanized ways, while those in the lower and middle classes struggle to survive and establish themselves, and at the same time preserve the cultural identity of their children. A member of the Ramallah Club in Washington (a Christian cultural and social association) told me that they raised their children according to the traditions of Ramallah in the 1960s or 1970s when they left. When they got scared that they could not protect them, they sent them back to Palestine. But both parents and children alike were disappointed with the society they found there. Ibtisam was concerned that Palestine would change so much and so fast that by the time she came back from college she would not recognize her country anymore. She was hoping that Palestinians could preserve their traditions and their culture.

Upon their return, these young Palestinians were immersed in a Palestinian society, not just exposed to a scattered community, which helped them see their own cultural traditions and the role of religion in a different light. It confirmed the rules and norms by which they had lived and made being a Muslim (for those who were Muslim) the societal norm. They witnessed the debates within the society and the different interpretations of religion and tradition, and through this found their own position. Being Muslim gave Muslim returnees common ground with many local Palestinians and was somewhat more reliable in uniting them than were the debates about politics.

For the Amrikan, immersion in Palestinian society confirmed those aspects of their identity that were emphasized by their parents, culture, and tradition—being Arab, more than being Palestinian. The older members of the group had developed an identity before coming to Palestine so that they felt more like "political Palestinians." In coming back on their own to learn more about Palestine, they had taken a step away from their parents. They could reject religion to an extent, although even they had to negotiate norms of behavior and adjust to local expectations. But, as Palestinian society also has a secular segment, it was not difficult for them to find acceptance and people with whom to replace close family ties.

When the returnees arrived, they felt like outsiders, just as they had felt in the diaspora, but this time it was a society that was supposedly their own. There was disappointment and tension on both sides, but also an adjustment and re-socialization process that changed returnees and locals alike.[14]

As identities are constantly rewritten and renegotiated, as well as applied to different contexts and situations, the description and study of the rewriting process itself is methodologically difficult. At any point in time, I could ask the respondents about changes in their identity, but the answers would be determined by their current state and construction of identity, and thus subject to an adjustment of memory that gave meaning to the change. In addition, an adolescent's memories of childhood tend to picture the past as an easier and less troubled time than the present. The identity change that the return process caused was perceived as the upheaval of a familiar life and surroundings, an experience of both loss and gain. The gains became clearer during the return process, and as time passed, it was rare that a respondent could not cope with the current situation at all. All respondents appreciated the gain in knowledge and life experience despite the painful start and the other disappointments.

How Do You See Yourself Now?

To get an idea where they saw themselves in terms of identity labels, I asked all respondents who and what they thought they were at that point in time. For the Aideen, "Who are you?" seemed to be a rather easy question to answer. Most of them, without reluctance or doubt, said they were Palestinian. For some of them, being Muslim came before being Palestinian or Arab, because it is a broader category. Those with only one Palestinian parent, such as Qasim and Nimr, considered the Palestinian aspect of their identity more important:

> Yes, I am half Palestinian and half Lebanese. But I feel closer to Palestine because it is threatened, under occupation. Lebanon is not; the

situation is much better than in Palestine. You always feel closer to the endangered. (Nimr)

At one point, Basma told me about her pride in being Palestinian when she showed her passport at a border post, but then later she said:

Honestly? I feel I am not totally Palestinian; I feel that I am not only Palestinian, and sometimes I feel that I have more experience than others. I have seen lots of different things, and sometimes I feel happy because I have that experience. People think that kind of experience is something that isn't nice; they tell me it is the worst thing you have. But I think it is the best thing I have; I have seen everything in my life. I don't feel that I have to see something new; I am never astonished about anything. I have everything; I saw everything: Now I can make good choices in my life.

For the Amrikan, the situation was more complicated. Growing up, they often perceived being Palestinian and being Arab as being the same category. Baker describes many Palestinian American parents as having been "caught in a time warp." She writes:

They hang on to the social norms of their village from 20 years ago and force their children to live by them. Religion, usually Islam, is drilled into them more than nationality. Many of these children accept being Muslim but altogether reject being Arab. Religion is a nonnegotiable subject and being Muslim is one source of intense pride, partly because it is now seen as "cool" among their age group in the United States. (BAKER 1998, 4)[15]

The importance of religious identity is supported by the interviews, but I could not find what Baker called rejection of being Arab. The younger Amrikan sometimes called themselves Americans and distinguished their group from Arabs or *'Arab*. However, that was a response to being labeled Amrikan and being marginalized as a group. They noticed the differences between themselves and local Palestinians. In this context, it made sense for them to stress those aspects of their identity that made them different from those around them. In the United States, and elsewhere, they could not be like all the others, and in Palestine they were still not like the others. The emphasis on one's identity within the group set the boundaries of self-definition. Those who answered my question about how they saw themselves after their return to Palestine ultimately put "Palestinian" first:

I have a white complexion so people think I might be pure American, so they ask me, "What nationality are you?" And I am very proud to say

that I am Palestinian and when I went back it was very good for me to
say I have been here and I have seen it. Speaking Arabic with the older
people, they really like that, and I really like it too; I am really proud to
be a Palestinian. I would never change what I am.   ('AZIZ)

Palestinian . . . Palestinian who grew up in America. People call me Palestinian American. And I don't mind, but I would rather just be called
Palestinian, because that is who I am.   (RAMI)

Others acknowledged the different layers and aspects of their identity:

I am 100 percent Muslim, I can tell you that. Muslim, Arab, and American, that is all for people who know that stuff. My parents come from
Palestine and I lived in America most of my life. I have Palestinian blood
in me; everybody's heart is usually the same, and I just have an American
brain.   (MUKHLIS)

Well, I guess, technically I am a full-blood Palestinian: My mother is
Palestinian, my father is Palestinian, my whole family is Palestinian. But
I don't consider myself fully Palestinian. I mean, I was born and raised
in America and Canada, so that is the way I look at things, from their
point of view. So I guess I wouldn't call myself an American Palestinian,
I call myself Palestinian American, because my blood is Palestinian, but
culturally I am American. Mentally, I am American, because I don't
think like the people here. That is how all of us think, all my friends in
Ramallah and my brother and my cousins who are American, they think
that they are Palestinian Americans, because they are proud of their
culture but they also stick to the way they were taught in America.
                                                                (JANE)

Rayda spoke very eloquently about her experience and reflected on who
she was and what had happened to her during her journey to find her
roots, her self-perception, and the Palestinian people. She explained to me
how being in Palestine had changed her self-definition:

In a way I feel more comfortable calling myself Palestinian, because I
used to call myself a Palestinian without being able to speak to someone in Arabic. I think it is almost ridiculous when it comes down to it;
if you don't know at least that much, there is something wrong. I feel
more comfortable calling myself a Palestinian, but I don't necessarily feel
more Palestinian or less American or whatever, because I've always been
Palestinian American.

If we see identity building as a process, a stream of changes, adjustments to changing environments and experiences, what then could the future of Palestinian identity be? The young Palestinians have different plans for the near- and long-term future, but the political, social, and economic situation in Palestine and in the diaspora will have an impact on whether Palestinians will survive as a people and achieve national independence or not. Will a Palestinian state, in whatever form, resolve the struggle to find a Palestinian identity?

CHAPTER 7

Home and the Future of Palestinian Identities

> *I have never felt any loyalty to any place. It is as if being homeless has been my homeland, a kind of transnational place where I, along with other Palestinians of my generation, have felt the same sense of at-homeness that other folk, with a state of their own have had.* (TURKI 1988, 129)

Has being without a home and homeland become the home of the Palestinian diaspora? This chapter is "returning" to the question of home and homeland touched upon throughout this study. Have the young Palestinians interviewed for this study really returned? Do they feel at home now? How can these feelings be translated into a future of Palestinian identities? Is feeling at home equivalent to integration in Palestine? And, finally, what options do the young Palestinians have if the return process does not result in integration?

Rayda's Story

Rayda was twenty-four and had been in Palestine for eight months when I interviewed her. Her parents were originally from a village near Ramleh located in the area that Palestinians fled in 1948. Both families became refugees for the first time in 1948 and lived near Jericho until 1967, when they again fled, this time to Jordan.

Rayda's parents were the first in both extended families to leave the Arab world for a new life in America. Because of that, Rayda felt as different from her Palestinian relatives as from the Americans with whom she grew up. Of her upbringing in America she said:

> I enjoyed being a Palestinian who grew up in America. There are things that I wish were different and there are things that I am very happy about the way they are. . . . The other day somebody asked me if I would have

rather been born here in Palestine or outside. My answer to that was that as a woman I am really thankful that I grew up outside, because it gave me the chance to evolve my own character and my independence and personality, which are things I see really lacking in many women here. So as a woman I am glad that I grew up outside. But I think that if I was a boy I would have rather grown up here. Now that I am here I hear stories about prison; I hear stories about the Intifada and about growing up in different neighborhoods. These are things I really envy and I miss that as a part of my life. Or when I hear people singing songs and I don't know a word of them, that hurts me.

Rayda recalled realizing more about her Palestinian identity when she went to college. Like many other Palestinian Americans of her generation, she was confronted with pro-Israeli activities on campus and felt that she had to respond in some way. Through these counter-activities, lectures, demonstrations, and protests, she learned more about the Palestinian issue and about herself. She realized that she needed to come to Palestine to find out for herself what her connection to Palestine was. The other purpose of her "return" was to improve her Arabic, as she felt that her lack of fluency was an obstacle to feeling Palestinian. The "return visit" was not her first trip to Palestine. When she was eleven, her father had taken the entire family to visit the village that his family came from and the camp in Jericho where he grew up.

After she finished college, Rayda felt uncertain about what she wanted to do, so she decided to go to Palestine. She recalled the decision not as an attempt to escape, but as taking a year off to think about her future while studying Arabic and learning about her place of origin.

She realized that she knew very little about her parents' history, aside from the fact that they had been trying to raise their children as Palestinians, with Palestine's culture, language, and moral values. There were Palestinian movies, books, and newspapers in the house, and conversation occasionally centered on Palestine, but looking back, she felt that she knew very little:

> I don't know exactly what life was like for them growing up, which is strange because I don't know why I never asked them or why they never told me. But a lot of the things we would hear growing up would come from when my parents hated the country they were in. When they hated the way we were turning out, they would say, "If only we had never left Palestine and if only. . . ." My father is still very connected to the situation here through writing letters, through speaking in places, through

keeping strong contact with the Arab and Muslim community wherever he is, through charity funds, because thankfully he has the opportunity to do that.

They would talk to us about it, but no details of their personal situation. I don't know if they were so personal that they couldn't talk about them, or if they thought that we were not ready to hear them, or if they were just waiting for us to ask. And my father was willing to have every opportunity for you to understand at your fingertips. If any one of my brothers and sisters wants to come here, he is the first to say, "How can I help you?" They are very adamant about keeping their morals and their culture and their religion a part of our lives. Sometimes it works and sometimes it doesn't, but it is there and they try.

Assessing her time in Palestine, she told me that she was proud of knowing the people better, of knowing the language better, and understanding things from her own perspective. She also said that it hurt her that people still called her a foreigner or even a Jew. Rayda dressed very casually and had not adjusted to Palestinian expectations of female dress.

And there are people who refuse to believe, refuse to believe that I am Palestinian. And I say, "But look at my eyes; you see Arab eyes don't you?" And someone actually said to me, "But if you are an Arab woman, you wouldn't look straight in my eyes." I couldn't even believe that came out of his mouth. But then most people who find out that I am Palestinian figure that, okay, so my father married an American woman; you know they need an excuse for all these earrings, for the way that I walk down the street, or that I feel free to walk down the street at whatever time and with whoever. Yes, they keep you feeling very American.

At the time of the interview Rayda had a relationship with a Palestinian from the West Bank who, as a musician, helped her relate to Palestinian culture through the music she had grown up with. He told her that the music was in her blood and soul, even if she was not conscious of it and did not know where she had learned it. Her relationship with him was very close, and I asked her if she wanted to stay in Palestine and marry him.

That is a difficult question, because right now there [are] a lot of places in the world that I want to see before I can decide where I want to spend my life. But there is a big part of me that would want to live my life here. But [only] as long as I got to live in the way that I would like to live my life, and sometimes I feel that that might be really difficult. And in this time that is coming I think that I will be leaving, probably by the summertime, and, hopefully, sometime later coming back here, always for sure for visits, hopefully, to live for a longer period of time.

You know, I never ever thought that I would find someone who had the same ideas that I had, who has the same hopes, who I could speak to; this was always my problem. I thought I would never be able to marry an Arab man, because we would have such a huge problem in communication, not only because of the language, because of the way of thinking. I totally surprised my whole family by being the one who actually found a Palestinian Muslim man to hopefully share my life with, and that was a big surprise for me and for my whole family.

Rayda and Ziyad got married in Al-Bireh and left for America before I left Palestine in the summer of 1999. Rayda had a baby girl the following year, and when I last saw her at a rally for Palestinian rights in 2001, she was carrying her daughter who was wearing a T-shirt that said: Third-generation refugee!

She had already mentioned that she would leave Palestine again, so I asked how she defined home and where she thought she felt at home:

Thankfully, for me, I have the ability to feel at home almost wherever I am. I can make a home in America, I can make a home where I am going to school, I can make a home here. If I'd have to leave today and go somewhere else, I think I could make my home there. But I think that comes from the feeling that you don't fit anywhere, and when you think about it you can fit in everywhere. Like being Palestinian American, I fit in very well in America and I fit in here as well. And I can fit in well in Italy, I am sure. So home is where I am.

Rayda saw her own life connected to Palestine: She wanted her children to learn Arabic and be Palestinians, but she did not necessarily want to settle in Palestine. She believed that the problems Palestinians would have in the future would be as much internal as external ones. No matter what kind of state might be created, Palestinian society would have to evolve to provide a homeland and security for its citizens. She realized that it would be difficult for her to be accepted the way she was, and knew that this acceptance would be a precondition for her living there. For Rayda, return to Palestine was a journey into culture, language, politics, and her own personality, and she left with the feeling of being reassured of her Palestinian identity, but settling there for good seemed difficult.

Marwan's Story

Marwan was twenty-four and had returned to Palestine in 1994. He came back with his mother and siblings as part of the official Aideen. His father had been killed in an Israeli attack in Tunis in 1985. Marwan's father was originally from a village in the 1948 area. The village was depopulated in 1948, but the inhabitants returned after the war. It was destroyed in 1967, and his father left Palestine to become a member of the Palestinian resistance in Jordan. His mother came from a refugee family from Hebron but was born and raised in Syria where she and Marwan's father met and married.

Marwan spent his childhood and youth in various Arab countries, following the PLO and his father from Lebanon to Syria, to Tunisia, and then to Jordan. A Palestinian community always surrounded him, and both parents worked for the PLO. He had no questions about his identity as a Palestinian and shared his family's dream of one day returning to Palestine.

> Whenever we would see someone who came from here, we knew that we couldn't come here, and we wanted it so much, so we would envy him. When the peace process started, it became possible to return to our country. I didn't feel very comfortable in any country. I was okay in Tunis, and also in Jordan; my friends were there and all that, but I still wanted to come back here. And when we found out that we could return, we were very happy.

His parents had conveyed an image of Palestine as a wonderful, naturally beautiful, and hospitable homeland. His father spoke of the trees in the village and the special smell of the earth, his mother of the peaceful life before occupation. When I asked him if he found what he had expected he said:

> No, of course not how I imagined it; the picture was very beautiful, it was imagination and it was impossible to find that in the reality in any country. Until now there are some problems in this country, but it is your country: If you don't take care of it and build it, who will do it? It can't be that some outsider comes and fixes it for you.

> We thought of the Palestinians here, the people of the Intifada, as an amazing people. So when you come here, you expect to find a special people, very civilized politically and socially. And then you discover that that is not true, the Intifada had a lot of negative consequences. The culture and the education of the people suffered.

He had problems coping with his disappointment as well as with the way people approached the returnees as a group. But his worldview and his feeling about Palestine had not changed.

I won't tell you I never have days when I am sick of the country, sick of the people. Sometimes I walk on the streets and that alone makes me tired, from the people I see there. Sometimes I do say, Why do I have to live here? But at the same time, I say, No, I live here and I must live here. And our children and their children will be here, so that we never end. But it needs a lot of work, and we will get tired of it and our children will have to work hard and get tired as well, and maybe my grandchildren will start feeling comfortable here. I don't expect to feel too good here.

Because he had traveled out of Palestine on occasion after 1994, he was sure about his relation to Palestine:

And every time I traveled I felt my connection to here, and not love for the family, but for the place. Because from Jordan I traveled as well; I went to Romania, to other countries, and I never had that same feeling for Jordan. I don't know why. I would miss a particular friend, or I would long for my family, my sister, brother, and my mum. But I wouldn't feel love for the country itself. Here I feel that I miss the country; I am angry about many things here and at the same time I feel love for it. I guess it is not the fault of the people; they lived through the Intifada and the occupation: They need to learn; they need to develop. It needs effort from the people who are themselves educated, civilized, and understanding.

He had clear plans for his role in the efforts to change Palestine. He thought he might leave temporarily to get a higher degree after he finished his bachelor's degree at Birzeit University, but planned to return to work for the foreign ministry or as a diplomat. He considered that political work, but emphasized that he was not committed to any of the political parties. He sometimes worked at the Orient-House in Jerusalem and was active in university politics.

His intention to work in foreign policy was an attempt to integrate his migration experience into his life plan. It would allow him to identify himself with Palestine as a homeland but would simultaneously open the door to traveling or living abroad. Movement was a part of his childhood experience, so this choice would reconcile the two opposing longings for change and stability.

The two stories have shown two different ways of coping with the return experience and translating this experience into plans for the future.

If feeling at home is a condition for staying, what exactly does it mean to be at home?

Feeling at Home and Having a Homeland

"Home" is a term we all invest with meaning. A traditional definition of home might read: "the stable physical centre of one's universe — a safe and still place to leave and return to, and a principal focus of one's concern and control" (Rapport and Dawson 1998b, 6). In this understanding, home organizes space and time to provide the human being with a sense of stability. Such a definition is not compatible with the concept of the modern world as a "world of movement." One has to work with a broader understanding, emphasizing change and movement over routine and stability. In essence, we must rely on a conception of home that permits much more mobility, conceiving it as "plurilocal," something to be taken along whenever one decamps (Rapport and Dawson 1998b, 7).

Most people expect home to be a place in which one can be at ease, but, in reality, homes are civic, constructed institutions, producing bodies, borders, subject positions, discourses and ideologies, and mechanisms of surveillance and discipline (Sagar 1997, 237).

Clearly, defining what home is or can be is not unproblematic, and it is not always the safe haven for our being that we imagine it to be. Making a place a home is often considered a female task and may be used as a reason to confine women to the home. Thus, home is a gender issue as well. We could define home as a place "where one best knows oneself" (Rapport and Dawson 1998b, 9), keeping in mind that such a definition of home is somewhat paradoxical, both ambiguous and transgressing in attempting to fix something that is in itself in constant negotiation.

Home can also be related to the larger concept of homeland, taking the idea and reality of home from the individual into the collective sphere of cultural norms. And even if we identify home as one of the "fictions that we employ to feel at home" (Sagar 1997, 238), we must recognize that people have different needs and perceptions in this respect. There are people in this "world of movement" who can comfortably live with a cosmopolitan identity and a home that they carry with them. But others, economically and culturally not as privileged, perceive homelessness not as an opportunity for new experiences and a challenge but as a burden and a source of suffering. Refugees are not only alone when forced to move again and again but their options for improving their lives are limited and dependent on others.

The increasing fluidity and motion of the modern world has as its counter-development an urge for stability, be it in the form of various "fundamentalisms" or in the emergence of particular nationalisms. Universalistic notions of cosmopolitanism are challenged by nationalist constructions and "there is no objective middle ground or postmodern freedom to construct one's own virtual home space" (Fog Olwig 1998, 227).

The interviews in this study reflect vague definitions of what home means to the interviewees. One common definition of home is "where my family is." It goes beyond the individualistic idea of "home is where I am, or is within me" and considers blood relations the most stable bonds between human beings. It also reflects on the age of my respondents, for whom home was still a place their parents made and not something that they had to create on their own.

Concepts of homeland and home, the feeling of belonging somewhere and being relatively comfortable and safe, are subjective and individual, though they can be shared and shaped by groups as well. Ideology plays an important role, as does one's upbringing and socialization. To ask the respondents in this study if Palestine felt like home to them would have amounted to demanding a loyalty statement, and as we have seen, the ideological meaning of homeland in the Palestinian context cannot be overestimated. To avoid eliciting such a statement, I asked them where they felt their home was and how they would explain this feeling to me. The answers reveal their disappointments and frustrations, but also their longing to be at home.

For Basma, the place that she called home was a place in the past; she had not found a similar place or feeling in Palestine, a fact that might explain why she wanted to leave again:

> Yes, I have such a place, my grandma's house. It's the place I really love. I used to sit in the sun there; it is a typical Syrian house. It's open, the sun enters, and there are trees all around. My grandmother used to prepare things for cooking, and I used to sit with her in the sun, and then my aunties would come and my cousins and my uncles. I feel that's the house of the whole family. And I was part of that family. That is the reason I love that place.

Najma was reluctant to admit that she did not feel at home in Palestine. The nationalist discourse she supported had little room for such confessions, but she explained why she felt that way:

That was always a question for us, and I personally all my life felt at home in the place where I was. If the people there loved us and we loved the people and we were comfortable there, then I felt at home. I have to say the people we met here so far and the way they treated us didn't give us the feeling to be at home or in our homeland. And until now I don't have the feeling that this is my country, my home, or what I expected it to be. I am ready to live here in sweet and bitter days. But I feel like a stranger in my own country.

Feeling at home can be expressed in personal terms, through family, stability, and a house. Homeland is an ideological term, and many respondents had difficulty using it. Those of the Aideen who expressed discontent with the homeland they found were reluctant to tell me that openly, and expressed hope that both this feeling and the homeland would change in time.

For the Amrikan, it was less of a political question, and for many there was also less of a choice to be made. For them the statement "home is where my family is" proved to be even more true. When I asked them which place they considered home, about half of them said Palestine. Some added that this feeling had changed over time, as we saw in Ibtisam's graduation speech, because feeling at home in a place had as much to do with knowing that place as with other bonds that one might feel. Rami said about home:

> I think two places should be home: Your home is where your family is. And home is where your background is, where your ancestors are from. But, see, that definition splits where home is for me. My family, everyone I grew up with, two of my brothers and two of my sisters live in the States, so that is home for me. And also over here is a home for me, because here is my family; it is where my dad was born, my dad's dad, and everybody. That is very important, after you come here.

In choosing between the two places they knew, and after spending considerable time in Palestine, many of the respondents clearly pointed to Palestine as their home. Ayat explained to me why she though it was an easy choice:

> I feel at home when I am comfortable with my surroundings, like when I am satisfied with what is going on around me. I consider this place my home, because I don't consider America home. I consider it some place where people go and get as much as they can from it and then go back to where they consider home. That is what usually happens: You go there,

and you make whatever you want to make, and then you go back to your own country and build a nice house and have a nice car and things like that. It is just a place to work.

The young respondents had many plans, and the decision to stay in or leave Palestine had implications for professional choices, but also translated into expressions of attachment to Palestine.

Adjustments: Changing the Homeland, or Home Is Where You Make It

None of the young returnees found what he or she had expected upon return. The realities of Palestine were more complex, less glorious, and in everyday life more difficult than they had imagined. One had three choices at a certain point in the return process. The first option was to accept Palestine as a homeland and adjust to its circumstances and challenges by rewriting one's own identity. The second option was to accept Palestine as one's homeland but to attempt to change those things that caused one discontent and were considered wrong, disruptive, and bad for the future, not only for the individual, but also for the society. The third option was to leave again—in some cases for good, and in others to return later in life.

All the respondents had learned from their time in Palestine and had, in various ways, developed an attachment to the country. I asked them what they would change in Palestine, and it was in their answer to this question that they expressed their connection or attachment most explicitly.

Jane and Janet told me that they wanted to study something related to psychology or teaching, because Palestinian society needed professionals who could counsel people with problems and help them "be more open about things and develop." Ayat said that she wanted to go to the United States to study law and then, after some years of professional experience, to come back and help people in Palestine and improve society. She, like many other girls in the Amrikan group, spoke about gender inequality and how developing the confidence of women and supporting their rights was necessary and would change Palestinian society for the better.

The ideas about changes in Palestine that came from the Aideen sounded more "political," and the Aideen were, to an extent, more outspoken. They felt more Palestinian, while most of the Amrikan were at least bicultural. Palestinians who lived in Arab countries did not become Lebanese, Syrian, Jordanian, or Tunisian, even if they adopted certain values and lifestyles. They perceived themselves as strictly Palestinians.

The return to Palestine might have challenged their definition of what Palestinian is, but their national identity was deeply embedded in their consciousness. Thus, they were also more cautious in their criticism, and they delivered criticism from both an outsider's and insider's position, depending on the situation and topic.

Majid said about changing Palestine:

> I would change the minds of people first, their way of thinking. You have to look ahead, because it doesn't help you to look back all the time. There is a life and it is beautiful. . . . This land is not going to change; the land itself is beautiful, but we don't understand the country. We don't know what it needs to work with it and develop it. It cannot be that someone rules here with the logic of money or power. This is my country and I am free in it, but I know that my freedom is built on the freedom of the others and has to cooperate with it. If all people would live according to that rule, we could have the best life.

Muna, Hanadi, and Najma planned to finish their studies and then work in one or another way for the country. Najma wanted to work as a PLO representative, possibly for the foreign ministry; Hanadi and Muna wanted to work as journalists. Hanadi was also interested in environmental issues. Nimr already worked for the PA and did political work on refugee questions.

Because of their legal documents, many of the Aideen had little choice but to stay in Palestine. Palestinian passports and Arab legal documents meant similar restrictions on travel in many parts of the world. Their commitment to Palestine was clearly more political in nature and translated directly into plans for the future. For most of them, the choice they made for the future (or were planning to make) was a synthesis of adjusting to the homeland they had found and attempting to change aspects of it that displeased them. The adjustment process between Aideen and locals was mutual, thus this choice was possible.

The Amrikan had different opportunities to leave, although many depended on their parents as a source of financial support for their education and as an authority. The majority of the Amrikan were planning to leave Palestine, at least temporarily, but many intended to return. They had adjusted to Palestine, and Palestinian society had at least gotten used to their presence. As more Palestinian American families sent their kids back for high school, and a new group of volunteers started working for NGOs in the area every year, they were a familiar sight, at least in Ramallah.

Whether they stayed or left, the future of Palestinian identities would depend on their decisions about whom to marry and where to raise their children.

Spouses and Children: The Next Palestinian Generation

Endogamous marriage is assumed to have been the norm for Palestinian society before 1948. Historical developments and, in the Palestinian case especially, migration and the concomitant disruption of traditional social structures have considerably changed the conditions under which one chooses a spouse.

In the 1980s Alqudsi-Taghreed found that not only the choice of spouses but also the celebration of weddings had changed considerably in the Palestinian community in Kuwait. Intermarriage between Palestinians from rural and urban backgrounds had increased in numbers because of exile, especially because younger Palestinians had opportunities to meet in workplaces. Alqudsi-Taghreed asserts that when they, like many others, chose to celebrate their weddings in pre-1948 rural style, their choice was "a political statement that affirm[ed] their Palestinian identity" (Alqudsi-Taghreed 1990, 40).

Into the 1980s, studies of Palestinian communities found that young Palestinians tended to marry people from their former villages, thus keeping the traditional arrangements alive. But marital patterns have changed considerably, with new forms evolving in some parts of the community while other parts of the community keep the traditions alive. Change therefore reveals itself in the number of choices about how to find a spouse.

The decision to marry a Palestinian, for the fact that he or she is Palestinian, has important implications for the identity of the next generation. According to the PLO charter and the draft of Palestinian citizenship law, a person is only considered Palestinian if his or her father is Palestinian, that is, if he is a descendant of those Palestinians who lived in Palestine before 1948 (see Davis 1996, 66).[1] Following this logic, it is essential for a Palestinian woman to marry a Palestinian man in order to have Palestinian children.

But exile has changed patterns in choosing a spouse. Palestinian communities in Arab countries, and the close social communities of the refugee camps enable Palestinians to choose a spouse from within the extended family or village. However, with women in the camps working outside the home and taking part in political organizations and other activities, and with young Palestinians — men and women — studying in universities, there are more possibilities to meet people outside the traditional social circle. The same is true for Palestinian society in Israel, the West Bank, and Gaza. As a result, one finds many different variations of matchmaking and/or choosing a partner.

Because of the patrilineal character of the Palestinian family, it is easier and certainly more socially acceptable for a Palestinian man to marry a non-Palestinian woman. There were many such marriages in Lebanon, Syria, Egypt, and Jordan. It is also not uncommon for Palestinian women —for example, in Lebanon—to marry Lebanese men. Palestinian men in Western countries, where a Palestinian community was mostly absent, chose non-Palestinian wives even more often.

Because they are raised according to a different standard from Palestinian men, Palestinian women face considerable problems in marriage. Palestinian American men can and do marry American women, because they can date them before marriage, which is often not possible with Palestinian women. Palestinian American women are expected to marry Palestinian men of the same religion, and as the men of the community often marry outside the community, the women have to look for Palestinian men in Palestine or among recent immigrants. "The problem here is that most immigrant Palestinian men think Palestinian-American women are 'too American.' They see them as too independent, too strong, and unable adequately to pass on Palestinian culture and language to their children" (Cainkar 1990, 59).

The same author, based on an extended study of the lives of Palestinian American women, also describes the marital patterns of Palestinian men who studied or worked abroad and were without a network of family members in the same country or area. These men often go back to Palestine to find a wife through matchmaking, and after getting married there, bring their new wife back to the United States (Cainkar 1990, 62).[2]

All these different patterns can be found in the families of my respondents and demonstrate the variety of options for Palestinian marriages. The significance of having a Palestinian mother, but not a Palestinian father, is exemplified in the stories of Paul, Sandy, and Nigel. All three of them grew up feeling part of their father's culture and only in late adolescence reached a point where they started questioning themselves and their parents about the Palestinian aspects of their identity. It is no coincidence that they all voluntarily returned to Palestine.

Paul was born in Lebanon; his father was a Lebanese Maronite and his mother a Christian Palestinian from 1948. He explained to me how his mother tried to hide the Palestinian aspects of his identity and dialect, because of fears during the civil war. Only after the family migrated to the

United States, after which pictures of and news about the Intifada triggered empathy in Paul, did Paul feel that he had a connection to Palestinians. His interest grew, and he applied for an internship in Palestine, initially for a summer. He ended up staying for more than a year working for an NGO. During that time he grew closer to Palestine, although he was still a Lebanese nationalist. He left in 1999 but felt a stronger connection to Palestine and the Palestinian part of his heritage than he had before.

Sandy and Nigel were raised in Britain as children of a British father and a Palestinian mother who had grown up outside Palestine. Since Sandy came to Palestine to work for an NGO, I could see her attitude slowly changing. Before she decided to come to Palestine, she worked for a pro-Palestinian organization in London where she learned about the conflict, Palestinian history, and the present situation. Her presence in Palestine subsequently inspired her younger sister and her brother to visit Palestine for the first time, and, more importantly, motivated her mother to come to discover the country with her daughter. In our talks, Sandy insisted that in Palestine she had found her place and an explanation for those things in her that never seemed to fit in Britain, things that reflected her Palestinian side. She recognized her "outsider" position more in Palestine than in Britain, but she was comfortable with this distance. Her way of expressing her commitment to Palestinians was through her work. She found it difficult to learn Arabic. However, she found it even more difficult to leave, and in 2002 she was still living in Ramallah.

One of the questions about the future that I asked my young respondents, all but one of whom were single when I first met them, was whether or not they wanted to marry a Palestinian. The young men reported that they had more freedom to choose, while the young women said that they were expected by their parents to marry Palestinian men. Many agreed that it was necessary to marry within the community.

Kamila told me that her father felt very strongly about this and that he was not really joking when he said that if she married a foreigner she would not be his daughter anymore. She was determined to make her own choice, but admitted that in a past relationship that she had had with a non-Palestinian, she felt that some of the "natural" understanding about Palestine and its culture, music, and traditions was missing.

Most of the Aideen women, with the exception of Basma and Kamila, had no doubt that they would marry a Palestinian man of their own choosing when the time came. They planned to continue the marital pattern of their parents, many of whom had met in exile while studying or doing political work, rather than through family networks. Only Amina said that she did not want to marry because she wanted to achieve professional success and retain her independence, and if she married, she would do it late in life.

The young men all planned to get married; Mamduh already had a Tunisian fiancée, and Marwan said that it was a strong possibility that his future wife would be Palestinian.

For the Amrikan, marriage was more of an issue because of family expectations, and although many of them were younger, they had clear plans and images concerning marriage. Jane told me that she had not wanted to marry a Palestinian but rather an American who had been raised like her. Then she met a Palestinian American who was visiting his family. She found that they communicated so well that she now thought that she would rather marry a Palestinian American. "He is just like me. I wouldn't think that he is Palestinian, because of the way he acts; he acts in things like me, and I like that American mentality."

For Amira there was no doubt that her future husband was going to be an Arab, if not a Palestinian, and she hoped that he would be "an honest guy." Most of the girls said that they wanted to marry a Palestinian American, someone with a similar upbringing and background, so that they could understand each other. Only Ibtisam said exactly the opposite, arguing that another Arab American would have the same gaps in language and cultural knowledge, so she wanted to marry an Arab man in order to learn from him and become more Arab herself.

At seventeen, 'Aziz was planning to marry his Palestinian girlfriend because he was "very much in love with her." Mukhlis thought nationality did not matter as long as the girl was pretty and nice to him. Munzir thought that his wife was likely to be Palestinian, unless he fell in love with somebody else. He said:

> Traditionally the parents pick the person you are going to marry. But now it is kind of changing down here, people fall in love and then they get married. So either thing might happen to me.

Rami did not want an arranged marriage but considered it keeping Palestinian tradition to marry a Palestinian woman.

Hiyam explained to me how her ideas about marriage had changed since she had come to Palestine and had a relationship with a Palestinian man, whom she had considered marrying. In the end she decided against it, but for personal reasons, not because he was Muslim and she was Christian, and not because they were culturally too different.

Before that I had sort of decided that I wasn't going to marry any Palestinian, or that I wasn't going to be involved with anybody Palestinian. Which was something new; he was the first Palestinian man that I was involved with. Before that the only thing close was someone half Palestinian, and he grew up in Canada, so it was different. I think that it is a problem because it opened up a door for me; it is acceptable for me now and I know I can do it. I'd like to be married and have children; I don't know if necessarily soon, and it depends on what happens and who comes in line if they come in line. I realize now that I can be married to a Palestinian. I would have to be married to someone who would understand being here and who would want to be here as well, because I see myself always being here. If I am to decide to go to Canada or live somewhere else I will always come here as well. But he would not, as a principle, have to be Palestinian.

If and how the next generation is going to define themselves as Palestinian will to a large extent depend on the decisions of this generation of young Palestinians.

For those of the Aideen who were planning to stay in Palestine, this was not really a question. They assumed that their children would grow up as Palestinians in Palestine, with no outside challenge to their national identity. Ideally, they might grow up in a Palestinian state with institutions and symbols to teach them pride in being Palestinian citizens.

To those who wanted to leave again and considered remaining abroad, the question was more complicated. But as they confirmed their own Palestinian identity, developed in exile and undergoing adjustments since their return, they would have something to pass on to their children, even if they married someone who was not Palestinian. Kamila's statement about her future children may sum up these expectations:

> I think, whoever I marry, they will be half Palestinian at least, and I will teach them everything about Palestine, definitely. I have to teach them the history of this land; they definitely have to learn. And this is why I think the children in this society, they should really know everything: They should know about all the history and all the massacres that happened; they should know about all our writers, people that got killed, important people; they should learn about all this stuff, and I will teach my kids definitely. They will be half Palestinian.

The Amrikan, many of them already Palestinian American in their own eyes, were faced with a different challenge in raising their children. Most planned to live a comfortable life in the United States and only settle in Palestine later in their lives. This decision to return later was closely linked to the idea of raising their children in a Palestinian environment. Despite the fact that many of them had found being sent back to Palestine a difficult experience, most of them planned on doing the same with their own children. Many also said that it would be better to teach their children Arabic and the Palestinian culture at an earlier age, when they were still flexible, more open, and less Americanized. Hiyam sums this issue up for the Amrikan:

> They will grow up Palestinian, and I will teach them Arabic, which is something my parents didn't do. They will go and they will learn how to read and write, and depending on where they grow up, I'd want them to learn both, because I am Canadian as well, and I value that very much.

Palestinian Identities and a Future Palestinian State

The Oslo process has not only allowed for a limited number of Palestinians to return to Palestine but has also fundamentally altered the circumstances of defining Palestinian national identity on a number of levels.

The establishment of the Palestinian Authority left the PLO's organizations and institutions in a shambles at the time of the Oslo agreement, rendering it nothing more than a symbolic institution to represent Palestinians. In principle, the Palestinian Authority speaks and negotiates on behalf of all Palestinians, but in reality it cannot even govern those Palestinians in the West Bank and Gaza. That the focus of Palestinian political activity is on the West Bank and Gaza has, within just a few years, made most of the Palestinian diaspora feel like outsiders in Palestinian politics. The early hope for a right to return and the euphoria of imagining this hope realized is gone. Many diaspora Palestinians feel that the peace deal has been made at their expense, without their consent, and without any benefit to them.

A reevaluation of the meanings of Palestinian identity has taken place on two main levels. The Oslo agreements have led to the gradual redefinition of Palestinian identity, mainly because the agreement and the creation of the PA led to a de-legitimization of the Palestinian resistance (Andoni 1998, 17). By accepting guarantees of Israeli security as the guiding principle of the peace process and abandoning the legitimate right of the Palestinians to resist the occupation until they achieve their own nation-state, the process has made Palestinians hostage to Israel and subject to its punishment and control. Based on the security discussion, the legitimate resistance of Palestinians (from the 1960s to the First Intifada) had been redefined as a punishable criminal activity. As a result, Palestinians have been divided into those who enforce Israeli security measures and those who are punished and oppressed by the same measures. A new rift in Palestinian society has appeared. On the one hand, there are those who work for the PA and its security network and who have a history of being heroes of the resistance outside the Intifada. Their function is reduced to controlling "their own neighbors in the refugee camps" (Andoni 1998, 18). The other group consists of those who did not join the security forces or the PA; they have lost a sense of direction and feel demoralized by the new conditions.

Thus, a unified Palestinian identity is threatened by the process of individualization of interests in the context of the new Palestinian Authority. Instead of a single goal—Palestinian independence—there are the daily difficulties of building a quasi-state that may never be a real state. Institution building entails the awarding of resources and posts, distributing power, and dealing with corruption.

The second important rift is between Palestinians in the West Bank and Gaza, and those in the diaspora. While the PA is responsible for Palestinians already in the West Bank and Gaza, it is also responsible for negotiating the borders of a Palestinian state and the conditions for a right of return, thus speaking on behalf of all Palestinians. The events since August 2002 have made it seem very unlikely that Israel will ever recognize the right of return for all Palestinians.

Even if a Palestinian state were, at some point, allowed a law of return comparable to that of Israel, many Palestinians would most likely not return and settle in Palestine.[3] Palestinian citizenship might have symbolic value and also provide some protection to those who carry Palestinian passports, which would then be recognized internationally. The right of return would have to be an internationally recognized principle that could individually be translated into different life decisions.

If this point were ever reached, Palestinian identity might have to be renegotiated by Palestinian individuals and communities. But as long as the Palestinians are in exile and are not just economic migrants, the national and political aspects of Palestinian identity will translate into national demands and can act to unify Palestinians. These political aspects of Palestinian national identity are of existential importance for Palestinian refugees in Lebanon and can have a very different meaning for Palestinians there than, for example, for a Palestinian businessman in Chicago. Both have the right to choose.

The question here is the future of Palestinian identities; thus, the discussion will be taken a step further and will relate Palestinian identity to global developments of transnational identities, global movement, and migration as a way of life.

Diaspora, Homeland, and Transnational Identities

Appadurai, in arguing for a transnational anthropology, has remarked that group identities, and their social, cultural, and territorial reproduction, are increasingly influenced by migration, regrouping in new locations, and the reconstruction of group histories (Appadurai 1991, 191). This adds a new non-localized quality to ethnic and national projects. Thus, perceptions of home, diaspora, and national identity are redefined by people living in a "world of movement" and by those studying them.

By defining Palestinian migration as a particular case, but still in relation to general global processes of migration and movement, the future of the Palestinian people as one between homeland and diaspora is inevitable. Many authors advance the argument that members of diaspora communities live their lives between homeland and diaspora, concerned with developments in the homeland as well as the diaspora country. Both places can in different ways be considered home, and in fact this being between two homes can be experienced as a comfortable space to inhabit.

The term "at home in diaspora" (Pattie 1994, 185) was coined to describe Armenians outside Armenia. Pattie points out that their concept of home is mobile and nomadic, in that they define home less as the place in which they live than as the place where their family is. Some members of a diaspora can accept the diaspora as a permanent condition, while others in the same group or community insist on conserving nationalism across borders and so support social and political organizations in order to maintain the ideal of an Armenian nation and the dream of return to the homeland (Pattie 1994, 186).

For part of the Palestinian diaspora, similar patterns are apparent, while the national aspirations and the absence of a secure homeland keep the largest part of the Palestinian diaspora under unacceptable conditions. Thus, they are less able to accept the permanence of their exile, and see return as the only desirable solution.

And yet, as this study shows, even for those who do return, settling in Palestine is not the only option. Many younger Palestinians, especially those who are educated, develop more and more professional and personal mobility and consider it possible to live abroad and still be Palestinian.

The respondents of this study, by virtue of their privileged situation in terms of social and economic background and available education, are part of Palestine's future elite. They will be or are already lawyers, journalists, scholars, teachers, and politicians and can thus influence the development of Palestine whether from within the homeland or from the diaspora. Some of them already have a transnational identity and feel connected to more than one place in the world. They also possess the cross-cultural skills to navigate different societies and cultural settings.

The creation of a Palestinian state, like the Oslo process itself, would be a new, but temporary challenge to Palestinian identity. In the future, Palestinians may become part of international diaspora communities and may join the global network of migrants.

Conclusion

> It is impossible to "go home" again, for neither home nor migrant stayed the same.   (CHAMBERS 1994, 74)

This study has presented examples of Palestinian return experiences as part of the larger scheme of Palestinian migration, which, over the last century, has been described as a form of "conflict migration," thus placing individual return experiences into the context of flight, exile, diaspora, and work migration.

Most Palestinians today are not living within the borders of historical Palestine. They are refugees and continue to live in host countries under a variety of legal and economic conditions. Each of them has different plans and opportunities for the future. Despite their diverse situations, Palestine remains the most important reference point for their lives.

Historically, Palestinian national identity emerged as a result of political changes in the Middle East in the first half of the twentieth century and was further developed in the aftermath of the Nakba in 1948. The uprooting of a large segment of Palestinian society from their homeland, and their subsequent experience as refugee exiles in neighboring Arab countries hindered the initial stages of the development of a Palestinian national movement. Within two decades this experience proved to be the single most important factor in the emergence of a Palestinian national consciousness. Palestinian historiography and the memories of

Palestinian society and life before 1948 have played a vital role in preserving Palestinian heritage and identity and passing it on to new generations. For those in exile, collective memory, literature, and visual arts were important sources for learning what it means to be a Palestinian. More recently, media and the Internet have become alternative sources of knowledge about Palestine and the Palestinians. Media coverage of the First Intifada (1987–1991) in particular helped young Palestinians identify with their fellow Palestinians in Palestine and generated a new sense of pride in being Palestinian. As this media coverage was often not favorable to the Palestinians (reflecting Israeli and pro-Israeli politics), Palestinians have learned to read between the lines and have also turned to independent sources of information, as is evident through the proliferation of Web sites and e-mail lists.

Palestinian identities have developed differently in different host countries. Many factors influence the formation of identities. This study has built on a concept of changing identities and has argued for recognizing the multiple nature of personal, political, and cultural identities within every individual. The empirical material demonstrates that the situation in the host country, the existence of a Palestinian community, the initial circumstances for leaving Palestine, and the involvement in Palestinian politics are some factors that are crucial to a sense of Palestinian identity. The young respondents of this study substantiate this claim.

As discussed earlier, Palestinians have been called a diaspora, a term originally applied only to Jews. More recently, the term diaspora has been applied to other dispersed and scattered peoples. In the context of this discussion, diasporas appear as a feature of modern life. And although the centrality of the homeland for the diasporic imagination is stressed in most of these approaches, they tend to take the dispersal as a fact of life, or, to go further, as a chance for cultural development. Yet, and certainly in the Palestinian case, this runs the risk of devaluing national aspirations and denying the right to historical justice and a national homeland. Thus, the term "Palestinian diaspora" should be used cautiously.

To look at the Palestinian diaspora as merely a case of migrancy and globalization runs the risk of misrepresenting the collective and individual suffering of countless Palestinians over the last century. Yet, it far more comprehensively explains the emergence of hybrid and diverse identities. Palestinian identity is, especially among the younger generation studied here, only one of their identities. However, only the Palestinians have the right to declare a post-national state of existence or declare that the search for the homeland is now over.

Philosophical insight into injustice, uprooting, and the postmodern homelessness of the individual cannot make redundant the need for protest, resistance, and demands for change. What it can offer is understanding, the emergence of other voices, and the achievement of an awareness about how we can change our "realities."

Palestine as a symbolic, imagined, and real homeland is central to Palestinian self-definitions. The image of a homeland to which to return from exile shaped the expectations of Palestinians in the diaspora countries and was thus a defining factor for the possible return experience itself. One has to distinguish between images that are based on the personal memories of those who emigrated from Palestine and those of the following generations who do not have such personal memories. Parts of the Palestinian diaspora communities were able to visit Palestine, while others (and in fact the majority of the exile Palestinians) were barred from visiting. Thus, there is a clear distinction between images of Palestine that were entirely imagined and those that were based on memories. The distinction largely coincided with their different reasons for leaving Palestine and with their level of political engagement in the diaspora. The images of Palestine can be categorized as those of a cultural as opposed to those of an imagined national homeland, *al-balad* on the one hand, and *al-watan,* on the other.

The return of a considerable number of Palestinians has turned the dream of returning to the homeland into a possibility. But the return of selected Palestinians, those who were to work for the Palestinian Authority and those who could afford to return, has also been perceived as a betrayal of the right of return of all Palestinian refugees. Simultaneously, the installation of Palestinian pseudo-state institutions, led by the "outside" leadership, challenged the leadership aspirations of the Palestinian "inside" elite that had gained influence and power during the Intifada. The popular sentiments of local Palestinians against returnees reflected this shift in power distribution. The PA is the pillar of the Oslo process and one of its most important results. Thus, criticism of the process, discontent with the PA, and disagreements between local Palestinians and returnees were often expressed in one breath. The return of a segment of the Palestinian diaspora community has resulted in the clash of different definitions of Palestinian identity in Palestine, and thus the return process entailed negotiating these contradicting identities. This negotiation was further complicated by the fact that the young respondents of this study were not in positions of power in Palestinian society. They perceived the negative images of returnees and the tension and occasional conflicts as unfair to them, while displaying considerable understanding and patience for the attitude of local Palestinians.

But far more importantly, the return process took place inside the returnees, taking the form of a challenge to the identity that they formed in exile. This return process has been described in pre-liminal, liminal, and post-liminal stages. The concept of liminality allows us to recognize return as taking place in different steps, and stresses the fluidity of the process. Upon arrival in Palestine, the young returnees temporarily lost their social identities and had to negotiate their position in the newly found Palestinian society. They were forced to recognize the realities of Palestine, to compare them to their images, and to cope with the discrepancies. Options for closing the gap included adjusting their concepts of their own identity as well as attempting to change the reality of Palestine. The respondents of this study exercised both options, in many cases combining the two through a long and painful process of negotiation. Ultimately, recognition of Palestine as a real homeland, and integration into Palestinian society was possible for some, while others had to cope with "eternal liminality."

This state of being a transnational with a floating idea of "home" and nationality can be as much a blessing as a burden. Where it was perceived as a burden, the young returnees tended to have future plans that were supposed to provide the stability and certainty they longed for. They hoped to settle down, either in Palestine or somewhere else, start a family, and build a career to ensure that they might feel at home somewhere someday. Those who saw their transnationalism as a blessing stressed the choices and opportunities that were also a characteristic of their youth.

For the respondents, the return experience resulted in a process of rewriting aspects of their Palestinian and other identities. The confrontation with the realities of Palestine and other Palestinians has for all of them resulted in strengthening their Palestinian identity, whether politically, culturally, or even religiously. Even for those who left again, to study or live elsewhere, the image of Palestine has been transformed into a more realistic picture, enhanced by individual memories. The return process was a mutual adjustment process between locals and returnees that simultaneously altered both groups' previous definitions of Palestinian identity. The realities of Palestine, the ongoing occupation, the difficult economic and social conditions, and the problems with the Palestinian Authority replaced the idealized image with a complex picture of Palestinian society.

Epilogue

Since I left Palestine in the summer of 1999, much has happened to Palestine, the Palestinians in general, and the respondents of this study in particular. I pointed to the events and developments of the Second Intifada and its impact on Palestinian society in the preface.

I have been back only once: In the summer of 2001 I went on a brief trip to Jerusalem to lecture to Palestinian and Israeli students. I had been planning on going to Ramallah to meet and speak with some of the many young Palestinians I had met through my fieldwork, but it turned out to be impossible. The West Bank was completely closed off, and I was not brave enough to try to sneak in and out, given the Israeli checkpoints and unreliable transportation. Even my visit to the Old City of Jerusalem was short: What was a ten-minute drive from Tantour (between Bethlehem and Jerusalem) and back now took two hours each way because of the many Israeli checkpoints.

The situation in Palestine has made it impossible for me to stay in touch with many of the interviewees. I have, over the years, heard from some of them, either through e-mail or through Palestine-related activities, but I have lost contact with many. This is particularly true for those I spoke with in Arabic, as many of them did not use e-mail.

No numbers are available on how many Palestinians might have left the West Bank and Gaza since the outbreak of the Second Intifada. The daily hardships, the economic depression, and the ongoing attacks on Palestinian towns and villages, combined with the utter lack of Palestinian control over any aspect of their situation, has forced many to consider leaving their homeland to seek safety and stability for their families. Jordan has put additional restrictions on Palestinians trying to enter that country. The Jordanian government was concerned that the situation in the West Bank would create a new wave of refugees, and Jordan felt incapable of absorbing any more Palestinians.

I knew in 1999 that many of the young Amrikan were planning to leave Palestine to attend college in the United States and elsewhere. One of them, Zaynab, has stayed in touch. She started college in the United States, but a few months into the Second Intifada she decided that she needed to be with her family in Ramallah and went back. She wrote to me that she felt that her country needed her and that it was worse for her to look at the destruction from afar than to be there. Back in Ramallah she continued to write about the destruction, the despair, and the loss of friends. The last time I heard from her, she had gone to Jordan for safety.

Some of the voluntary returnees have chosen to stay on and share the suffering of their people, while trying to help in different ways. Kamila is working as an independent journalist and sends out news briefings to the world. Allen, Tariq, and Hiyam are working for different NGOs and are among those who document developments in the Occupied Territories and call for the attention of the international community and the solidarity movement.

Sandy wrote to me to tell me that she had left Palestine but had married a Palestinian man and had had a daughter. She said:

> The effect of leaving Palestine and getting the horrors out of my system has made it very difficult for me to imagine going back there at the moment, especially with the little one, although of course she has to meet her grandparents at some point. . . . I feel sorry for her sometimes that she couldn't just be Spanish or Chinese or something definable; instead she is condemned to a lifetime's awareness of the oppression of her people. My husband thinks it doesn't matter and that life there can be beautiful anyway.

She also said that she found it hard to be in the United Kingdom, where people could not even begin to imagine the situation in Palestine and did not have a sense of what oppression was. Doubtlessly, her return to Palestine has helped her discover and reassert the Palestinian aspects of her identity and has resulted in her creating a new Palestinian family.

That the right of return is not likely to disappear from the Palestinian agenda and is in fact the central demand of many Palestinians in considering any kind of solution to the Israeli-Palestinian conflict may be illustrated by an incident in July 2003. The Palestinian Center for Policy and Survey Research (PCPSR), one of the Palestinian institutions that carries out regular public opinion polls among Palestinians in the West Bank and Gaza, had gathered journalists for a news conference on a recent study that the center had conducted on attitudes toward the right of return. On the day the findings were supposed to be announced, Palestinians attacked the office of the director of the center and distributed a news release conveying that the right of return was sacred and could not be given up either by the Palestinian leadership or through the findings of any researcher. Western journalists were quick in lauding the poll as demonstrating that the Palestinian refugee issue might disappear with less effort than expected after all. The *New York Times* described the incident under the headline: "Palestinian Mob Attacks Pollster over Study on 'Right of Return'" (*New York Times*, July 14, 2003). The article pointed out that the crowd was trying to send a message to the Palestinian prime minister, Mahmud Abbas, that he must not compromise on the issue of return, but it also contended that the incident illustrated the state of lawlessness in the Palestinian territories. The opinion poll, conducted among fewer than five thousand Palestinian refugees in Lebanon, Jordan, the West Bank, and Gaza, had found that 95 percent of respondents demanded that Israel recognize the right of return (see www.pcpsr.org). Given particular and very limited choices regarding a final settlement of the return issue, only 10 percent of respondents chose permanent residence in Israel, and even fewer respondents would have accepted Israeli citizenship as a precondition for their return. More than half of the respondents were reportedly willing to accept compensation and would return to homes in the West Bank and Gaza. Khalil Shikaki, the director of the PCPSR concluded that "refugees were less interested in being nationalist standard-bearers than in living fuller lives" (*New York Times*, July 14, 2003). The attack on him, and the responses that followed the press release about the poll, show that many Palestinians do not agree with his assessment. The poll did recognize the need to address the realities of Palestinian refugees and was carried out in agreement with the Palestinian Authority, but it can also be read as an attempt to make the refugee issue disappear by pointing to statistics. However, the conflict over the right of return and the search for a solution remain a question of principles versus realities.

The respondents of this study are but a small group of the Palestinian people. They were young at the time of the interviews and all of them still had to make many choices about their future. It is safe to assume that more than half of them have left Palestine since I spoke to them. Others have chosen to stay, and some are among the activists and intellectuals who work to keep the fate of the Palestinians in the public eye and in the headlines. All the returnees and those respondents who are part of the Palestinian diaspora will carry some of the responsibility for achieving justice and finding a solution as well as for living their lives as Palestinians.

List of Respondents

I have used pseudonyms for all interviewees throughout the study. The following list provides the age of the respondent at the time of the interview (year of birth in parentheses) and date, place, and language of the interview. I have chosen Arabic pseudonyms for Arabic names and English pseudonyms for English names.

'Adil, 32 years old (1967), 2/22/99, Chicago, English
Allen, 26 years old (1973), 5/11/99, Ramallah, English
Amin, 26 years old (1973), 2/20/99, Chicago, English
Amina, 22 years old (1976), 4/01/99, Ramallah, Arabic
Amira, 18 years old (1980), 1/26/99, Al-Bireh, English
Amy, 16 years old (1983), 4/01/99, Ramallah, English
Ayat, 17 years old (1982), 4/29/99, Al-Bireh, English
'Aziz, 17 years old (1981), 11/24/98, Ramallah, English
Basma, 19 years old (1980), 3/06/99, Ramallah, English
Dalia, 23 years old (1975), 11/30/98, Ramallah, English
Halima, 20 years old (1979), 5/28/99, Ramallah, Arabic/English
Hamdi, 18 years old (1980), 11/05/98, Ramallah, English
Hanadi, 19 years old (1980), 3/13/99, Ramallah, Arabic
Hiyam, 27 years old (1971), 6/06/99, Ramallah, English
Ibtisam, 17 years old (1982), 4/08/99, Ramallah, English
Jane, 17 years old (1981), 11/08/98, Ramallah, English
Janet, 15 years old (1983), 11/08/98, Ramallah, English
Jimmy, 19 years old (1979), 11/03/98, Ramallah, English
Kamila, 24 years old (1975), 2/09/99 and 25/05/99, Ramallah, English
Lana, 17 years old (1981), 3/12/99 Ramallah, Arabic
Majid, 27 years old (1971), 11/23/98, Ramallah, Arabic
Mamduh, 25 years old (1973), 5/05/99, Ramallah, Arabic
Mansur, 28 years old (1970), 5/30/99, Ramallah, English
Marwan, 24 years old (1975), 4/11/99, Ramallah, Arabic
Mukhlis, 17 years old (1981), 1/12/99, Ramallah, English

Muna, 20 years old (1979), 3/07/99, Ramallah, Arabic
Munir, 20 years old (1978), 5/08/99, Ramallah, English
Munzir, 17 years old (1982), 4/09/99, Ramallah, English
Nabila, 15 years old (1984), 4/11/99, Ramallah, English
Nadir, 28 years old (1970), 8/21/98, Maryland, English
Najma, 21 years old (1977), 3/25/99, Birzeit, Arabic
Nigel, 23 years old (1976), 5/25/99, Ramallah, English
Nimr, 29 years old (1971), 3/10/99, Ramallah, Arabic
Nizar, 31 years old (1966), 8/25/98, Virginia, English
Paul, 26 years old (1972), 6/08/98, Jerusalem, English
Qasim, 29 years old (1970), 3/04/99, Ramallah, Arabic
Rami, 17 years old (1982), 4/09/99, Ramallah, English
Randa, 24 years old (1974), 8/24/98, Washington, D.C., English
Ranya, 16 years old (1983), 5/11/99, Ramallah, English
Rayda, 24 years old (1975), 3/05/99, Al-Bireh, English
Sa'ad, 34 years old (1964), 8/20/98, Virginia, English
Salim, 19 years old (1979), 8/20/98, Washington, D.C., English
Sandy, 25 years old (1974), 4/01/99, Ramallah, English
Shuruq, 16 years old (1983), 4/01/99, Ramallah, English
Sulayman, 19 years old (1980), 4/06/99, Ramallah, English
Susan, 28 years old (1970), 8/11/98, Washington, D.C., English
Tanya, 22 years old (1976), 2/22/99, Chicago, English
Tariq, 23 years old (1976), 5/26/99, Ramallah, English
Yasin, 17 years old (1981), 11/04/98, Ramallah, English
Zaynab, 18 years old (1981), 4/11/99, Ramallah, English

Notes

1. Introduction: Palestinian Migration, Refugees, and Return

1. Shiblak in 1997 estimated that there were sixty thousand returnees; Tansley speaks of there having been fifty-two thousand then. See Tansley 1997, 5 and 51. Robinson, in 2000, estimated that there were a hundred thousand returnees. None of these numbers includes Palestinians who came to Palestine with foreign passports and tourist visas and decided to stay (Robinson 2000).

2. The situation of Palestinian refugees in Lebanon, Jordan, Syria, and Egypt has been well studied (see works by Sayigh, Peteet, Brand, CERMOC, and FAFO). Growing up and spending one's whole life in a refugee camp in any Arab country is key to the identities of the Palestinians who had this experience. The Palestinian refugees in the camps have to be seen as the counter-notion to the returnees, as these refugees are the ones who could not return until now, and they remain extremely marginalized and underprivileged as a group.

3. The collection of oral histories has become a focus of attention, and not only in the context of Palestine. Although personal memories tend to be affected by the interviewer, adjustments in memory, and the general wish that individuals have to give meaning to their own history, the method lends a voice to those who are not represented, or are only silently represented, by the official history.

4. I was working as a researcher at SHAML — The Palestinian Diaspora and Refugee Center in downtown Ramallah.

5. Palestinians refer to the events in 1947–48 as Nakba, which means catastrophe.

6. Salim Tamari has shown how research projects and funding have shaped Palestinian Studies in Palestine and often reinforce the imbalance of power between locals, local researchers, and foreigners (Tamari 1994, 1997).

7. This approach is not unproblematic either and reproduces some of the imbalance of power between researcher and "subject" (Abu-Lughod 1986, 1993).

8. These are phrases taken from different Palestinian authors: "songs for a country no longer known" from Barghouti 1998, 59; "sense of self as a people" from Said 1986b, 33; "woven from memories, from songs, from stories of elders, from pictures, from old coins and stamps" from Kanafani 1995, 40.

9. The number of Palestinian refugees in 1948 has been debated, and one finds a wide range of estimates. The UNRWA uses 726,000, and this can be taken as an average.

10. At the time, the United Nations adopted and thus reinforced a patriarchal ideology and has not changed this definition since its first formulation.

11. There are now detailed studies about the social structure, economic development, and political conditions in the refugee camps. Studies by Rosemary Sayigh (1977a, 1977b, 1979, 1994, 1998, and others), Peteet (1987, 1993), and Natur (1993) concern the camps in Lebanon. The Norwegian FAFO Foundation (Gilen et al. 1994; Endresen and Ovensen 1994; Pedersen and Hooper 1998) have studied the camps in Jordan. In the light of the peace process, Zureik (1994, 1996), Tamari (1996), and Rashad Khalidi (1999) have all published new work.

12. Rogge provides numerous examples of repatriation of refugees in Africa, including the case of Ugandans repatriated from neighboring countries between 1984 and 1987. In 1971, large numbers of Bangladeshis were repatriated from India. Van Hear cites cases of forced and voluntary repatriation, such as of Turks from Bulgaria in 1989 and Yemenis from Saudi Arabia in 1990. An important case of resettlement in a different country was the movement of Ugandans of Indian origin to the United Kingdom in 1972. Many of the Ugandans eventually tried to return to Uganda in 1993 after the political situation had changed (Van Hear 1997, 34).

13. For a concise overview of the civil and citizenship rights of Palestinians in Arab host countries, see Shiblak 1996b; for the policies and resolutions of Arab states, especially the Arab League, see Shiblak 1998.

14. In 1947 the Arab population of historical Palestine numbered approximately 1.3 million people. In 2000 it was estimated that there were between 7.7 and 9 million Palestinians around the world.

15. The draft of the Palestinian citizenship law has adopted a similar definition, thus declaring only the children of Palestinian *fathers* to be prospective citizens of a Palestinian state. See Davis 1996, 64.

16. The terms "return myth" and "return illusion," as applied to Turkish migrants in Germany, imply the insistence of migrants (especially those of the second generation) on their inevitable return to the homeland. This myth works as a defining factor of identity in differentiation from the German host society and can ease the tension between the old center of loyalty, Turkey, and the current center of life, Germany. See Mandel 1989, and Wolbert 1995, 25. For many work migrants a total cutoff from their home country would be too painful and disrupting to bear, and, thus, they keep the option of return open.

2. Palestinian National Identity, Memory, and History

1. After 1948 many of the Christian Palestinians who fled to Lebanon were naturalized, mainly for political consideration about the confessional balance of the country.

2. Quote from his senior thesis "Palestinianism — the Making of the Palestinian National Movement, 1870-1970," 1997. As much of the information in this story is

personal, I decided not to disclose Tariq's real name, although I quote from a scholarly text.

3. This overview only lists important steps in the the historical development of the Palestinian identity, relying on widely accepted "historical facts." Details and arguments about the history of the Palestinian national movement, especially the institutional and political history of the PLO, can be found in Cobban 1984, Y. Sayigh 1997, and Brand 1988a, among others.

4. Two religious figures, Hajj Amin al-Husseini and Izzadin Al-Qassam, were declared heroes of Palestinian history, and their narrative was developed into nationalist mythology. Budeiri also notes the use of religious terminology such as *jihad* (holy struggle), *shahid* (martyr), and *al-ard al-muqaddasa* (the Holy Land) for nationalist discourse. These and other terms are still important in the Palestinian discourse (Budeiri 1997, 196).

5. "Nationalist discourse thereby uses rural imagery to produce a powerfully holistic vision of Palestinian culture" (Swedenburg 1990, 25). This symbolism not only ties the image of the Palestinian population to the land of Palestine, but also allows to "paper over" social and class differences within the Palestinian national movement (26).

6. Both the Israeli and Palestinian versions of history, especially of the events of 1948, can be described as identity-founding national narratives. Recent Israeli historiography shows significant changes since new historians such as Benny Morris, Simha Flapan, and Ilan Pappe published the first studies. These scholarly contributions were followed by more publicly received contributions such as the TV documentary TKUMA describing the founding of Israel. It has to be remembered that the majority of Israelis still subscribe to the version of history that has dominated since 1948 and is so crucial to the "founding myth of Israel" (Flapan 1987a).

7. Much of the material written by Abu-Sitta in recent years has been made available through the Palestinian Return Committee (PRC), based in London; see their Web site at www.prc.org.uk. One can debate whether Abu-Sitta's work is in fact academic, as the materials he produces serve activist purposes and tend to be rather argumentative in tone.

8. Examples include the autobiography of Edward Said, *Out of Place,* published in 1999; reflective articles by Musa Budeiri, Salma Khadra Jayyusi, Yezid Sayigh, and others, published in 1998 in the *Journal of Palestine Studies* under the title "Reflections on al-Nakba"; and many others. For a discussion of Palestinian autobiographies, see Hammer 2003.

3. The Country of My Dreams

1. Cohen emphasizes the religious connotation of the term diaspora for the Jews, while at the same time pointing out that diaspora did not always suggest trauma, dis-

placement, and exile. Rather, the Jewish diaspora, in its dispersal, found space for the creative development of the community and successful trade relations.

2. The chapter on victim diasporas focuses on the African and Armenian diasporas. As editor of a subsequent series on global diasporas, Cohen invited the writing of a monograph on the Palestinian diaspora (Lindholm and Hammer 2003).

3. It seems ironic to put the colonizer and the colonized into the same diaspora category.

4. The center has published a number of monographs about the situation of the Palestinian communities in Syria, Egypt, and Iraq, including one dealing with the question and feasibility of return, and another one about the residency status and civil rights of Palestinian refugees in various Arab host countries. See Qudsiyeh 1997; Sahli 1996; Shiblak and Davis 1995; Shiblak 1998; and Yassin, Hanafi, and Saint-Martin 1995.

5. For these insights into Islamic philosophy I am grateful to Dr. Seyyed Hossein Nasr and the lecture on Suhrawardi that he gave in 2000. In his *Philosophical Allegories and Mystical Treatises,* the Islamic philosopher Shihabuddin Yahya Suhrawardi (1153–1191) tells the "Tale of Occidental Exile," in which *al-ghurba,* exile, is equated with being away from God, the source of everything. Thus, home, exile, and return take on different meanings, and truly being at home is not possible in this world.

6. Turki's oeuvre and the development of his ideas, thoughts, and style over the last three decades reflect so much of the Palestinian experience that I feel compelled to dedicate more than a footnote to him. This study is unfortunately not the place to discuss his work at length.

7. Examples are poems like "The Most Beautiful Love" (*Ajmal hubb*) from the collection "Olive Leaves" (*Awraq al-zaytun*), published in 1964; "Lover of Palestine" (*'Ashiq min Filastin*); and "Poems about an Old Love" (*Qasa'id 'an hubbin qadim*), published in 1966.

8. In two other translations, the Arabic title "Al-laji" was translated into "The Exile." See Hijjawi 1968, 23, and al-Messiri 1970, 76.

9. I have developed these thoughts in more detail in an essay on the recreation of the lost homeland Palestine. See Hammer 2000.

10. Sulayman Mansur was born 1947 in Birzeit, Palestine. He studied Fine Arts in Jerusalem (1967–1970), was the head of the League of Palestinian Artists (1986–1990), and, since 1995, has been the director of the Al-Wasiti Art Center in Jerusalem. He has presented his work at numerous international exhibitions, and won the Palestine Prize for the Arts (1998). (I am grateful to Al-Wasiti Art Center in Jerusalem for providing biographical information on the Palestinian painters.)

11. Fathi Ghabin was born 1947 in Heribia, Gaza. He is a self-taught artist committed to literature, politics, and culture, and was head of the Fathi Ghabin Center for the Arts (est. 1995).

12. Nabil 'Anani was born 1943 in Latrun, Palestine. He holds a bachelor's degree in fine arts from Alexandria, Egypt, and a master's in archaeology from Al-Quds University in Jerusalem. He has been the head of the League of Palestinian Artists since 1998. He has had solo exhibitions in Palestine, has participated in nu-

merous group exhibitions all over the world, and received the Palestine Prize for the Arts (1997).

13. The distinction between political and economic is, in the Palestinian case, rather difficult to make. JanMohamed identifies four main categories of people who cross borders: exile, immigrant, colonialist, and scholar. The two categories relevant to us are exile and immigrant, which he differentiates as follows: "While both the exile and the immigrant cross the border between one social or national group and another, the exile's stance toward the new host culture is negative, the immigrant's positive" (JanMohamed 1992, 101). In Palestinian life, the lines are not clearly drawn, and much work migration is planned to be temporary but later becomes permanent emigration.

4. Return to Palestine: Dreams and Realities

1. "Poetry is not the exclusive idiom of the educated elite among Palestinians. Rather, the opposite is true. Poetry to us is a currency of everyday exchange, a vital starting point to meaning. A child recites poetry. A politician quotes a line in poetry, to prove a point. A personal letter contains, always, at least one line of poetry. Moments of despair in everyday life, moments of joy, are celebrated or defined in poetry. . . . People define themselves and their environment in verse" (Turki 1988, 45).

2. The novel is a thought-provoking parable about contradicting loyalties, and poses the question of whether relation by blood is more important than cultural and human aspects of life, a concept that deeply challenges the notion of roots. The end of the novel indicates that social parenthood and care can overrule blood relation, whatever the circumstances may be. Kanafani also portrays Israelis as humans like Palestinians, with the same feelings of responsibility, care, and love toward the child. In raising these questions, the novel can be seen as a contribution to the discussion about identity and loyalty and thus central to this study.

3. It includes names such as Haidar Abdul Shafi, Ibrahim Abu-Lughod, Salman Abu-Sittah, Naseer Aruri, Hanan Ashrawi, Azmi Bishara, Noam Chomsky, Marc Ellis, Norman Finkelstein, Muhammad Hallaj, Shafiq al-Hout, Faysal al Husseini, Ali Jarbawi, Fouad Moughrabi, Ilan Pappe, Hasib Sabbagh, Edward Said, Susan Akram, Atif Kubursi, and Suhail Natur.

4. The question is "whether individual human rights recognized under international law can be protected and promoted in the Palestinian refugee case when such rights collide with collective rights under international law—in this case, the right to self-determination" (Akram 2000, 8). The Palestinian position in the Oslo I and II negotiations and beyond has been rife with such contradictions.

5. Clearly, the Palestinian leadership is unwilling or incapable of openly discussing these ideas. As a result, the Palestinian negotiating position, apart from being politically weak in general, reacts to political developments instead of offering a clear framework for a solution. The fragile balance between representing the Palestinian people and their best interests, and the Palestinian leadership's struggle to increase its

own power prevents a fruitful dialogue and a consistent stand. Too many concessions can and will be interpreted as betrayal, while insisting on principles can prevent any solution at all.

6. Interview with Ali Jarbawi, April 15, 1999, Birzeit University (together with Betty Dhamers).

7. Interview with Sharif Kanaana, April 18, 1999, Ramallah.

8. The survey conducted by Dr. Yussif Abdelhaqq in conjunction with the Center for Palestine Research and Studies (CPRS) in Nablus led to a workshop at the center, but the study was never published in its entirety and was not available at the center. However, a summary of the workshop was published in Arabic.

9. The English texts include Moughrabi 1997, Karmi 1994, M. A. Khalidi 1995a, Kanafani 1995, and Abunimah 1998. Examples of Arabic reflections are Muhammad 1997, Zaqtan 1997, M. Barghouti 1997, and Khadr 1997. All the Arabic texts appeared in one issue of the cultural journal *Al-Carmel* published in Ramallah. The texts by Barghouti and Khadr have been partly translated into English and published by the *Journal of Palestine Studies;* see Khadr 1997 and Barghouti 1998.

10. When talking about the young respondents of this study who returned from Arab countries, I will use the spelling Aideen. The correct transliteration would be *'Aidun,* or, colloquially, *'Aidin.* I find Aideen easier to read in text.

11. A national number (*raqam watani*) was assigned to Palestinians who applied to return and work for the PA. The compiled lists of these people had to be approved by Israel before any of these Palestinians could enter the country. The "return permits" also included dependent family members.

12. Quote from Ibtisam's graduation speech at the Friends Boys School in Ramallah on May 23, 1999.

5. The Return Process in Comparison

1. Her unpublished essay was based on fieldwork at Birzeit University in 1995. I am grateful for the opportunity to read this essay and acknowledge here the inspiration I took from it.

2. Interview with Jim Fine, March 31, 1999. He was the principal of the Friends Boys School, where I conducted a number of interviews.

3. This quote is taken from a text that Hiyam wrote after this trip. I am grateful for the opportunity to work with the essay. I have only changed her name to grant her anonymity.

4. For Muslims, Jerusalem is the third holiest place (*thalith al-haramayn*) after Mecca and Medina. *Masjid al-Aqsa,* the farthest mosque, is mentioned in Sura 17, verse 1 of the Qur'an, as referring to *Isra',* the night journey of Muhammad from Mecca to Jerusalem. As mentioned in Sura 53, verse 12, Muhammad ascended in body and spirit from Jerusalem to heaven. *Al-isra' wa-l mi'raj,* the night journey and ascension to heaven, are considered by Muslims a miracle or sign from God. The Dome of the Rock,

Qubbat as-Sakhra, is believed to have been built on the rock from which Muhammad ascended to heaven.

5. Moughrabi 1997, 10: "A kind of social Darwinism seems to dominate Palestinian society, where a crude individualism prevails and where only the fit, the clever, and the well-connected survive. The weak and the poor, along with those who are without *wasta* [influence and contacts in high places] are the losers. During the occupation . . . so many Palestinians have become imbued with the culture of the occupier, becoming rude, aggressive, lacking in common courtesy, and totally unconcerned about anything beyond their own personal welfare. Lying and cheating has become standard operating procedure for many people. These are not the same people I left behind many years ago. . . . No common courtesy or mercy in public transport or on the street is shown older people, women with children, or people with obvious disabilities. Driving behavior reflects both the lack of common courtesy and the absence of an authority that punishes violations of basic rules."

6. The article states: "Conflicts often erupt in extended families, with the returnees criticized by their West Bank-bred relatives for not speaking enough Arabic or [for] dressing improperly. Elderly Palestinians accustomed to complete obedience suddenly encounter back talk from Palestinian American youngsters used to defending their views. The Americans sometimes refuse to eat the Arabic dishes prepared at home, offending relatives" (Associated Press July 30, 1999).

7. The article also gives a figure of three hundred thousand Palestinian Americans living in the United States and thirty thousand having returned from the United States to the West Bank and Gaza. The source of these figures is not specified, and both seem extremely high to me.

8. Many of the issues of gossip, social control, and the use of public spaces apply to locals as well, in particular to Palestinian women, and are negotiated in similar ways. Here these issues are approached from the perspective of the returnees.

9. In the Palestinian context, the Intifada has played an important role in clarifying these two positions. For a more detailed discussion on this topic, see Hammami 1990, and Heiberg and Ovensen 1993, 250–270. In the Palestinian context, the hijab as a symbol has been invested by different groups of women with religious, nationalistic, social, and cultural meanings.

10. That does not mean that it never happens but rather that the respondents did not tell me about it.

11. Information about Birzeit and the election results can be found at www.birzeit .edu.

12. English-speaking returnees participated in the Arabic language program for foreigners, though they needed intense classes in modern standard Arabic, including grammar and writing. These returnees spoke enough Arabic to understand instruction but had problems taking exams and writing papers. During my research I did not come across English-speaking Birzeit students, but Wernefeldt recognized them as a distinct group in her study.

13. FBS has been operating in Ramallah/Al-Bireh for more than a hundred years.

14. Interview with Jim Fine, March 31, 1999.

15. Al-Urduniyya, Al-Jenan School, Bridge Academy, and others, all of them in the Ramallah/Jerusalem area. This fact could be explained by the fact that there is a concentration of returnees with only English-speaking children in this area, but some of the respondents told me that their parents decided to live in or around Ramallah to allow their children into these schools.

16. Though a Christian school, the student population of FBS was 70 percent Muslim. According to the new PA curricula, Muslims are instructed in Islam and Christians in Christianity, while both Muslims and Christians attend ethics classes to learn about and discuss questions of morality and ethics.

6. Rewriting of Identities in the Context of Diaspora and Return

1. The PLO had a representative office in Kuwait and was allowed to run schools and social institutions, but they had no military forces there.

2. Both studies are now historical. The situation of Palestinians in Kuwait has changed dramatically since the Gulf War in 1991, when a large number of them were expelled in response to PLO support for Saddam Hussein.

3. With the American media highly focused on domestic politics and tending to disregard foreign policy issues, many Palestinian Americans get their information from the Internet and satellite TV.

4. Muslims consider Palestine a holy place, thus explaining Muslim organizations' commitment to Palestine. Rational considerations, such as representation in the American context as a minority, support choosing the larger Muslim community over the Arab American one. The secular orientation of Arab American organizations has, for more religiously inclined Palestinian Americans, always posed a problem. Also, religious-political identity interferes less with loyalty to the United States than does a competing national identity. Palestinian American Muslims are not losing their Palestinian identity; instead, they create a set of overlapping identities. The events of September 11, 2001, have changed the experiences of Arabs and Muslims in the United States and have driven identity debates in a whole new direction.

5. The first term indicates a speaker who can clearly distinguish the two languages and apply the appropriate grammatical rules. Mixing the languages (or even code switching) is conscious and is only used when the communication partner can also understand both languages. A naive bilingual would apply the grammatical rules of one language to the other and would not be capable of recognizing and correcting mistakes in either language.

6. In the United States, instruction in mosques and Islamic centers usually takes place on Sunday. Many respondents recall that these mosques and Islamic centers were far away, and they could not deal with the strict atmosphere and mode of teaching. At their young age, their interest in religious instruction seemed to have been low as well. Arabic tutors were often described as boring and not motivating.

7. Arabic is not easy for speakers of Indo-European languages to learn. Palestinians in the Arab world and in Palestine itself have high expectations about the ability of Palestinians everywhere to be able to speak their native language. The result is a lack of appreciation for any progress made along the way to learning it, and constant pressure on Palestinians outside the Arab world to learn more. Many young exile Palestinians in Western countries seem to feel that they will never live up to these high expectations and thus give up on the whole project.

8. The importance and distribution of literary works in a particular society is often overestimated, and social realities are not considered at all. Palestinians have a higher literacy rate than other Arabs, but literacy does not imply the interest or ability to read poems, novels, and short stories.

9. These statements were always a bit apologetic and made me wonder if it was my anthropological projection that gave these issues their importance, as though I somehow assumed that because literature and reading was an important part of my childhood, the same would be true for my interviewees.

10. In the context of Arab American literature, book titles such as Orfalea's *Wrapping the Grape Leaves* (1982) and *Grape Leaves* (1988), and Joanne Kadi's *Food for Our Grandmothers* (1994) reflect the importance assigned to Arabic food for preserving cultural identity.

11. What may be considered "unnecessary" or "excessive" by Western standards is a way of demonstrating higher socioeconomic status. The display of such virtues is a mark of respect and honor in many societies.

12. Interview with Ali Jarbawi, April 15, 1999.

13. Jane told me during the interview that she thought less than 50 percent of the Palestinians in Palestine were Christians (the actual number is 3 percent). She also thought that there were hardly any Muslims in Lebanon, which is why she would want to live there rather than in Palestine. I do not know if this was just her personal misinformation, or if it reflected the perceptions of Christians in Palestine.

14. Interview with Ali Jarbawi, April 15, 1999.

15. I agree with Baker's observations but deeply resent her use of language, which implies that some kind of injustice is done to these children by teaching them religion and tradition. This approach does not consider the difficulties immigrant parents face in childrearing, and it dwells on the idea that religion and tradition contradict the Western idea of individualism and compromise the best interests of the children.

7. Home and the Future of Palestinian Identities

1. Jad, Johnson, and Giacaman noted in 2000 that the Palestinian Election Law, which governed the 1996 elections in the West Bank and Gaza, defined Palestinian nationality through either parent. The latest draft of a basic law states that this question will be addressed later. The authors conclude: "The council thus avoids separating Palestinian nationality and Palestinian citizenship, which would be a very difficult

turning point for the Palestinian national movement. Further debates on a nationality law may raise these very prickly questions in which gender issues are subsumed" (Jad, Johnson, and Giacaman 2000, 143).

2. Many male "return visitors" end up spending their vacations in Palestine, not only visiting relatives but being introduced to prospective brides. Also, arranged marriage often take place between Palestinian American returnee girls and young men who come to Palestine for the purpose of choosing a bride to take back to the United States. This is somewhat different from the pattern that Cainkar describes.

3. Passed in 1950, the Israel Law of Return grants citizenship to every descendant of a Jewish parent anywhere in the world.

Bibliography

Abd Rabbeh, Salah. 1996. *The Refugees and the Dream of Return to the Land of the Sad Oranges* [*Al-laji'un wa hulm al-ʿauda ila ard al-burtuqal al-hazin*]. Bethlehem: Badil-Alternative Information Center-Project for Palestinian Refugee and Residency Rights.

Abdelhaqq, Yousif. 1997. A Workshop on the Economic Situation of the Returnees [*Nadwa hawla-l-audaʿa al-iqtisadiyya li-l-ʿaidin*]. *Al-Siyasah al-Filastiniya* 4 (14): 195–201.

Abdulhadi, Mufid. 1998. *The Other Side of the Coin: A Native Palestinian Tells His Story.* Jerusalem: PASSIA.

Abdulrahim, Dima. 1990. Islamic Law, Gender, and the Politics of Exile: The Palestinians in West Berlin. A Case Study. In *Islamic Family Law,* edited by Chibli Mallat and J. Connors, 181–201. London: Graham and Trotman.

Abdul-Shafi, Mustafa. 2000. Of Remembrance and Forgiveness. *Palestine Chronicle,* www.palestinechronicle.com.

Abraham, Nabeel. 1989. Arab American Marginality: Myth and Praxis. *Arab Studies Quarterly* 11 (2–3): 17–44.

Abraham, Sameer Y., and Nabeel Abraham, eds. 1983. *Arabs in the New World: Studies on Arab American Communities.* Detroit: Center for Urban Studies, Wayne State University.

Abu-Laban, Baha, and Michael W. Suleiman. 1989. *Arab Americans: Continuity and Change.* Belmont: Arab American University Graduates Press.

Abu-Lughod, Ibrahim. 1973. Educating a Community in Exile: The Palestinian Experience. *Journal of Palestine Studies* 2 (3): 94–111.

———. 1998. The Last Day Before Jaffa Fell [*Al-yawm al-akhir qabla suqut Yafa.*] *Al-Carmel* 55–56 (Spring/Summer): 117–129.

———, ed. 1971. *The Transformation of Palestine.* Evanston, Ill.: Northwestern University Press.

Abu-Lughod, Janet. 1983. Demographic Consequences of the Occupation. *MERIP Reports,* no. 115: 13–17.

———. 1989. A Rift in Their Souls: The Palestinians in Exile. In *Palestinians under Occupation: Prospects for the Future,* edited by P. E. Krogh and M. C. McDavies. Washington D.C.: CCAS, Georgetown University.

Abu-Lughod, Lila. 1986. *Veiled Sentiments: Honor and Poetry in a Bedouin Society.* Berkeley: University of California Press.

————. 1993. *Writing Women's Worlds: Bedouin Stories.* Berkeley: University of California Press.

Abunimah, Ali. 1998. Dear NPR News . . . *The Link* 31 (5): 1–14.

Aburish, Said K. 1989. *Children of Bethany: The Story of a Palestinian Family.* Bloomington: Indiana University Press.

Abu Sharif, Bassam, and Uzi Mahnaimi. 1995. *Tried by Fire: The Searing True Story of Two Men at the Heart of the Struggle between the Arabs and the Jews.* London: Little, Brown.

Abu-Sitta, Salman. 1996. The Right of Return: Sacred, Legal, and Possible Too. Web site of the Palestinian Return Committee. www.prc.org.uk.

Ahmed, Hisham. 1995. Realism Misperceived: Arab-American Discourse and the Question of Palestine. In *Discourse and Palestine,* edited by Annelies Moors et al., 237–252. Amsterdam: Het Spinhuis.

Akram, Susan. 2000. Reinterpreting Palestinian Refugee Rights under International Law. *News from Within* 16 (4): 8–14.

Alqudsi-Taghreed, Ghabra. 1990. City and Village in the Palestinian Wedding Song: The Palestinian Community in Kuwait. In *Images and Reality: Palestinian Women under Occupation and in the Diaspora,* edited by Suha Sabbagh and Ghada Talhami, 35–54. Washington: Institute for Arab Women's Studies.

American-Arab Anti-Discrimination Committee, Western Regional Task Force. 2000. *PRIMER: The Palestinian Right of Return.* September.

Anderson, Benedict. 1994. *Imagined Communities: Reflections on the Origin and Spread of Nationalism.* London: Verso.

Andoni, Lamis. 1998. Preserving the Palestinian Identity after Oslo. In *The Legitimacy of Resistance: Options for Palestinian Survival,* 17–20. Washington, D.C.: Center for Policy Analysis on Palestine.

Anthias, Floya. 1998. Evaluating "Diaspora": Beyond Ethnicity? *Sociology* 32 (3): 557–580.

Antonelli, Alessandra. 1998. From the Battleground to the Table. *Palestine Report,* 10–11. February 27.

Appadurai, Arjun. 1991. Global Ethnoscapes: Notes and Queries for a Transnational Anthropology. In *Recapturing Anthropology: Working in the Present,* edited by Richard G. Fox, 191–210. Santa Fe: School of American Research Press.

Associated Press. 1999. Palestinian Americans Leave Their Mark on West Bank Culture. Posted at www.idrel.com.lb. July 30.

Aql, 'Abd al-Salam. 1995. Palestinian Refugees of Lebanon Speak. *Journal of Palestine Studies* 25 (1): 54–60.

Arab Resource Center for Popular Arts. 1998a. *Al-Jana* [*The Harvest,* Arabic], no. 6. February.

————. 1998b. *Al-Jana* [*The Harvest,* English]. May.

Aruri, Naseer, and Samih Farsoun. 1980. Palestinian Communities and Arab Host Countries. In *The Sociology of the Palestinians,* edited by Khalil Nakhleh and Elia Zureik, 112–116. New York: St. Martin's.

Arzt, Donna E. 1997. *Refugees into Citizens: Palestinians and the End of the Arab-Israeli Conflict.* New York: Council of Foreign Relations Books.

Ashkar, Ahmad. 1995. Internal Refugees: Their Inalienable Right to Return. *News from Within* 6 (8): 14–17.

Ata, Ibrahim Wade. 1986. *The West Bank Palestinian Family.* London: Routledge.

Aulas, M. C. 1984. The Daily Life of Palestinians in South Lebanon and the Beirut Area. *Arab Studies Quarterly* 6:228–231.

Badil. 1998a. New Israeli-Palestinian Position Paper on the Refugee Question. *Article 74,* 25 (www.badil.org).

———. 1998b. Refugees: Five Years after Oslo. *Article 74,* 25 (www.badil.org).

Bailey, Clinton. 1984. *Jordan's Palestinian Challenge, 1948–1983: A Political History.* Boulder: Westview.

Baker, Joharah. 1998. Palestinian-Americans: Where Do They Belong? *Palestine Report,* 4–5. January 23.

Baransi, Salih. 1982. The Story of a Palestinian under Occupation. *Journal of Palestine Studies* 11 (1): 3–30.

Barbeau, Rose-Marie. 1998a. Remembrance of Things Lost. *Palestine Report,* 10–11. March 6.

———. 1998b. Something Other Than Stones . . . The Memory Project. *Palestine Report,* 10–11. May 8.

Bardenstein, Carol B. 1999. Trees, Forests, and the Shaping of Palestinian and Israeli Collective Memory. In *Acts of Memory: Cultural Recall in the Present,* edited by Mieke Bal et al., 148–168. Hanover: Dartmouth College.

Barghouti, Iyad. 1988. *Palestinian Americans: Socio-Political Attitudes of Palestinian Americans towards the Arab-Israeli Conflict.* Durham: University of Durham, Center for Middle Eastern and Islamic Studies.

Barghouti, Mourid. 1997. The Sojourn in Time [*Al-iqama fi-l-waqt*]. *Al-Carmel* 51 (Spring): 146–158.

———. 1998. Songs for a Country No Longer Known. *Journal of Palestine Studies* 27 (2): 59–67.

———. 2000. *I Saw Ramallah.* Cairo: American University in Cairo Press.

Baroud, Ramzy. 2000. Remembrance: Connecting Past Catastrophe to the Present. *Islam Online.* Posted at www.islam-online.net. May 20.

Barron, Andrea. 1988. Jewish and Arab Diasporas in the United States and Their Impact on U.S. Middle East Policy. In *The Arab-Israeli Conflict: Two Decades of Change,* edited by Jehuda Lukacs and Abdallah M. Battah, 238–262. Boulder: Westview.

Basisu, Muin. 1980. *Descent into the Water: Palestinian Notes from Arab Exile.* Wilmette: Medina.

Battisti, Francesca, and Alessandro Portelli. 1994. The Apple and the Olive Tree: Exiles, Sojourners, and Tourists in the University. In *Migration and Identity,* edited by Rina Benmayor and Andor Skotnes, 35–53. Oxford: Oxford University Press.

Bauman, Zygmunt. 1996. From Pilgrim to Tourist—or a Short History of Identity. In *Questions of Cultural Identity,* edited by Stuart Hall and Paul du Gay, 18–36. London: Sage.

Baumgarten, Helga. 1991. *Palästina: Befreiung in den Staat. Die palästinensische Nationalbewegung seit 1948.* Frankfurt: Suhrkamp.

Bendt, I., and J. Downing. 1982. *We Shall Return: Women of Palestine.* Westport: Lawrence Hill.

Benmayor, Rina, and Andor Skotnes. 1994. Some Reflections on Migration and Identity. In *Migration and Identity,* edited by Rina Benmayor and Andor Skotnes, 1–18. Oxford: Oxford University Press.

Bennani, Nen. 1980. Mahmoud Darwish: The Experience of a Poet of Experience. *Leviathan* 3 (1): 33–38.

Bhabha, Homi. 1996. Culture's In-between. In *Questions of Cultural Identity,* edited by Stuart Hall and Paul du Gay, 53–60. London: Sage.

Bisharat, George. 1994. Displacement and Social Identity: Palestinian Refugees in the West Bank. In *Population Displacement: Development and Conflict in the Middle East,* edited by Seteney Shami. New York: Center for Migration Studies.

Black, Richard, and Khalid Koser. 1999. *The End of the Refugee Cycle? Refugee Repatriation and Reconstruction.* New York: Berghahn.

Boullata, Kamal, Irene Ghossein, and Naseer Aruri. 1979. *The World of Rashid Hussein: A Palestinian Poet in Exile.* Detroit: Association of Arab-American University Graduates.

Bowman, Glenn. 1994. A Country of Words: Conceiving the Palestinian Nation from the Position of Exile. In *The Making of Political Identities,* edited by Ernest Laclau, 138–170. London: Verso.

Brand, Laurie A. 1988a. *Palestinians in the Arab World: Institution Building and the Search for State.* New York: Columbia University Press.

———. 1988b. Palestinians in Syria: The Politics of Integration. *Middle East Journal* 42 (4): 621–637.

———. 1995. Palestinians and Jordanians: A Crisis of Identity. *Journal of Palestine Studies* 24 (4): 46–61.

Brynen, Rex. 1989. PLO Policy in Lebanon: Legacies and Lessons. *Journal of Palestine Studies* 18 (2): 48–70.

———. 1990. *Sanctuary and Survival: The PLO in Lebanon.* Boulder: Westview.

———. 1995. The Neopatrimonial Dimension of Palestinian Politics. *Journal of Palestine Studies* 25 (1): 23–36.

———. 1997. Statehood Key to Refugee Solution: Low Priority. Interview conducted by Stephanie Nolan. *Palestine Report,* 10–12. April 25.

Budeiri, Musa. 1997. The Palestinians: Tensions between Nationalist and Religious Identities. In *Rethinking Nationalism in the Arab Middle East,* edited by James Jankowski and Israel Gershoni, 191–206. New York: Columbia University Press.

Budeiri, Musa, Inea Bushnaq, Shafiq al-Hout, Salma Khadra Jayyusi, Mamdouh Nofal, Yezid Sayigh, Haidar Abdel Shafi, and Fawaz Turki. 1998. Reflections on al-Nakba. *Journal of Palestine Studies* 28 (1): 5–35.

Busailah, Reja-e. 1981. The Fall of Lydda, 1948: Impressions and Reminiscences. *Arab Studies Quarterly* 3 (2): 123–151.

Cainkar, Louise. 1990. Palestinian Women in the U.S.: Who Are They and What Kind of Lives Do They Lead? In *Images and Reality: Palestinian Women under Occupation and in the Diaspora,* edited by Suha Sabbagh and Ghada Talhami, 55–66. Washington, D.C.: Institute for Arab Women's Studies.

———. 1996. Immigrant Palestinian Women Evaluate Their Lives. In *Family and Gender among American Muslims,* edited by Barbara C. Aswad and Barbara Bilge, 41–58. Philadelphia: Temple University Press.

Center for Policy Analysis on Palestine. 1993. *Facts and Figures about the Palestinians: A Special Report.* Washington, D.C.

———. 1994. *Palestinian Refugees: Their Problems and Future.* Washington, D.C.

———. 1998. *The Legitimacy of Resistance: Options for Palestinian Survival.* Washington, D.C.

Chambers, Ian. 1994. *Migrancy, Culture, Identity.* London: Routledge.

Christison, Kathleen. 1989. The American Experience: Palestinians in the U.S. *Journal of Palestine Studies* 18 (4): 18–36.

———. 2001. *The Wound of Dispossession: Telling the Palestinian Story.* Santa Fe: Sunlit Hills.

Clarke, Richard. 1999. "Palestine over the Sea": Interview with Suheir Hammad. *Palestine Report,* 6–7. April 16.

Clifford, James. 1994. Diasporas. *Cultural Anthropology* 9 (3): 302–338.

Cobban, Helena. 1984. *The Palestinian Liberation Organization: People, Power, and Politics.* Cambridge: Cambridge University Press.

Cohen, Robin. 1997. *Global Diasporas: An Introduction.* London: University College.

Cohen, Yinon, and Andrea Tyree. 1994. Palestinian and Jewish Israeli-Born Immigrants in the United States. *International Migration Review* 28 (2): 243–255.

Cohen, Yinon. 1996. Economic Assimilation in the United States of Arab and Jewish Immigrants from Israel and the Territories. *Israel Studies* (1996): 75–97.

Cohen, Yinon, and Yitchak Haberfeld. 1997. The Number of Israeli Immigrants in the United States in 1990. *Demography* 34 (2): 199–212.

Cole, Carleton. 2000. Kawash's Greatest Desire Is to Go Home, a Home He Has Never Visited. *Palestine Chronicle.* Posted online at www.palestinechronicle.com.

Collins, John. 1996. Exploring Children's Territory: Ghassan Kanafani, Njabulo Ndebele, and the "Generation" of Politics in Palestine and South Africa. *Arab Studies Quarterly* 18 (4): 65–85.

Conner, Walker. 1986. The Impact of Homelands upon Diasporas. In *Modern Diasporas in International Politics,* edited by Gabriel Sheffer, 16–46. London: Croom Held.

Dajani, Maha Ahmed. 1986. *The Institutionalisation of Palestinian Identity in Egypt.* Cairo: American University in Cairo Press.

Dallal, Shaw J. 1998. *Scattered Like Seeds.* Syracuse, N.Y.: Syracuse University Press.

Darwish, Mahmoud. 1980. *The Music of Human Flesh: Poems of the Palestinian Struggle.* Washington, D.C.: Three Continents.

Darwish, Mahmud, Samih al-Qasim, and Adonis. 1984. *Victims of a Map.* London: Al Saqi.

Darwish, Mahmoud. 1995. Mahmoud Darwish Returns to the Homeland: An Interview. *Palestine Report*, 16–17. September 29.

———. 1997. *Diwan Mahmud Darwish*. Vol. 1. Beirut: Dar-al-ʿAwda.

———. 1998. In the Words of a Poet . . . Address to the Palestinian People on the Occasion of the Fiftieth Anniversary of the Nakba. *Palestine Report*, 10–12. May 8.

Davis, Uri. 1994. Return to Palestine from Exile: Implications of the Israeli-Palestinian Accord. *Arab Review* 3 (1): 5–10.

———. 1996. Palestine Refugees at the Crossroads of 1996 Permanent Status Negotiations. In *Civil and Citizenship Rights of Palestinian Refugees*, edited by Abbas Shiblak and Uri Davis, 2–79. Monograph Series no. 1. Ramallah: SHAML.

Deeb, Mary-Jane, and Mary E. King. 1996. *Hasib Sabbagh: From Palestinian Refugee to Citizen of the World*. Lanham, Md.: Middle East Institute and University Press of America.

Dodd, Peter. 1970. Palestinian Refugees of 1967: A Sociological Study. *Muslim World* 123 (2): 60–70.

Dodd, Peter, and Halim Barakat. 1969. *River without Bridges: A Study of the Exodus of the 1967 Palestinian Arab Refugees*. Beirut: Institute for Palestine Studies.

Drake, Laura. 1998. Re-constructing Identities: The Arab-Israeli Conflict in Theoretical Perspective. *Middle East Affairs Journal* 4 (1–2): 39–92.

Edy, Jill A. 1999. Journalistic Uses of Collective Memory. *Journal of Communication* (Spring): 71–85.

Efrat, Moshe. 1993. *The Palestinian Refugees: The Dynamics of Economic Integration in Their Host Countries*. Tel Aviv: Israeli International Institute for Applied Economic Policy Review.

Eisenlohr, Charlene Joyce. 1996. Adolescent Arab Girls in an American High School. In *Family and Gender among American Muslims*, edited by Barbara Aswad and Barbara Bilge, 250–270. Philadelphia: Temple University Press.

Elmessiri, Abdelwahab, and Kamal Boullata. 1982. *The Palestinian Wedding: A Bilingual Anthology of Contemporary Palestinian Resistance Poetry*. Washington, D.C.: Three Continents.

Elmessiri, Nur, and Abdelwahab Elmessiri. 1996. *Land of Stone and Thyme: An Anthology of Palestinian Short Stories*. London: Quartet.

Endresen, Lena C., and Geir Ovensen. 1994. *The Potential of UNRWA Data for Research on Palestinian Refugees: A Study of Administrative UNRWA Data*. Report 176. Oslo: FAFO.

Escribano, Marisa, and Nazmi El-Joubeh. 1981. Migration and Change in a West Bank Village: The Case of Deir Dibwan. *Journal of Palestine Studies* 11 (1): 150–160.

Farah, Randa. 1997. Crossing Boundaries: Reconstruction of Palestinian Identities in al-Baqʿa Refugee Camp, Jordan. In *Palestine, Palestiniens*, edited by Riccardo Bocco, Blandine Destremau, and Jean Hannoyer, 259–298. Beirut: CERMOC.

Farah, Tawfic. 1977. Political Socialization of Palestinian Children in Kuwait. *Journal of Palestine Studies* 6 (4): 90–102.

———. 1987. Learning to Support the PLO: Political Socialization of Palestinian Children in Kuwait. In *Political Socialization in the Arab States,* edited by Tawfiq E. Farah and Yasumasa Kuroda, 171–183. Boulder: Lynne Rienner.

Farsoun, Samih K., and Christina E. Zacharia. 1997. *Palestine and the Palestinians.* Boulder: Westview.

Fischbach, Michael. 2003. *Records of Dispossession: Palestinian Refugee Property and the Arab-Israeli Conflict.* New York: Columbia University Press.

Flapan, Simha. 1987a. *The Birth of Israel: Myths and Realities.* New York: Pantheon.

———. 1987b. The Palestinian Exodus of 1948. *Journal of Palestine Studies* 16 (4): 3–26.

Flores, Alexander. 1984. *The Palestinians in the Arab-Israeli Conflict: Social Conditions and Political Attitudes of the Palestinians in Israel, the Occupied Territories and the Diaspora.* Bonn: Forschungsinstitut für Auswärtige Politik.

Fog Olwig, Karen. 1998. Epilogue: Contested Homes—Home-Making and the Making of Anthropology. In *Migrants of Identity,* edited by Nigel Rapport and Andrew Dawson, 225–236. Oxford: Berg.

Frangi, Abdallah. 1982. *PLO und Palästina.* Frankfurt: Fischer Verlag.

Frisch, Hillel. 1997. Ethnicity, Territorial Integrity, and Regional Order: Palestinian Identity in Jordan and Israel. *Journal of Peace Research* 34 (3): 257–269.

Gellner, Ernest. 1983. *Nations and Nationalism.* Oxford: Blackwell.

Gennep, Arnold van. 1909. *The Rites of Passage.* London: Routledge.

Ghabra, Shafeeq. 1987. *Palestinians in Kuwait: The Family and the Politics of Survival.* Boulder: Westview.

———. 1988. Palestinians in Kuwait: The Family and the Politics of Survival. *Journal of Palestine Studies* 17 (2): 62–83.

Giacaman, Rita, Islah Jad, and Penny Johnson. 1996. For the Common Good? Gender and Social Citizenship in Palestine. *Middle East Report* (January–March): 11–16.

Gilen, Signe, Are Hovdenak, Rania Maktabi, Jon Pedersen, and Dag Tuastad. 1994. *Finding Ways: Palestinian Coping Strategies in Changing Environments.* Report 177. Oslo: FAFO.

Gillis, John R. 1994. Memory and Identity: The History of a Relationship. In *Commemorations: The Politics of National Identity,* edited by John R. Gillis, 3–24. Princeton, N.J.: Princeton University Press.

Gilmour, David. 1988. *Dispossessed: The Ordeal of the Palestinians.* London: Sphere.

Glazer, Steven. 1980. The Palestinian Exodus in 1948. *Journal of Palestine Studies* 9 (4): 96–118.

Gonzalez, Nancie L. 1989. The Christian Palestinians of Honduras: An Uneasy Accommodation. In *Conflict, Migration, and the Expression of Ethnicity,* edited by Nancie L. Gonzalez and Carolyn S. McCommon, 75–90. Boulder: Westview.

Gonzalez, Nancie L. Solien. 1992. *Dollar, Dove, and Eagle: One Hundred Years of Palestinian Migration to Honduras.* Ann Arbor: University of Michigan Press.

Graham, Mark, and Shahram Khosravi. 1997. Home Is Where You Make It: Repatriation and Diaspora Culture among Iranians in Sweden. *Journal of Refugee Studies* 10 (January): 115–133.

Graham-Brown, Sarah. 1989. Impact on the Social Structure of Palestinian Society. In

Occupation: Israel over Palestine, edited by Naseer Aruri, 223–254. Belmont, Mass.: Association of Arab-American Graduates.

Gresh, Alain. 1999. In the Shadow of Their Homeland: Palestinian Dreams and Anger. *Le Monde Diplomatique.* Posted on FOFOGNET, March 25–26, 1999. February.

Grossberg, Lawrence. 1996. Identity and Cultural Studies—Is That All There Is? In *Questions of Cultural Identity,* edited by Stuart Hall and Paul du Gay, 87–107. London: Sage.

Hadawi, Sami. 1988. *Palestinian Rights and Losses in 1948: A Comprehensive Study.* London: Saqi.

———. 1990. *Bitter Harvest: A Modern History of Palestine.* New York: Olive Branch.

Haddad, Toufic. 2000. No Time to Lose: An Interview with Susan Akram. *News from Within* 16 (4): 14–18.

Hagopian, Edward, and A. B. Zahlan. 1974. Palestine's Arab Population: The Demography of the Palestinians. *Journal of Palestine Studies* 3 (4): 32–73.

Haj, Majid al-. 1988. The Arab Internal Refugees of Israel: The Emergence of a Minority within the Minority. *Immigrants and Minorities* 7 (2): 149–165.

Hall, Stuart. 1990. Cultural Identity and Diaspora. In *Identity: Community, Culture, Difference,* edited by Jonathan Rutherford, 222–237. London: Lawrence and Wishart.

———. 1993. Cultural Identity in Question. In *Modernity and its Futures,* edited by Stuart Hall, David Held, and Tony McGrew, 273–316. Cambridge, U.K.: Polity.

Hallaj, Muhammad. 1994. The Refugee Question and the Peace Process. In *Palestinian Refugees: Their Problem and Future,* 3–8. Washington, D.C.: Center for Policy Analysis on Palestine.

Hammad, Suheir. 1996a. *Born Palestinian, Born Black.* New York: Harlem River.

———. 1996b. *Drops of This Story.* New York: Harlem River.

Hammami, Rema. 1990. Women, the Hijab, and the Intifada. *Middle East Report* 20: 24–28.

Hammer, Juliane. 2002. Homeland Palestine: Lost in the Catastrophe of 1948 and Recreated in Memory and Art. In *Crisis and Memory in Islamic Societies,* edited by Angelika Neuwirth and Andreas Pflitsch, 453–481. Beirut/Stuttgart: Steiner Verlag.

———. 2003. A Crisis of Memory: Homeland and Exile in Contemporary Palestinian Memoirs. In *Crisis and Memory: The Representations of Space in Modern Levantine Narrative,* edited by Ken Seigneurie and Samira Aghacy, 177–198. Wiesbaden: Reichert.

Hamzeh-Muhaisen, Muna. 1998a. 50 Years of Nakba: Commemorating the Catastrophe. *Palestine Report,* 6–7. February 27.

———. 1998b. Remembering—50 Years of Nakba. *Palestine Report,* 8–9. March 6.

———. 1998c. Return to Palestine: Nostalgia vs. Reality. *Palestine Report,* 6–7. March 27.

———. 1998d. When Time Came to a Standstill . . . *Palestine Report,* 6–7. May 1.

———. 1998e. Where Do We Belong? *Palestine Report,* 8–9. May 15.

Hanafi, Sari. 1996. *Between Two Worlds: Palestinian Workers in the Diaspora and the Building of the Palestinian Entity [Bayna ʿalamayn: rijal al-ʿamal al-filastiniyun fi-l-shatat wa binaʾ al-kiyan al-filastini].* Cairo: Dar al-Mustaqbal al-ʿArabi.

Handler, Richard. 1994. Is "Identity" a Useful Cross-Cultural Concept? In *Commemorations: The Politics of National Identity*, edited by John R. Gillis, 27–39. Princeton, N.J.: Princeton University Press.

Harik, Iliya. 1986. The Palestinians in the Diaspora. In *Modern Diasporas in International Politics*, edited by Gabriel Sheffer, 315–332. London: Croom Held.

Harlow, Barbara. 1992. The Palestinian Intellectual and the Liberation of the Academy. *Edward Said: A Critical Reader*, edited by Michael Sprinker, 173–193. Oxford: Blackwell.

———. 1998. Palestine: Kan Wa-Ma Kan? *Diaspora* 7 (1): 75–85.

Hart, Jason. 1999. Growing Up "Mukhayyamji": Boyhood in Hussein Camp, Amman. Paper presented at "The Uncertain State of Palestine: Futures of Research" conference at the University of Chicago, February 1999.

Hassan, Bilal al-. 1974. The Palestinians in Kuwait: A Statistical Study [*Al-filastiniyun fi Kuwayt*]. *Dirasat Filastiniya*, no. 97. Beirut: Palestine Liberation Organization Research Center.

Hasso, Frances S. 2000. Modernity and Gender in Arab Accounts of the 1948 and 1967 Defeats. *International Journal of Middle East Studies* 32 (4): 491–510.

Heacock, Roger. 1999. Al-Mahalliune wal 'aidune: Locals and Returnees in the Palestinians National Authority PNA: A Historical Perspective. In *The Becoming of Returnee States: Palestine, Armenia, Bosnia*. Birzeit: Graduate Institute of International Studies. Posted at www.birzeit.edu.

Heiberg, Marianne, and Geir Ovensen. 1993. *Palestinian Society in Gaza, West Bank and Arab Jerusalem*. Oslo: FAFO.

Hijjawi, Sulafa. 1968. *Poetry of Resistance in Occupied Palestine*. Baghdad: Ministry of Culture.

Hilal, Jamil. 1993. PLO Institutions: The Challenge Ahead. *Journal of Palestine Studies* 2 (1): 46–60.

Hobsbawm, Eric. 1990. *Nations and Nationalism since 1780: Programme, Myth, Reality*. Cambridge: Cambridge University Press.

Hobsbawm, Eric, and Terence Ranger, eds. 1983. *The Invention of Tradition*. Cambridge: Cambridge University Press.

Hooglund, Eric, ed. 1985. *Taking Root: Arab American Community Studies*. Washington, D.C.: ADC.

Hourani, Faisal. 1998. War at Night and Day [*Harb al-layl wa-l-nahar*]. *Al-Carmel* 55–56 (Spring/Summer): 149–161.

Hovdenak, Are. 1997. On the Gulf Road: Palestinian Adaptations to Labour Migration. In *Constructing Order: Palestinian Adaptations to Refugee Life*, edited by Are Hovdenak et al., 19–78. Oslo: FAFO.

Hovdenak, Are, Jon Pedersen, Dag H. Tuastad, and Elia Zureik. 1997. *Constructing Order: Palestinian Adaptations to Refugee Life*. Report 236. Oslo: FAFO.

Hovsepian, Nubar. 1992. Connections with Palestine. In *Edward Said: A Critical Reader*, edited by Michael Sprinker, 5–18. Oxford: Blackwell.

———. 1994. Universal versus Particular Identity: Reflections on a Visit to Palestine. *Arab Studies Quarterly* 16 (1): 43–53.

Hudson, Michael C. 1997. Palestinians and Lebanon: The Common Story. *Journal of Refugee Studies* 10 (3): 243–60.

Husseini, Hassan Jamal. 1989. *Return to Jerusalem.* London: Quartet.

Huzzayin, Salah. 1998. The Village I Did Not Visit [*Al-balda al-lati lam azurha*]. *Al-Carmel* 55–56 (Spring/Summer): 162–174.

Ismael, Jaqueline S. 1981. The Alienation of Palestine in Palestinian Poetry. *Arab Studies Quarterly* 3 (1) (Winter): 43–55.

Issa, Mahmoud. 1998. Resisting Oblivion: Decoding the Silencing Process in Modern Palestinian Historiography. Paper presented at "50 Years of Human Rights Violations: Palestinians Dispossessed" conference in Jerusalem.

Jaafari, Lafi Ibrahim. 1973. The Brain-Drain to the United States: The Migration of Jordanian and Palestinian Professionals and Students. *Journal of Palestine Studies* 3 (1): 119–131.

Jabbour, Hala Deeb. 1994. An Answer Waiting for a Question. In *Women in Exile,* edited by Mahnaz Afkhami, 50–63. Charlottesville: University of Virginia Press.

Jad, Islah. 1998. Patterns of Relations within the Palestinian Family during the Intifada. In *Palestinian Women of Gaza and the West Bank,* edited by Suha Sabbagh, 53–62. Bloomington: Indiana University Press.

Jad, Islah, Penny Johnson, and Rita Giacaman. 2000. Transit Citizens: Gender and Citizenship under the Palestinian Authority. In *Gender and Citizenship in the Middle East,* edited by Suad Joseph, 137–157. Syracuse, N.Y.: Syracuse University Press.

JanMohamed, Abdul R. 1992. Worldliness-without-World, Homelessness-as-Home: Toward a Definition of the Specular Border Intellectual. In *Edward Said: A Critical Reader,* edited by Michael Sprinker, 96–120. Oxford: Blackwell.

Jarrar, Najeh. 1994. *The Palestinian Refugees: Referential Introduction and Exploration for the Future* [*Al-laji'un al-filastiniyun: madkhal li-l-muraja'a wa istiqra' li-l-mustaqbal*]. Jerusalem: PASSIA.

———. 1997/1998. Camp Refugees and the Peace Process. *Palestine-Israel Journal* 6 (3–4). Special Issue, *The USA and the Conflict,* 110–117.

Jayyusi, Salma Khadra. 1992. *Anthology of Modern Palestinian Literature.* New York: Columbia University Press.

Johnson, N. 1979. Palestinian Refugee Ideology: An Inquiry into Key Metaphors. *Journal of Anthropology Research* 34:534–553.

Jordan Times. 2001. Palestinian Refugees in Syria Still Hope to Return. Posted at FOFOGNET. January 16.

Kadi, Joanne, ed. 1994. *Food for Our Grandmothers: Writings by Arab-American and Arab-Canadian Feminists.* Boston: South End.

Kanaana, Salwa. 1996. Laila and Abu Ali: Will They Come Home? *Palestine Report,* 8–9. February 23.

Kanaana, Sharif. 1992a. *The House Is Our Father's: Studies in Palestinian Folklore* [*Al-dar dar abuna: dirasat fi-l-turath al-sha'bi al-filastini*]. Jerusalem: Jerusalem International Center for Palestinian Studies.

———. 1992b. *Still on Vacation! The Eviction of the Palestinians in 1948.* Jerusalem: Jerusalem International Center for Palestinian Studies.

Kanaaneh, Rhoda Ann. 2002. *Birthing the Nation: Strategies of Palestinian Women in Israel.* Berkeley: University of California Press.

Kanafani, Ghassan. 1984. *Palestine's Children.* London: Heinemann.

———. 1987a. *Ghassan Kanafani: Complete Writings [Al-athar al-kamila].* Vol. 2. *Short Stories.* Beirut: Mu'assasa al-Abhath al-ʿArabiya.

———. 1987b. *Return to Haifa [ʿA'id ila Hayfa].* Beirut: Mu'assasa al-Abhath al-ʿArabiya.

Kanafani, Noman. 1995. Homecoming. *Middle East Report* 25 (3-4): 40-42.

Karmi, Ghada. 1994. The 1948 Exodus: A Family Story. *Journal of Palestine Studies* 23 (2): 31-40.

———. 1999. After the Nakba: An Experience of Exile in England. *Journal of Palestine Studies* 28 (3): 52-63.

Karmi, Ghada, and Eugene Cotran, eds. 1999. *The Palestinian Exodus: 1948-1998.* Reading, UK: Ithaca.

Katz, Sheila H. 1996. Shahada and Haganah: Politicizing Masculinities in Early Palestinian and Jewish Nationalisms. *Arab Studies Journal* 4 (2): 79-94.

Khadr, Hassan. 1997. Confessions of a Palestinian Returnee. *Journal of Palestine Studies* 27 (1): 85-95.

———. 1998. The Bread of the Arabs [*Khubz al-ʿArab*]. *Al-Carmel* 55-56 (Spring/ Summer): 140-148.

Khalidi, Muhammad Ali. 1995a. A First Visit to Palestine. *Journal of Palestine Studies* 24 (3): 74-80.

———. 1995b. Palestinian Refugees in Lebanon. *Middle East Report* 25 (6): 28-29.

Khalidi, Rashid. 1994. Toward a Solution. In *Palestinian Refugees: Their Problem and Future,* 21-26. Washington, D.C.: Center for Policy Analysis on Palestine.

———. 1995. The Palestinian Refugee Problem: A Possible Solution. *Palestine-Israel Journal* 2 (4): 73-78.

———. 1997. *Palestinian Identity: The Construction of Modern National Consciousness.* New York: Columbia University Press.

———. 1998. Fifty Years after 1948: A Universal Jubilee? *Palestine-Israel Journal* 5 (2): 8-17.

———. 1999. Truth, Justice, and Reconciliation: Elements of a Solution to the Palestinian Refugee Issue. In *The Palestinian Exodus, 1948-1998,* edited by Ghada Karmi and Eugene Cotran, 221-241. Reading, UK: Ithaca.

Khalidi, Walid. 1959. Why Did the Palestinians Leave? An Examination of the Zionist Version of the Exodus of 1948. *Middle East Forum* 35 (7): 21-24.

———. 1984. *Before Their Diaspora: A Photographic History of the Palestinians, 1876-1948.* Washington, D.C.: Institute for Palestine Studies.

———. 1988. Plan Dalet: Master Plan for the Conquest of Palestine. *Journal of Palestine Studies* 18 (1): 4-19.

———, ed. 1992. *All That Remains: The Palestinian Villages Occupied and Depopulated by Israel in 1948.* Washington, D.C.: Institute for Palestine Studies.

Khouri, Mounah A., and Hamid Algar, eds. 1974. *An Anthology of Modern Arabic Poetry.* Berkeley: University of California Press.

Kimmerling, Baruch. and Joseph S. Migdal. 1993. *Palestinians: The Making of a People*. New York: Free Press.

Kjorlien, Michele L. 1993. The Evolution of Palestinian National Identity. Unpublished paper, Georgetown University.

Kleiman, E. 1986. Khirbet Khiz'ah and Other Unpleasant Memories. *Jerusalem Quarterly* 40 (1986): 102–118.

Klein, Menachem. 1997. Quo Vadis? Palestinian Authority Building Dilemmas since 1993. *Middle Eastern Studies* 33 (2): 383–404.

———. 1998. Between Right and Realization: The PLO Dialectics of the Right of Return. *Journal of Refugee Studies* 11 (1): 1–19.

Kodmani-Darwish, Bassma. 1997. *La diaspora palestinienne*. Paris: Presses Universitaire de France.

Kossaifi, George F. 1980. Demographic Characteristics of the Arab Palestinian People. In *The Sociology of the Palestinians*, edited by Khalil Nakhleh and Elia Zureik, 13–46. London: Croom Held.

———. 1996. *The Palestinian Refugees and the Right of Return*. Washington, D.C.: Center for Policy Analysis on Palestine.

Kubursi, Atif. 1996. *Palestinian Losses in 1948: The Quest for Precision*. Washington, D.C.: The Center for Policy Analysis on Palestine.

Kuroda, Alice, and Yasumasa Kuroda. 1978. *Palestinians without Palestine: A Study of Socialization among Palestinian Youths*. Washington, D.C.: University Press of America.

———. 1987. Palestinians and World Politics: A Social-Psychological Analysis. In *Political Socialization in the Arab States*, edited by Tawfiq E. Farah and Yasumasa Kuroda, 161–170. Boulder: Lynne Rienner.

Lanehart, Sonia L. 1996. The Language of Identity. *Journal of English Linguistics* 24 (4): 322–331.

Latte Abdallah, Stephanie. 1995. Palestinian Women in the Camps of Jordan. *Journal of Palestine Studies* 24 (4): 62–72.

Lavie, Smadar, and Ted Swedenburg. 1996. *Displacement, Diaspora, and Geographies of Identity*. Durham, N.C.: Duke University Press.

Le Monde Diplomatique. 1999. The Palestinian Refugees: Facts and Figures. February 1999. Posted at www.idrel.com.lb.

Le Troquer, Yann, and Rozenn Hommery al-Oudat. 1999. From Kuwait to Jordan: The Palestinians' Third Exodus. *Journal of Palestine Studies* 28 (3): 37–51.

Lesch, Ann Mosley. 1991. Palestinians in Kuwait. *Journal of Palestine Studies* 20 (4): 42–54.

Lindholm Schulz, Helena. 1999. *The Reconstruction of Palestinian Nationalism: Between Revolution and Statehood*. Manchester: Manchester University Press.

Lindholm Schulz, Helena, and Juliane Hammer. 2003. *The Palestinian Diaspora: Formation of Identities and Politics of Homeland*. London: Routledge.

Lynd, Staughton, Alice Lynd, and Sam Bahour. 1994. *Homeland: Oral History of Palestine and Palestinians*. New York: Olive Branch Press.

Mahmoud, Lina. 1999. The Palestinian Diaspora Community in Britain: Whither Palestinian Identity? Master's thesis, London, SOAS.

Mandel, Ruth. 1989. Ethnicity and Identity among Migrant Guestworkers in West Berlin. In *Conflict, Migration, and the Expression of Ethnicity,* edited by Nancie L. Gonzales, 61–75. Boulder: Westview.

Maneie, Juliane El-. 1998. Exodus, Flucht, Vertreibung, Katastrophe: Die Entstehung des palästinensischen Flüchtlingsproblems in der palästinensischen und israelischen Historiographie der Ereignisse von 1948. In *Wessen Geschichte? Muslimische Erfahrungen historischer Zäsuren im 20. Jahrhundert,* edited by Henner Fürtig and Gerhard Höpp, 45–72. Berlin: Das Arabische Buch.

Mansur, Sulaiman. 1998. The Nakba and Palestinian Painting: An Interview With Sulaiman Mansur. *Palestine-Israel Journal* 5 (2): 91–95.

Marshood, Nabil, comp. 1997. *Palestinian Teenage Refugees and Immigrants Speak Out.* New York: Rosen.

Masalha, Nur. 1988a. On Recent Hebrew and Israeli Sources for the Palestinian Exodus, 1947–49. *Journal of Palestine Studies* 18 (1): 121–137.

———. 1988b. Refugee Interviews, 1948: Four Palestinians Describe the Period Leading Up to the Circumstances of Their Expulsion and Departure. *Journal of Palestine Studies* 18 (1): 158–171.

———. 1992. *Expulsion of the Palestinians: The Concept of "Transfer" in Zionist Political Thought, 1882–1948.* Washington, D.C.: Institute for Palestine Studies.

———. 1996. *Israeli Plans to Resettle the Palestinian Refugees, 1948–1972.* Monograph Series No. 2. Ramallah: SHAML.

———. 1999. The 1967 Palestinian Exodus. In *The Palestinian Exodus, 1948–1998,* edited by Ghada Karmi and Eugene Cotran, 63–109. Reading, UK: Ithaca.

Masriyeh Hazboun, Norma. 1996. *Israeli Resettlement Schemes for Palestinians in the West Bank and Gaza Strip since 1967.* Monograph Series No. 4. Ramallah: SHAML.

Massarueh, Abdul-Salam Y. 1986. The Palestinians: Exiles in the Diaspora. *Middle East Insight* 4 (6): 26–30.

Maswada, Tayseer Abdel-Hafez. 1994. The Demographic Characteristics of Palestinian Refugees in Syria, 1949–1992. Ph.D. diss., University of London.

Mattar, Philip. 2000. *Encyclopedia of the Palestinians.* New York: Facts on File.

McCarus, Ernest, ed. 1994. *The Development of Arab-American Identity.* Detroit: University of Michigan Press.

Messiri, Abdul Wahab al-, ed. 1970. *A Lover from Palestine and Other Poems.* Washington, D.C.: Free Palestine.

Mojahid, Daud. 1989. Growing Up Arab in America. *Arab Studies Quarterly* 11 (2–3): 173–180.

Moors, Annelies, Toine van Teffelen, Sharif Kanaana, and Ilham Abu Ghazaleh. 1995. *Discourse and Palestine: Power, Text and Context.* Amsterdam: Het Spinhuis.

Morris, Benny. 1987. *The Birth of the Palestinian Refugee Problem, 1947–49.* Cambridge: Cambridge University Press.

———. 1990. *1948 and After: Israel and the Palestinians.* Oxford: Clarendon Press.

Moughrabi, Fuad. 1997. A Year of Discovery. *Journal of Palestine Studies* 26 (2): 5–15.

Moughrabi, Fuad, and Pat Al-Nazer. 1989. What Do Palestinian Americans Think? Results of a Public Opinion Survey. *Journal of Palestine Studies* 19 (4): 91–101.

Muhammad, Zakariya. 1997. Bone and Gold [*Al-'azm wa-l-thahab*]. *Al-Carmel* 51 (Spring): 125–140.

Muneef, Abdarrahman. 1998. Palestine in Memories [*Filastin fi-l-dhakira*]. *Al-Carmel* 55–56 (Spring/Summer): 216–227.

Muslih, Muhammad. 1988. *The Origins of Palestinian Nationalism, 1856–1920.* New York: Columbia University Press and Institute for Palestine Studies.

———. 1993. Palestinian Civil Society. *Middle East Journal* 47 (2): 258–274.

Mustafa, Mohammed. 1996. The Palestinian Diaspora. Paper presented at "The Palestinian Economy: Towards a Vision" conference. June.

Naff, Alixa. 1999. *The Arab Americans: The Immigrant Experience.* Philadelphia: Chelsea House.

Nakhleh, Issa. 1991. *Encyclopedia of the Palestine Problem.* New York: Intercontinental Books.

Nakhleh, Khalil. 1975. Cultural Determinants of Palestinian Collective Identity. *New Outlook* 18 (November): 31–40.

Nakhleh, Khalil, and Elia Zureik, eds. 1980. *The Sociology of the Palestinians.* New York: St. Martin's.

Natur, Suhail Mahmud. 1993. *The Conditions of the Palestinian People in Lebanon* [*Auda'a al-sha'ab al-filastini fi lubnan*]. Beirut: Dar al-Taqaddum al-'Arabi.

Nazzal, Nafez. 1978. *Palestinian Exodus from the Galilee, 1948.* Beirut: Institute of Palestine Studies.

Nour, Amer. 1993. *Coming Home: A Survey of the Socioeconomic Conditions of West Bank and Gaza Strip Returnees after the 1991 Gulf War.* Jerusalem: Palestine Human Rights Information Center.

Ofteringer, Ronald. 1997. *Palästinensische Flüchtlinge und der Friedensprozess, Palästinenser im Libanon.* Berlin: Das Arabische Buch.

Orfalea, Gregory. 1982. *Wrapping the Grape Leaves: A Sheaf of Contemporary Arab American Poets.* Washington, D.C.: ADC.

———. 1988a. *Before the Flames: A Quest for the History of Arab Americans.* Austin: University of Texas Press.

———. 1988b. *Grape Leaves: A Century of Arab American Poetry.* Salt Lake City: University of Utah Press.

———. 1989. Sifting the Ashes: Arab-American Activism during the 1982 Invasion of Lebanon. *Arab Studies Quarterly* 11 (2–3): 207–226.

Palestine-Israel Journal of Politics, Economics, and Culture. 1995. *Refugees* 2 (4).

———. 1998. *1948: A Tale of Two Peoples* 5 (2).

Palestine Human Rights Information Center (PHRIC). 1993, October. A Bittersweet Coming Home: The Experience of Palestinians Returning from the Gulf. *From the Field: A Monthly Report on Selected Human Rights Issues,* 1–7.

Palestine Report. 1996. Dormant Diaspora Wealth Awakens. *Palestine Report* 1 (32): 16–17. January 5.

Palestinian Central Bureau of Statistics. 1999. *Population, Housing, and Establishment Census—1997.* Web site www.pcbs.org.

Palestinian Refugee ResearchNet (PRRN). 1997a. Palestinian Refugees: An Overview. Posted at PRRN, www.arts.mcgill.ca.

————. 1997b. Palestinian Refugees and Final Status: Key Issues. Posted at PRRN, www.arts.mcgill.ca.

Palestinian Return Committee. 1999. The Palestinians in Lebanon: Between the Impotency of Oslo and the Weariness of Their Hosts. Web site of the PRC, www.prc.org.uk.

Palumbo, Michael. 1989. *The Palestinian Catastrophe: The 1948 Expulsion of a People from Their Homeland.* London: Quartet.

Pappe, Ilan. 1992. *The Making of the Arab-Israeli Conflict, 1947–1951.* London: Tauris.

————. 1999. Were They Expelled? The History, Historiography, and Relevance of the Palestinian Refugee Problem. In *The Palestinian Exodus, 1948–1998,* edited by Ghada Karmi and Eugene Cotran, 37–63. Reading, UK: Ithaca.

Parmenter, Barbara M. 1994. *Giving Voice to Stones: Place and Identity in Palestinian Literature.* Austin: University of Texas Press.

Pattie, Susan. 1994. At Home in Diaspora: Armenians in America. *Diaspora* 3 (2): 185–198.

Pedersen, Jon. 1997. Introduction: Migration, Homecoming, and Community Organization. In *Constructing Order: Palestinian Adaptations to Refugee Life,* edited by Are Hovdenak et al., 7–18. Oslo: FAFO.

Pedersen, Jon, and Rick Hooper, eds. 1998. *Developing Palestinian Society: Socio-Economic Trends and Their Implications for Development Strategies.* Report 242. Oslo: FAFO.

Peretz, Don. 1993. *Palestinians, Refugees, and the Middle East Peace Process.* Washington, D.C.: United States Institute of Peace.

————. 1994. The Question of Compensation. In *Palestinian Refugees: Their Problem and Future,* 15–20. Washington, D.C.: Center for Policy Analysis on Palestine.

Peteet, Julie Marie. 1987. Socio-political Integration and Conflict Resolution in the Palestinian Camps in Lebanon. *Journal of Palestine Studies* 16 (2): 29–63.

————. 1992. *Gender in Crisis: Women and the Palestinian Resistance Movement.* New York: Columbia University Press.

————. 1993. Authenticity and Gender: The Presentation of Culture. In *Arab Women: Old Boundaries, New Frontiers,* edited by Judith Tucker, 49–62. Bloomington: Indiana University Press.

————. 1994. Transforming Trust: Dispossession and Empowerment Among Palestinian Refugees. In *MisTrusting Refugees,* edited by E. V. Daniels and J. Knudsen, 168–188. Berkeley: University of California Press.

Plascov, Avi. 1981. *The Palestinian Refugees in Jordan, 1948–1957.* London: Frank Cass.

Qudsiyeh, Labeeb. 1997. *The Palestinian Refugees in Iraq (Al-laji'un al-filastiniyun fi-l-'iraq)*. Monograph Series No. 7. Ramallah: SHAML.

Quigley, John. 1999. The Right of Displaced Palestinians to Return to Home Areas in Israel. In *The Palestinian Exodus 1948–1998*, edited by Ghada Karmi and Eugene Cotran, 151–170. Reading, UK: Ithaca.

Rabinowitz, Dan. 1997. *Overlooking Nazareth: The Ethnography of Exclusion in Galilee*. Cambridge: Cambridge University Press.

Rapport, Nigel, and Andrew Dawson. 1998a. Home and Movement: A Polemic. In *Migrants of Identity*, edited by Nigel Rapport and Andrew Dawson, 19–38. Oxford: Berg.

———. 1998b. *Migrants of Identity: Perceptions of Home in a World of Movement*. Oxford: Berg.

Rimawi, Mahmoud. 1998. The Culture of Silence [*Thaqafat al-samt*]. *Al-Carmel* 55–56 (Spring/Summer): 227–231.

Robinson, Glenn E. 1997. *Building a Palestinian State: The Incomplete Revolution*. Bloomington: Indiana University Press.

———. 2000. Succession and Authoritarianism in Palestine: What Next after Arafat? Report from a CPAP Briefing. *For The Record*, No. 58. Washington, D.C.: Center for Policy Analysis on Palestine. October 25.

Rogge, John R. 1994. Repatriation of Refugees: A Not So Simple Optimum Solution. In *When Refugees Go Home: African Experiences*, edited by Tim Allen and Hubert Morsink, 14–49. Trenton, N.J.: Africa World Press.

Rooke, Tetz. 1996. The Most Important Thing Is What Happens Inside Us: Personal Identity in Palestinian Autobiography. In *Identity in Asian Literature*, edited by Lisbeth Littrup, 232–254. Richmond: Curzon.

Rothenberg, Celia E. 1999. Proximity and Distance: Palestinian Women's Social Lives in Diaspora. *Diaspora* 8 (1): 23–50.

Rouchdy, Aleya. 1974. Research on Arab Child Bilinguals. In *Arabic Speaking Communities in American Cities*, edited by Barbara Aswad, 169–180. New York: Center for Migration Studies.

Rouhana, Nadim N. 1997. *Palestinian Citizens in an Ethnic Jewish State: Identities in Conflict*. New Haven: Yale University Press.

Rouhana, Nadim N., and As'ad Ghanem. 1998. The Crisis of Minorities in Ethnic States: The Case of the Palestinian Citizens in Israel. *International Journal of Middle East Studies* 30 (3): 321–346.

Rouleau, Eric. 1985. The Palestinian Diaspora in the Gulf. *MERIP Reports*, no. 132 (1985): 13–15.

Rubinstein, Danny. 1991. *The People of Nowhere: The Palestinian Vision of Home*. New York: Random House.

———. 1994. The People of Nowhere: The Right of Return as Reflected in Israeli and Palestinian Eyes. *Palestine-Israel Journal* 2 (Spring): 79–85.

———. 1995. A Material and Spiritual Homeland. *Palestine-Israel Journal* 2 (4): 15–19.

Rushdie, Salman, and Edward Said. 1991. On Palestinian Identity: A Conversation with Edward Said. In Salman Rushdie, *Imaginary Homelands,* 166–186. New York: Granta Books.

Rutherford, Jonathan. 1990. A Place Called Home: Identity and the Cultural Politics of Difference. In *Identity: Community, Culture, Difference,* edited by Jonathan Rutherford, 9–27. London: Lawrence and Wishart.

Sabbagh, Suha, and Ghada Talhami. 1990. *Images and Reality: Palestinian Women under Occupation and in the Diaspora.* Women of Palestine Monograph Series. Washington, D.C.: Institute for Arab Women's Studies.

Safieh, Afif. 1997. *Children of a Lesser God?* London: Palestinian General Delegation to the UK.

Safran, William. 1991. Diasporas in Modern Societies: Myths of Homeland and Return. *Diaspora* 1 (1): 83–99.

Sagar, Aparajita. 1997. Homes and Postcoloniality. *Diaspora* 6 (2): 237–252.

Sahli, Nabeel. 1996. *The Palestinians in Syria [Al-filastiniyun fi suriya].* Monograph Series No. 3. Ramallah: SHAML.

Said, Edward. 1984. The Mind of Winter: Reflections on Life in Exile. *Harper's* 269:50–59. September.

———. 1986a. *After the Last Sky. Palestinian Lives.* New York: Pantheon.

———. 1986b. The Burdens of Interpretation and the Questions of Palestine. *Journal of Palestine Studies* 15 (1): 29–37.

———. 1990. Reflections on Exile. In *Out There: Marginalization and Contemporary Cultures,* edited by Russell Ferguson et al., 357–366. Cambridge: MIT Press.

———. 1992. *The Question of Palestine.* New York: Vintage.

———. 1994. *The Politics of Dispossession: The Struggle for Palestinian Self-Determination, 1969–1994.* New York: Pantheon.

———. 1999. *Out of Place: A Memoir.* New York: Knopf.

Said, Edward W., Ibrahim Abu-Lughod, Janet Abu-Lughod, Muhammad Hallaj, and Elia Zureik. 1990. *A Profile of the Palestinian People.* New York: International Progress Organization.

Salam, Nawaf. 1993. Between Repatriation and Resettlement: Palestinian Refugees in Lebanon. *Journal of Palestine Studies* 24 (1): 18–27.

Salim, Walid. 1997. *The Right of Return: Palestinian Alternatives [Haqq al-'awda: bada'il filastiniya].* Panorama: Palestinian Centre for Democracy Building and Education of Society.

Samhan, Helen Hatab. 1987. Politics and Exclusion: The Arab American Experience. *Journal of Palestine Studies* 16 (2): 11–28.

Sanbar, Elias. 1982. The Long Return to the Homeland. *Arab Studies Quarterly* 4 (4): 291–300.

Sayigh, Rosemary. 1977a. The Palestinian Identity among Camp Residents. *Journal of Palestine Studies* 6 (3): 3–22.

———. 1977b. Sources of Palestinian Nationalism: A Study of a Palestinian Camp in Lebanon. *Journal of Palestine Studies* 6 (4): 17–40.

———. 1979. *Palestinians: From Peasants to Revolutionaries.* London: Zed.

————. 1993. Palestinian Women and Politics in Lebanon. In *Arab Women: Old Boundaries, New Frontiers*, edited by Judith Tucker, 175–192. Bloomington: Indiana University Press.

————. 1994. *Too Many Enemies: The Palestinian Experience in Lebanon*. London: Zed.

————. 1995. Palestinians in Lebanon: Harsh Present, Uncertain Future. *Journal of Palestine Studies* 24 (3): 37–53.

————. 1998. Palestinian Camp Women as Tellers of History. *Journal of Palestine Studies* 27 (2): 42–58.

Sayigh, Yezid. 1997. *Armed Struggle and the Search for State: The Palestinian National Movement, 1949–1993*. Oxford: Clarendon Press.

Sayigh, Yezid, and Rosemary Sayigh. 1987. The Politics of Palestinian Exile. *Third World Quarterly* 9:28–66.

Sayre, Ward, and Jennifer Olmstedt. 1999. Economics of Palestinian Return Migration. *MERIP Report* 212 (Fall).

Schiff, Benjamin N. 1995. *Refugees onto the Third Generation: UN Aid to Palestinians*. Syracuse, N.Y.: Syracuse University Press.

Seitz, Charmaine. 1998a. Ramallah's Coffee Crowd. *Palestine Report* 5 (10): 6. August 21.

————. 1998b. Still Sitting at the Table . . . *Palestine Report* 5 (10): 16. August 21.

Shain, Yossi. 1996. Arab-Americans at a Crossroad. *Journal of Palestine Studies* 25 (3): 46–59.

Shakhshir, Bilal, and Na'ima Ahmad. 1995. Return Is Our Right . . . But It Can Be Painful. *Palestine Report*, 12–13. March 19.

Shakir, Evelyn. 1997. *Bint Arab: Arab and Arab American Women in the United States*. Westport, Conn.: Praeger.

Sharabi, Hisham. 1978a. *Embers and Ashes: Memoirs of an Arab Intellectual* [*Al-jamr wa-l-ramad: dhikrayat muthaqqaf ʿarabi*]. Beirut: Dar at-Taliʿa li-l-Tibaʿa wa-l-Nashr.

————. 1978b. *The Palestinians: 30 Years After*. Washington, D.C.: CCAS, Georgetown University.

————. 1998a. *The Palestinians: Fifty Years Later*. Washington, D.C.: Center for Policy Analysis on Palestine.

————. 1998b. *Pictures of the Past: An Autobiography* [*Suwwar al-madi: Sira dhatiyya*]. Beirut: Nelson.

Sharkawi, Rula. 1998. Said: No Hope for Peace until the Israelis Acknowledge Tragedy of Palestinian History. *Palestine Report*, 12–13. November 20.

Sheffer, Gabriel. 1995. Nationalism and Diaspora. *Migration* 2:50–104.

Shiblak, Abbas. 1996a. Residency Status and Civil Rights of Palestinian Refugees in Arab Countries. *Journal of Palestine Studies* 25 (3): 36–45.

————. 1996b. Residency Status and Civil Rights of Palestinian Refugees in Arab Countries. In *Civil and Citizenship Rights of Palestinian Refugees*, 7–22. Monograph Series No. 1. Ramallah: SHAML.

————. 1998. *The League of Arab States and Palestinian Refugees' Residency Rights*. Monograph Series No. 11. Ramallah: SHAML.

Shlaim, Avi. 1986. Husni Za'im and the Plan to Resettle Palestinian Refugees in Syria. *Journal of Palestine Studies* 15 (4): 68–80.

Shohat, Ella. 1995. Exile, Diaspora, and Return: The Inscription of Palestine in Zionist Discourse. In *Discourse and Palestine,* edited by Annelies Moors et al., 221–236. Amsterdam: Het Spinhuis.

Shuaibi, Issa. 1979/1980. The Development of Palestinian Entity Consciousness. *Journal of Palestine Studies.* Part 1, 9 (1): 67–84; Part 2, 9 (2): 50–70; Part 3, 9 (3): 90–124.

Sirhan, Nimer. 1998. The Nakba in Palestinian Folk Literature. *Palestine-Israel Journal* 5 (3/4): 153–160.

Slyomovics, Susan. 1994. The Memory of Place: Rebuilding the Pre–1948 Palestinian Village. *Diaspora* 3 (2): 157–168.

———. 1995. Discourses on the Pre–1948 Palestinian Village: The Case of Ein Hod/Ein Houd. In *Discourse and Palestine,* edited by Annelies Moors et al., 41–54. Amsterdam: Het Spinhuis.

———. 1998. *The Object of Memory: Arabs and Jews Narrate the Palestinian Village.* Philadelphia: University of Pennsylvania Press.

Smith, Anthony D. 1991. *National Identity.* New York: Penguin.

Smith, Pamela Ann. 1984. *Palestine and the Palestinians, 1876–1983.* London: Croom Held.

———. 1986a. The Exile Bourgeoisie of Palestine. *Middle East Report* 16 (5): 23–27.

———. 1986b. The Palestinian Diaspora 1948–1985. *Journal of Palestine Studies* 15 (3): 90–108.

Stratton, Jon. 1997. Displacing the Jews: Historicizing the Idea of Diaspora. *Diaspora* 6 (3): 302–329.

Sukarieh, Mayssoun, ed. 1999. Through Children's Eyes: Children's Rights in Shatila Camp. *Journal of Palestine Studies* 29 (1): 50–57.

Sulaiman, Jaber. 1994. The Palestinians in Syria: Data and Testimonies [*Al-filastiniyun fi suriya: bayanat wa shahadat*]. *Majallat al-Dirasat al-Filastiniya* 20 (Autumn 1994): 136–162.

Susskind, Yifat. 2000. *The Crisis of Palestinian Refugees and the Right of Return: A MADRE Backgrounder.* New York: MADRE, An International Human Rights Organization. September.

Swanson, Jon S. 1996. Ethnicity, Marriage, and Role Conflict: The Dilemma of a Second Generation Arab-American. In *Family and Gender among American Muslims,* edited by Barbara C. Aswad and Barbara Bilge, 241–249. Philadelphia: Temple University Press.

Swedenburg, Ted. 1990. The Palestinian Peasant as National Signifier. *Anthropological Quarterly* 63 (January 1990): 18–30.

———. 1991. Popular Memory and the Palestinian National Past. In *Golden Ages, Dark Ages: Imagining the Past in History and Anthropology,* edited by Jay O'Brian and William Rosenberry, 152–179. Berkeley: University of California Press.

———. 1995. *Memories of the Revolt: The 1936–1939 Rebellion and the Palestinian National Past.* Minneapolis: University of Minnesota Press.

Takkenberg, Lex. 1998. *The Status of Palestinian Refugees in International Law.* Oxford: Clarendon Press.

Tamari, Salim. 1991. The Palestinian Movement in Transition: Historical Reversals and the Uprising. *Journal of Palestine Studies* 20 (2): 57–70.

———. 1994. Problems of Social Science Research in Palestine: An Overview. *Current Sociology* 42 (1): 69–86.

———. 1996. *Return, Resettlement, Repatriation: The Future of Palestinian Refugees in the Peace Negotiations.* Beirut: Institute for Palestine Studies, posted on Palestinian Refugee Research Net.

———. 1997. Social Science Research in Palestine: A Review of Trends and Issues. In *Palestine, Palestiniens,* edited by Riccardo Bocco et al., 17–40. Beirut: CERMOC.

———. 1999. Treacherous Memories. Paper presented at "The Uncertain State of Palestine: Futures of Research" conference, University of Chicago. February.

Tansley, Jill. 1997. *Adaptation in the West Bank and Gaza.* Monograph Series No. 6. Ramallah: SHAML.

Tarbush, Mohammad. 1985. *Reflections of a Palestinian.* Washington, D.C.: American Arab Affairs Council.

Tibawi, Ahmed L. 1963. Visions of the Return: The Palestine Arab Refugees in Arabic Poetry and Art. *Middle East Journal* 17 (5): 507–526.

Tölölyan, Khachig. 1996. Rethinking Diasporas: Stateless Power in the Transnational Movement. *Diaspora* 5 (1): 3–36.

Toubbeh, Jamil I. 1997. *Day of the Long Night: A Palestinian Refugee Remembers the Nakba.* Jefferson, N.C.: McFarland.

Turki, Fawaz. 1974a. *The Disinherited: Journal of a Palestinian Exile.* New York: Monthly Review Press.

———. 1974b. To Be a Palestinian. *Journal of Palestine Studies* 3 (3): 3–17.

———. 1975–1976. The Palestinians Estranged. *Journal of Palestine Studies* 5 (1–2): 82–96.

———. 1980. The Passions of Exile: The Palestine Congress of North America. *Journal of Palestine Studies* 9 (4): 17–34.

———. 1988. *Soul in Exile: Lives of a Palestinian Revolutionary.* New York: Monthly Review Press.

———. 1993. *Exile's Return: The Making of a Palestinian American.* New York: Free Press.

———. 1996. Palestinian Self-Criticism and the Liberation of Palestinian Society. *Journal of Palestine Studies* 25 (2): 71–76.

———. 1997. Palestine without Apologies: Reflections on the Decade. *Critique* (Spring): 91–108.

Turner, Victor. 1967. *The Forest of Symbols: Aspects of Ndembu Ritual.* Ithaca, N.Y.: Cornell University Press.

———. 1974. *Dramas, Fields, and Metaphors: Symbolic Action in Human Society.* Ithaca, N.Y.: Cornell University Press.

———. 1977. *The Ritual Process: Structure and Anti-Structure.* Ithaca, N.Y.: Cornell University Press.

Turner, Victor, and Edward Bruner, eds. 1986. *The Anthropology of Experience*. Chicago: University of Chicago Press.

Van Hear, Nicholas. 1997. *Reintegrating Refugees: Opportunities and Constraints*. Monograph Series No. 6. Ramallah: SHAML.

———. 1998. *New Diasporas: The Mass Exodus, Dispersal, and Regrouping of Migrant Communities*. Seattle: University of Washington Press.

Wehr, Hans. 1994. *Arabic-English Dictionary*. Ithaca: Spoken Language Services.

Weighill, Marie-Louise. 1999. Palestinians in Exile: Legal, Geographical and Statistical Aspects. In *The Palestinian Exodus 1948–1998*, edited by Ghada Karmi and Eugene Cotrane, 7–36. Reading, UK: Ithaca.

Wernefeldt, Magdalena. 1997. Outsiders, Halfies, and Ajanib: Young Returnees Repatriating Palestine. Master's thesis, University of Stockholm.

Wolbert, Barbara. 1995. *Der getötete Pass: Rückkehr in die Türkei, Eine ethnologische Migrationsstudie*. Berlin: Akademie-Verlag.

Yahya, Adel. 1998. *The Future of the Palestinian Refugee Issue in Final Status Negotiations: Palestinian Refugees: Their Past, Present, and Future*. Jerusalem: Israel/Palestine Center for Research and Information.

Yassin, Abdul-Kader, Sari Hanafi, and Olivier Saint-Martin. 1995. *The Palestinians in Egypt and North Sinai*. Monograph Series No. 5 Arabic and No. 9 English. Ramallah: SHAML.

Yehia, Karem. 1987. The Image of the Palestinians in Egypt, 1982–1985. *Journal of Palestine Studies* 16 (2): 45–63.

Zaqtan, Ghassan. 1997. The Negation of My Exile [*Nafyi al-manfiya*]. *Al-Carmel* 51 (Spring): 141–145.

Zetter, R. 1989. Challenging Research: The Palestinian Refugees, the Intifada and the Refugee Studies. *Journal of Refugee Studies* 2:5–9.

Zureik, Elia. 1994. Palestinian Refugees and Peace. *Journal of Palestine Studies* 24 (1): 5–17.

———. 1996. *Palestinian Refugees and the Peace Process*. Washington, D.C.: Institute for Palestine Studies.

———. 1997. The Trek Back Home: Palestinians Returning Home and Their Problems of Adaptation. In Are Hovdenak et al., *Constructing Order: Palestinian Adaptations to Refugee Life*, 70–102. Oslo: FAFO.

———. 1998. Palestinian Refugees and the Middle East Peace Process. Paper presented at "The Middle East Peace Process: Costs of Instability and Outlook for Insecurity" conference, Montreal. Posted at the Palestinian Refugee Research Net PRRN.

Index